TECHNĒ

"The gifted contributors to *Technē* have provided a path to a hermeneutic for the church's engagement with modern technology. Saving us from being both anti-technological monks and unbridled technological zealots, in *Technē* we have encounters with the use of technology that will allow pastor theologians and academic pastors to disciple believers to be tech-wise. I greatly enjoyed learning from them how to see technology as a significant part of the story of redemption."

—**Eric C. Redmond**, Moody Bible Institute

"Technology has invaded every aspect of our lives and yet has often evaded the theological reflection of the church. Rather than blindly embracing technology or attempting to reject it altogether, the church needs a distinctly Christian vision of technology that is grounded in God's wisdom and relevant for our contemporary context. *Technē* is a brilliant collection of essays that will equip followers of Jesus to be thoughtful and faithful in today's technological world. I highly recommend it."

—**Jeremy Treat**, pastor for preaching and vision, Reality Church of Los Angeles

"By defining technology broadly and theologically, *Technē* does not chase after any trend, but thoughtfully attends to the past, present, and possible future. All Christians, but especially those who bear responsibility for others, be they pastors, educators, authors, parents, or mentors, will find discussion of both questions they've puzzled over and also questions they haven't yet thought to ask. I look forward to returning to the wise principles in this volume for years to come."

—**Amy Peeler**, Wheaton College

"This volume of essays is a gift to the church. Refusing to take an either/or approach, these essays grapple with theological questions that accompany the growth of modern technology in all their complexity. As they do, the authors help us recover a theological vision of the embodied reality of creaturely life in which technology finds its rightful place and from which we can grapple with its dehumanizing effects."

—**Gayle Doornbos**, Dordt University

"In Genesis 11, God implies that through technology virtually nothing will be impossible for humans to achieve—and that this is not necessarily a good thing. How true this is turning out to be and therefore how necessary it is that Christians take time to think deeply, biblically, and wisely about technology. *Technē* is a wonderful book for doing this! You will be blessed by reading this book."

—**Jim Samra**, senior pastor, Calvary Church

"This is a strong collection of thoughtful essays addressing some of the most poignant moral and theological questions facing the church today. Drawing deeply on biblical, historical, and theological resources, these essays provide of wealth of insight for pastors, academics, and lay people seeking to navigate the complex world of technology and its manifold implications for living faithfully as Christians in the modern world."

—**Marc Cortez**, Wheaton College

TECHNĒ

CHRISTIAN VISIONS
of TECHNOLOGY

GERALD HIESTAND *and*
TODD A. WILSON, *editors*

CASCADE *Books* • Eugene, Oregon

TECHNĒ
Christian Visions of Technology

The Center for Pastor Theologians Series

Copyright © 2022 Wipf and Stock Publishers. All rights reserved. Except for brief quotations in critical publications or reviews, no part of this book may be reproduced in any manner without prior written permission from the publisher. Write: Permissions, Wipf and Stock Publishers, 199 W. 8th Ave., Suite 3, Eugene, OR 97401.

Cascade Books
An Imprint of Wipf and Stock Publishers
199 W. 8th Ave., Suite 3
Eugene, OR 97401

www.wipfandstock.com

PAPERBACK ISBN: 978-1-6667-0421-1
HARDCOVER ISBN: 978-1-6667-0422-8
EBOOK ISBN: 978-1-6667-0423-5

Cataloguing-in-Publication data:

Names: Hiestand, Gerald, 1974–, editor. | Wilson, Todd A., 1976–, editor.

Title: Technē : Christian visions of technology / edited by Gerald Hiestand and Todd A. Wilson.

Description: Eugene, OR : Cascade Books, 2022 | Series: The Center for Pastor Theologians Series | Includes bibliographical references and index(es).

Identifiers: ISBN 978-1-6667-0421-1 (paperback) | ISBN 978-1-6667-0422-8 (hardcover) | ISBN 978-1-6667-0423-5 (ebook)

Subjects: LCSH: Technology—Religious aspects—Christianity.

Classification: BR115.T42 T41 2022 (print) | BR115.T42 T41 (ebook)

11/16/22

Some Scripture quotations from the ESV (English Stand Version) Bible, copyright © 2001 by Crossway, a publishing ministry of Good News Publishers. Used with permission. All rights reserved.

Some Scripture quotations from the NASB (New American Standard Bible), copyright © 1995 by the Lockman Foundation. Used with permission. All rights reserved. www.lockman.org.

Some Scripture quotations from the RSV (Revised Standard Version) Bible, copyright © 1946, 1952, and 1971 by the National Council of the Churches of Christ in the United States of America. Used with permission. All rights reserved worldwide.

Some Scripture quotations from the NRSV (New Revised Standard Version) Bible, copyright © 1989 by the National Council of the Churches of Christ in the United States of America. Used with permission. All rights reserved worldwide.

"Digital Life and Social Media as Secular Liturgy: A Matter of Christian Formation" is adapted from material in *Restless Devices: Recovering Personhood, Presence, and Place in the Digital Age* by Felicia Wu Song. Copyright © 2021 by Felicia Wu Song. Used with permission of InterVarsity Press Academic, PO Box 1400, Downers Grove, IL 60515, USA. www.ivpress.com.

To Zach Wagner and Myndi Lawrence

An excellent editorial director and
an excellent editorial assistant

Contents

Acknowledgments | xi
Abbreviations | xiii
Introduction—Technē: Christian Visions of Technology | xv
  —Gerald Hiestand and Todd A. Wilson

Contributors | xvii

Part 1: Theological Reflections on Technology

1 Seeing the Inner Essence of Technology: Pastoral Reflections on Faithfulness to Christ in the Technological World | 3
   —Joel D. Lawrence

2 The Path More Traveled: The Place of the (Missing) Church in Christian Engagement of Technology | 16
   —Daniel J. Brendsel

3 The Alchemists' Dream: Three Judgments about Technology | 36
   —Andy Crouch

4 Why We Get Technology Wrong | 61
   —Douglas Estes

5 Sacrament and Technology | 77
   —Christopher J. Ganski

6 Proceed with Caution: Lessons from Saint Augustine, Jonathan Edwards, and Miroslav Volf | 92
—Jonathan Huggins

Part 2: Technological Reflections on Theology

7 A New Catechism for the Digital Age: Answering the Questions Posed by AI, Consciousness, and Transhumanism | 111
—Bruce Baker

8 Artificial Intelligence, the Ascension of Jesus Christ, and Human Flourishing | 129
—Neal D. Presa

9 On Human Transcendence, Artificial Intelligence, and the Gathering Gnostic Storm | 139
—Missy Byrd DeRegibus

10 In the Image of Our Choosing? Personhood, the Image of God, and the Ethics of Gene Editing | 151
—Nathan A. Barczi

11 Fearfully and Wonderfully Made? Christians and Embryos in an Era of Biotechnology | 172
—Jeff Hardin

12 The Technology of Reading | 187
—Karen Swallow Prior

13 Digital Life and Social Media as Secular Liturgy: A Matter of Christian Formation | 202
—Felicia Wu Song

14 Partnering with Pastors: How Early Modern Printers Advanced the Reformation | 221
—Jennifer Powell McNutt

Subject Index | 237
Name Index | 241

Acknowledgments

As in the past, we owe a debt of gratitude to the contributors of this volume. The subject of technology—and the church's engagement with it—is an ever-evolving field of reflection. We are grateful for the many able women and men who have thought, and continue to think, deeply on this important issue.

Likewise, we are grateful to the Center for Pastor Theologians, the organizer of the conference from which the papers in this book are drawn. The center has served as a catalyst for our work and has been a repository of wisdom and counsel on all things pastoral and theological. The staff of the center—Zach Wagner (editorial director) and Shelby Wagner (conference coordinator) did an amazing job of organizing and executing an outstanding conference. Joel Lawrence (executive director) and Rae Paul (managing director) have done a tremendous job continuing the ongoing work of the CPT.

In the same spirit, we are deeply grateful for the partnership of the CPT's five senior theological mentors: Scott Hafemann, Doug Sweeney, Peter Leithart, Kevin Vanhoozer, and Timothy George. Their commitment to the CPT's mission, their contribution to the fellowships, and their friendship and encouragement to the two of us have been an important catalyst for the CPT project and its associated publications.

Likewise, we continue to be profoundly grateful for Calvary Memorial Church in Oak Park, Illinois: the congregation where we have been privileged to serve as pastors. Calvary has graciously served as the host home for the CPT for more than a decade, and it is not an understatement to say that the CPT would not be what it is without Calvary's partnership and support.

And finally, Myndi Lawrence is owed a special commendation for her (extensive!) labors as our chief copy and production editor for this volume. Myndi did a tremendous job in organizing, copyediting, chasing down missing citations, and indexing (and beyond) in order to produce a completed manuscript ready for submission. It is no overstatement to say that this volume would not have happened without her excellent and dedicated work.

Abbreviations

TDNT *Theological Dictionary of the New Testament.* Edited by Gerhard Kittel and Gerhard Friedrich. Translated by Geoffrey W. Bromiley. 10 vols. Grand Rapids: Eerdmans, 1964–1976.

EDNT *Exegetical Dictionary of the New Testament.* Edited by Horst Balz and Gerhard Schneider. Translated by Virgil P. Howard et al. 3 vols. Grand Rapids: Eerdmans, 1990–1993.

Introduction

Technē: Christian Visions of Technology

GERALD HIESTAND *and* TODD A. WILSON, *editors*

THE CENTER FOR PASTOR Theologians is guided by a singular mission: to equip pastors to be theologians for today's complex world. We are deeply motivated by a desire to have theology return to its native habitat—the church—and to see pastors reclaim their fundamental calling—as theologians.

Each October, we host our annual theology conference at Calvary Memorial Church in Oak Park, Illinois, where we bring together a diverse group of evangelical pastors, theologians, nonprofit leaders, practitioners, and other Christian leaders to reason together about an area of pressing concern for Christians trying to live faithfully in the late modern world.

In October 2019, our theme was both timely and timeless. *Technē: A Christian Vision of Technology* was our conference focus, and it drew together an outstanding group of presenters and participants from all walks of life, academic disciplines, and fields of service. Many were pastors. But there were also scholars, technologists, missionaries, and many faithful lay Christians—all of whom were there to grapple with the meaning and significance of technology for the Christian.

Christians have an interesting relationship with technology. As Genesis 1 so succinctly yet profoundly declares, God created us in his image (v. 27),[1] and as part of that vocation, we are to make something of the world.

---

1. Unless otherwise indicated, all Bible quotes and references are taken from the Revised Standard Version (RSV).

Technology is one of the most important and powerful ways human beings exercise this dominion.

But while technology can extend our humanity in powerful and exciting ways, many of us feel that it can also compromise or fracture our humanity at its core. As a result, questions quickly emerge. What does it mean to be human? How does our creation in the image of God affect the way we use, design, and understand technology?

As Christians, we desire to use our technology to advance God's kingdom. We also wonder if some of the technologies we see being used in the world are running counter to the new world that God is making in Christ.

Technology enables us to reach the world with the good news of Christ in unprecedented ways. And yet it enables the enslavement of millions to the whims of worldly desire, greed, and consumerism.

Is the solution to reject technology? Or should we wholeheartedly embrace it? How does the Christian theological vision for the world affect our theological vision for the use of technology?

Put differently, technology connects us, and it separates us. It empowers us, and it enslaves us. It can heal us, and it can harm us. It can open new horizons of human potential and yet fracture and hamper our humanity in the process.

Virtually every church utilizes technology in its worship, communication, and ministries. But how many pastors have thought theologically about a Christian perspective and approach to technology? How can pastors shepherd and lead those in their congregations who work in technology industries?

We need to think hard and intentionally about these matters while also seeking the wisdom God has graciously given us in Scripture for navigating these issues. We need to reclaim the riches of the Christian tradition about creation and human identity.

As conveners of this conference, and now as editors of this volume of essays, we offer this collection of scholarly and pastoral contributions to you with both gratitude and hope. We are grateful for seasoned and substantive Christian reflection on a wide range of issues pertinent to casting a distinctly Christian vision for the God-honoring use of technology today—and in the future.

And we are hopeful that both pastors and congregations will be, even in some small way, better equipped to engage today's complex world, bearing the image of Christ, all for the sake of Christ.

Soli Deo gloria!

Contributors

BRUCE BAKER (PhD, University of St. Andrews) is an ordained PC(USA) pastor and teaches theological ethics in the School of Business, Government and Economics at Seattle Pacific University. His most recent publication is a chapter viewing AI through the lenses of sin and grace, in the book, *AI, Faith and the Future*.

NATHAN A. BARCZI (PhD, Nottingham; PhD, Massachusetts Institute of Technology) is pastor of preaching and teaching at Christ the King Church in Newton, MA, and the executive director of the Octet Collaborative, a Christian study center serving MIT. He has written numerous articles, including "In the Image of Our Choosing," published in *Christianity Today* (2017).

DANIEL J. BRENDSEL (PhD, Wheaton College) serves as pastor of First Presbyterian Church in Hinckley, MN. He is the author of *"Isaiah Saw His Glory": The Use of Isaiah 52–53 in John 12* (2014), has co-authored *An Interpretive Lexicon of New Testament Greek* (2014), and has written several articles and essays.

ANDY CROUCH (MDiv, Boston University School of Theology) is partner for theology and culture at Praxis. He is the author of numerous books, including *The Tech-Wise Family: Everyday Steps for Putting Technology in Its Proper Place* (2017), and *Strong and Weak: Embracing a Life of Love, Risk and True Flourishing* (2016).

Missy Byrd DeRegibus (GDCS, Regent College) is on staff with InterVarsity's Graduate and Faculty Ministry at Virginia Commonwealth University. She is author of the forthcoming book, *You're Going to Miss Me When I'm Gone: Why We'll Still Need the Body in an Age of AI*.

Douglas Estes (PhD, University of Nottingham) is associate professor of biblical studies and practical theology at Tabor College. Douglas has written or edited ten books and more than fifty essays. Recent books include *Journey Through James* (2021) and *Braving the Future* (2018). He is the editor of *Didaktikos*.

Christopher J. Ganski (PhD, Marquette University) is a pastor in the Christian Reformed Church. In 2011, Chris planted City Reformed Church in city-center Milwaukee, WI, where he continues to be the pastor.

Jeff Hardin (PhD, University of California-Berkeley) holds an MDiv and is chair of the Department of Integrative Biology, University of Wisconsin-Madison. In addition to numerous scientific research articles relating to embryonic development, Hardin is senior author of *World of the Cell*.

Jonathan Huggins (PhD, Stellenbosch University) is the chaplain at Berry College in Rome, GA, where he also teaches courses in biblical and theological studies. He is a priest in the Anglican Church in North America and author of *Living Justification* (2013). He has contributed articles to *Didaktikos*, *Anglican Compass*, and the Center for Pastor Theologians blog.

Joel D. Lawrence (PhD, Cambridge University) is the executive director of the Center for Pastor Theologians. He is the author of *Bonhoeffer: A Guide for the Perplexed* (2010), as well as numerous articles and chapters in books on a variety of theological and pastoral subjects.

Jennifer Powell McNutt (PhD, University of St. Andrews) holds the Franklin S. Dyrness Chair in Biblical and Theological Studies at Wheaton College and is an ordained minister in the PC(USA). She is the author of the award-winning book, *Calvin Meets Voltaire: The Clergy of Geneva in the Age of Enlightenment, 1685–1798* (2014), and lead editor of the forthcoming volume, *The Oxford Handbook of the Bible and the Reformation*.

NEAL D. PRESA (PhD, Drew University) is associate director of doctoral studies and visiting associate professor of preaching at New Brunswick Theological Seminary. He is also senior visiting professor at Union Theological Seminary (Philippines), adjunct professor of practical theology at International Theological Seminary (West Covina, CA), and research fellow for practical and missional theology of University of the Free State (Bloemfontein, South Africa). He previously served pastorates in New Jersey and California. His seventh book is *Worship, Justice, and Joy: A Liturgical Pilgrimage* (forthcoming).

KAREN SWALLOW PRIOR (PhD, State University of New York at Buffalo) is research professor of English and Christianity and culture at Southeastern Baptist Theological Seminary. She is the author of *Booked: Literature in the Soul of Me* (2012), *Fierce Convictions: The Extraordinary Life of Hannah More—Poet, Reformer, Abolitionist* (2014), and *On Reading Well: Finding the Good Life Through Great Books* (2018). She is co-editor of *Cultural Engagement: A Crash Course in Contemporary Issues* (2019).

FELICIA WU SONG (PhD, University of Virginia) is professor of sociology at Westmont College in Santa Barbara, CA. In addition to an early study of online communities (*Virtual Communities: Bowling Alone, Online Together* [2009]) and research on the mom-blogging industry, her latest book *Restless Devices: Recovering Personhood, Presence, and Place in the Digital Age* (2021) addresses digital practices and spiritual formation.

Part 1

THEOLOGICAL REFLECTIONS *on* TECHNOLOGY

1

Seeing the Inner Essence of Technology

Pastoral Reflections on Faithfulness to Christ in the Technological World

JOEL D. LAWRENCE

Pastoring in a World of Big Tech

THERE WAS A GENTLEMAN in the church I served recently named Clarence Bass. Clarence grew up in North Carolina in the 1920s and then served in World War II, training dogs to serve in the coast guard. After the war, Clarence attended Wheaton College, where he earned a master of arts in theology. From there, Clarence and his new wife traveled to Europe on the *Queen Mary* so Clarence could study in Edinburgh under T. F. Torrance and in Switzerland under Emil Brunner. While in Switzerland, Clarence attended Karl Barth's lectures in Basel. Clarence then moved back to the United States and taught theology at Bethel Seminary in St. Paul, Minnesota, for forty years. He has been attending our church for sixty-five years. Clarence and I went to lunch from time to time, and he told me stories of his life in theology and ministry. Through those conversations, I learned a great deal from Clarence about theology and pastoring. But there is one story that Clarence told that has shaped my understanding of the vocation of pastor-theologian more than any other.

When Clarence was growing up, his grandfather, who was blind, lived with his family. Every day after school, Clarence would take his grandfather for a walk, and as they walked, Clarence would describe for his grandfather the world as he saw it. He would describe the trees, the streams, a rainbow after a storm, the vibrant sunlight in the summer, or the muted colors on a cloudy day. On these walks, Clarence would illuminate the world for his grandfather, visualizing what his grandfather could not see so that he could have a vision of that which was hidden to his eyes. As pastor theologians, it is our calling to "take walks" with our congregations—describing to them the world as we see it theologically, looking beyond appearances, penetrating to the essence of the world's patterns, ideologies, and beliefs. Through this, we hope to enable the flocks entrusted to our care to better understand the dynamics of the world in which they are living, working, and raising children. We do this out of the pastoral burden we share, the burden of seeing our congregations walk faithfully with Christ and be witnesses of his Lordship.

We have been given the calling of pastor theologian in complex times, and as we live out our calling, we must be equipped to explore one of the great complexities of the world we inhabit: the massive expansion of technology in our day. We are all aware of the critical questions technological development is raising, questions regarding what technology is doing to our brains, to our relationships, to our children, and to our understanding of what it means to be human. Undoubtedly, we rejoice in many of the technological advances that have occurred in our days: How could we not be grateful that diseases that once took the lives of so many are now easily controlled through advances in medicine? How can we not be grateful for technology that allows us to speak with friends and family members who are living in far-off places, enabling us to stay in close relationship over great distances? We affirm that technology is among the good gifts of God, a gift that enables us to fulfill our role as stewards who are called to cultivate the world and bring order to God's creation.[1]

And yet the growth of modern technology produces significant pastoral challenges. We are told in book after book that we are standing on the

1. Many Christians view technology through the lens of the cultural mandate, rooted in the command of God in Genesis 1 to fill and subdue the world. While I appreciate this application of the cultural mandate, I do have concerns about the usefulness of this view of the mandate as we look to the future. As the ideology of technology, the main topic of this essay, has come to dominate our world, I am worried that the theological lens of the cultural mandate is insufficient for grappling with the challenges of modern technology. George Hobson's view of the technological ideology (see below)—rooted in the desire of humanity to control everything—lends a very different context to our understanding of the essence of technology, bringing with it the need to see the nature of human desire for controlling history through technology in new ways. This raises questions in my mind about the ability of a culture-mandate theology to adequately grasp the inner essence of technology and the all-encompassing demands it makes on our world and our lives.

precipice of a new world, one in which advances in technology have the potential to recreate our world in fundamental ways that none, even those who are at the forefront of developing these technologies, are fully able to grasp. We are told in one book that artificial intelligence (AI) will solve significant problems for human life,[2] and in another that AI could bring the end of humanity as we know it.[3] We are told that the use of smartphones is rewiring our minds and that social media is causing loneliness and depression in our society, leading to a spike in rates of teen suicide. So how should pastor theologians see the world of technology, and how should we guide our flocks to follow Christ in a world of technological hegemony?

I believe that, like Clarence walking with his grandfather, we are called to illuminate the technological world for our congregations. This is not to say that pastor theologians alone have sight; but it is to emphasize that our pastoral calling is to interpret the world theologically as best we can. To bring this illumination, it is essential that we penetrate below the surface of smartphones and tablets, VR goggles and Google, to see the "inner spiritual essence" of technology. I have borrowed this phrase from George Hobson, who writes, "As technology gains overwhelming momentum in our own day, its inner *spiritual essence*—the drive for human control over *everything*—is coinciding more and more with its actual *technical power*, thus giving rise to . . . the *technological ideology*."[4] Hobson calls us to see clearly that there is a technological ideology dominating our world, and this ideology is fundamentally spiritual. It is easy to miss this, accustomed as we are to thinking that technology is simply wires, screens, and routers. But the technological ideology is spiritual because it makes claims on our affections and promotes a particular vision of human purpose in the world. Because of this, I propose that we cannot evaluate technology properly unless we see the inner spiritual essence with clarity, evaluating theologically the claims it makes and the vision of humanity it contains. Only then will we be in a position to guide our flocks to follow Christ faithfully in a world shaped by the inner spiritual essence of technology.

So, how can we see the inner spiritual essence? In this essay, I am inviting you to come with me on a walk through the technological world. As we walk, I will make observations about three interrelated components that make up the inner spiritual essence of technology. First, in order for us to understand the historical context for the development of the inner spiritual essence, we will observe the rise of the technological ideology. Following this, we will

2. Topol, *Deep Medicine*.
3. Barrat, *Our Final Invention*.
4. Hobson, *Episcopal Church*, 52.

look at the influence of Western liberalism on the inner spiritual essence of technology, reflecting on how liberalism's vision of liberty has influenced the shape of the technological ideology. We will then observe the impact of humanism on the inner essence of technology. I will propose that humanism produces a messianic program that strives, through technological progress, to allow humans to attain our self-determined purposes. I will then conclude our walk by offering my pastoral reflections on leading our congregants to engage with the inner spiritual essence of technology.

So, let's go for a walk.

Observation 1: The Historical Rise of the Spiritual Essence of Technology

For millennia, humans have used technology to develop and support life in our world. For most of this history, technology consisted of tools that were extensions of human capacities, tools that enabled humanity to increase productivity in our labor. However, as history has moved into the modern world, a shift has occurred in the relationship between humanity and technology. In order to see clearly the inner spiritual essence of technology, it is critical that we understand this historical shift and how it has contributed to the development of the inner spiritual essence of technology.

One of the foremost observers of this shift was Jacques Ellul, a French sociologist and theologian who lived in the twentieth century and who investigated the technological ideology in penetrating ways. Ellul observed that, prior to the eighteenth century, the substance of technology consisted in the application of tools that were fashioned to support human labor in its work of cultivation and provision, tools like hammers and plows. These implements were extensions of human abilities and complemented human aptitudes, and so were under human control. But in the eighteenth century, with the rise of the scientific revolution and the Industrial Revolution it birthed, the inner essence of technology changed.[5] Moving from technologies that extend human capacities, technology has now grown into a total system that has come to dominate human life and reshape human experience of the world in fundamental ways.

Ellul calls this total system that dominates the modern world *technique*. In his best-known book, *The Technological Society*, Ellul states that "no social, human, or spiritual fact is so important as the fact of *technique* in the modern world."[6] For Ellul, *technique* is more than the sum of technologies;

---

5. See also Gay, *Modern Technology*, 27–29.
6. Ellul, *Technological Society*, 3.

it is, rather, a way of organizing the world that has come to dominate all aspects of human life. According to Jeff Greenman, *technique* is "the all-embracing consciousness of the mechanical world."[7] Ellul is describing a totalizing system of technicization that has mastery over the organization of human life in a way never before possible in history. For Ellul, what is critical about *technique* is that it reverses the relationship between technology and humanity. In all other eras of human history, humans utilized technology as a tool; in the age of *technique*, humans have become tools of the technical system, and *technique* has become the master of humanity.

The result of this is what Ellul calls "technical necessity," by which he means that we have no choice but to adopt the organizing methods of *technique*. This necessity inevitably leads to the loss of human freedom, an observation that lays bare the tragedy of *technique*: promising freedom, *technique* enslaves humanity. Ellul says it this way: "Today's technical phenomenon . . . has almost nothing in common with the technical phenomenon of the past . . . In our civilization technique is in no way limited. It has been extended to all spheres and encompasses every activity, including human activity."[8] The dominance of *technique* leads to a world that organizes human activity in order to maximize output and productivity, thereby creating a set of value judgments based on efficiency. In doing so, *technique* squeezes human beings into modes of productivity that alienate us from what have been vital historical resources of culture, transforming human labor into cogs in the economic machine.[9] *Technique* dominates our world as the spiritual essence that stands underneath and impels the growth of the technological system in our day.

In our first observation on our walk, we have engaged Jacques Ellul's understanding of the historic shift in technological dominance that has occurred in the modern era. Rather than simply analyzing the phenomena of technologies, Ellul calls us to see the totalizing system and methods of *technique* and the claims it makes on our lives. These claims can remain hidden if we don't look for them carefully, and our vision of modern technology will be blurred if we don't see the shift in technological development that has occurred in the modern world.

---

7. Greenman et al., *Understanding Jacques Ellul*, 23.

8. Ellul, *Technological Society*, 78.

9. There are echoes of the Marxist analysis of history here. In his early days, prior to his conversion to Christ, Ellul was a keen reader of Marx. Though he ultimately rejected Marxism, Marx's influence can be seen in Ellul's thought.

Observation 2: The Relationship of the Technological Essence and Liberalism

The second observation I want to make on our walk is the relationship between the technological ideology and Western liberalism.[10] In his book, *Why Liberalism Failed*, Patrick Deneen makes the connection between the modern technological system and liberalism when he writes, "You could say that our political (ideology) is the operating system that creates the environment in which various technological programs may thrive . . . Our deeper political commitments [shape] our technology."[11] For Deneen, we cannot grasp the nature of modern technology without understanding that it is rooted in the seedbed of the Western liberal political vision of humanity and the world.

The connection between Western liberalism and the modern technological ideology is rooted in liberalism's "new understanding of liberty."[12] Prior to the advent and growth of liberalism in the seventeenth century, liberty was conceived of as the ability for self-governance through the cultivation of virtue, formed in a reciprocal relationship between the individual and the structures of the family and the wider society to which the individual and family belonged. Ancient and medieval political structures, though differing in significant ways from each other, held a common vision in which the world was understood to be static and unchanging, a given to which human life must conform if humans are to thrive. In this vision, politics was organized in line with the revealed will of a deity (or deities) and according to the structures of a natural hierarchy.[13] Individuals and communities existed in light of this structure, and liberty was defined as the ability of the

---

10. By liberalism, I am referring to the political ideology that arose four hundred years ago and is the dominant political ideology of the Western world. I am not talking about "the left," i.e., the vision of statecraft that views social organization as best implemented by policies on the left-hand side of the spectrum as defined by Liberal to Conservative.

11. Deneen, *Why Liberalism Failed*, 103.

12. Deneen, *Why Liberalism Failed*, 95.

13. This is why democracy was held in contempt throughout most of political history until the time of the advent of liberalism. The vast majority of political thinkers in the history of political thought did not have a high view of democracy, for fear of the unlearned and reactive nature of the commoners and also the ever-present danger of factionalism that lurks in democratic societies. Even in the founding of the American experiment, which is supposed to be the shining example of democracy, James Madison writes concerning the necessity of representative democracy due to his contempt for the commoners. See Madison et al., *Federalist Papers*, especially Federalist 10. For a general description of the fear of democracy, see Grayling, *Democracy and Its Crisis*, 1–11.

human to develop a virtuous self-governance that would contribute to the common good of the family and the larger society.[14]

Liberalism arose as a rejection of this vision of the world and as a renewed vision of humanity.[15] Rather than seeing humans as dependent upon and organized by an unchanging natural order, liberalism viewed the world as malleable and therefore changeable through the application of human will. Anthony Pagden states this pointedly when he writes, "Man [is] the architect of his own social world."[16] Liberalism was a creed that no longer accepted the ancient vision of liberty as the formation of self-governing virtue in relation to the structured world, but rather "conceived humans as . . . individuals who could fashion and pursue for themselves their own version of the good life."[17] As such, liberalism created a world-encompassing project of humans liberating themselves from the errors and doctrines of the past, from the control of dogma and the clergy, and from the rule of kings and aristocrats who held their positions of power, not based on any kind of merit, but based on the accidents of birth and the appeal to God that reinforces their authority. Giambattista Vico, a seventeenth-century Italian philosopher, writes, "In this new history humans are not . . . the kind of plaything St. Augustine had imagined, dancing to the music . . . conducted by an omniscient deity. They are free. They have their origins in the state of nature . . . and . . . they progress; they improve. Their nature changes as their living conditions change."[18]

A key development of liberalism is what Larry Siedentop calls "the invention of the individual."[19] Defining humanity as autonomous, self-interested individuals, liberalism disconnects individuals from the structures and roots of communities that provide meaning and purpose to life. Instead of a communally determined notion of purpose that develops out of the family and society in which one was born, the liberal individualist would now be called to determine meaning and purpose for themselves.

---

14. For a description of the development of ancient and medieval political structures, see Fukuyama, *Origins of Political Order*.

15. ". . . the world of civil society has certainly been made by [humanity] and . . . its principles are therefore to be found within the modifications of our own human mind" (Giambattista Vico, quoted in Pagden, *Enlightenment*, 157).

16. Pagden, *Enlightenment*, 160.

17. Deneen, *Why Liberalism Failed*, 1.

18. Gianbattista Vico, quoted in Pagden, *Enlightenment*, 102.

19. See Siedentop, *Inventing the Individual*. Siedentop's book examines the new understanding of the individual that arose in the late-Medieval and Renaissance periods, which built the foundations upon which the Western liberal vison of humanity was constructed.

In the modern liberal expression of individualism, which Pankaj Mishra calls "selfie individualism," we are the determiners of our own individual meaning, and we give definition of our own purpose, a vision that has been inscribed in the American version of liberal individualism as "life, liberty, and the pursuit of happiness."[20] This view of humanity raises an important question: Who determines this happiness? The answer, of course, is the individual, who now pursues happiness by exercising their individual autonomous liberty, setting for themselves the *telos* of their life. Liberalism creates a new understanding of the purpose of human life, giving to each person the right to define happiness for the self.

What does this have to do with the inner spiritual essence of technology? Why do we need to understand liberalism if we are going to see the inner essence of modern technology? Having created this new vision of human liberty, liberalism must now encourage the creation of a world in which individual autonomous self-determination can be achieved. The invention of the individual demands a world in which the self-defined purposes of autonomous individuals are secured. But how can this world be created?

Observation 3: Humanism and the Messianic Mission of Technology

This question, rooted in the combined forces of the growth of *technique* as a total system and the Western liberal vision of humanity as autonomous, self-interested individuals, leads to the final observation I will make on our walk together: the messianic mission of the technological ideology.

In his book, *Age of Anger*, Pankaj Mishra writes that in the modern world, "[humanity] replaces God as the centre [sic] of existence and becomes the master and possessor of nature by the application of a new science and technology."[21] This vision of humanity as master over nature, and so as lord over history, is rooted in the dominant philosophical ideology of our day: humanism.[22] Arising from liberalism's vision of the liberty of the autonomous individual, humanism declares humanity to be the highest good.[23] Humanism is a vision of life and history in which humanity replaces the notion of a sovereign God with itself and therefore declares that our lives, and so history, are under our control. Because history is under our

---

20. Mishra, *Age of Anger*, 82.

21. Mishra, *Age of Anger*, 213

22. By humanism, I am referring to the philosophical vision that denies any good higher than the human. I am not referring to the humanism that was a movement in the Renaissance and that shaped the Reformation, the project of returning to the foundational texts of "the humanities," the Greek and Roman philosophers.

23. See Harari, *Homo Deus*, 65–68.

control, and because meaning is determined by the individual, it is our responsibility to shape history in a way that ensures we can achieve the meaning we desire. Humanism is driven to create a secure world in which we are free to pursue our self-created purposes. As such, humanism demands an application of the technological ideology that would ensure the elimination of anything that frustrates the advance of the humanist project.

This demand creates what Yuval Harari calls "the new human agenda."[24] For Harari, this agenda contains three items: seeking immortality, pursuing happiness, and achieving the status of divinity.[25] The humanist pursuit of technology is a project that trusts in the technological ideology as the means by which we can create solutions that remove the barriers to human happiness and limitation through the growth of the technical system. The desire to create this future is deeply rooted in the eschatological program of humanism that strives to overcome the world's problems. The danger in the technological ideology driving the technological development of our day is that it has faith in the soteriological myth that human control through technology can eliminate all that stands in the way of achieving the humanist goals we have created for ourselves.

This takes us back to Hobson's definition of the inner spiritual essence of technology that we heard at the beginning of our walk: "the desire for human control over everything." This desire is not new in human history; it goes all the way back to the Garden of Eden. But the ability for humans to exert this control is increasing in unprecedented ways. This drive, which enlivens the technological ideology, is one we must see clearly and, as pastor theologians, we must understand how this desire is deeply embedded in the technological world of our day. As we conclude our walk together, I want to offer my reflections on pastoring our congregations to see the inner spiritual essence of technology.

The Church's Presence in the World of Technological Dominance

There is a basic question that has animated my thoughts as we have taken our walk together: How can we as pastor theologians guide our churches to faithfully follow Christ in a world dominated by the technological ideology? I have suggested that to do so we must look below the surface of our world to see the inner spiritual essence of technology, and that only then can we truly guide our congregants in their relation to technology. But how can

24. Harari, *Homo Deus*, 1.
25. For more on this, see my "After *Sapiens*," 13–24.

these observations shape the way we pastor our congregations? What are the implications of our view of the inner spiritual essence of technology? And what does this view mean for our engagement with technology?

I want to begin my concluding pastoral reflections by returning once again to Jacques Ellul. In his work, Ellul offers a striking proposal for the church's relationship to the technological ideology. Ellul calls us, as the community whose fundamental identity is in Christ, to "profane technology."[26] For Ellul, to profane technology is not to reject the use of all technology. Rather, to profane technology is to see the claims that the technological system makes on our lives with clarity and be ever-vigilant to resist those claims that would conform us to the spiritual vision of technology, knowing as we do that our lives belong to another and are to be conformed to him alone.

Profaning technology, therefore, begins with the church having absolute clarity about our mission in the world. Ellul states that the Christian is to be present in the world as one who "has a part to play in this world which no one else can possibly fulfill."[27] According to Ellul, the part that the church has to play through our presence in the world is simple: to be salt and light by giving meaning to history through our witness to the Lordship of Jesus Christ.[28] Therefore, the presence of the church in the world is essential, but the church must be clear about the nature of our presence, especially with reference to the world's own self-saving work (or, in Hobson's language, the world's desire to control everything). Ellul writes,

> Christians must participate in the world's preservation. They really must work toward it. But . . . we must try to dispel serious misunderstanding on this subject. When we speak of the world's preservation, we immediately envision involvement in the activities that the world considers best for itself. The world chooses its paths and determines its plan of action for resolving its problems. It is often thought that Christians, to help preserve the world, should make efforts along these lines . . . The confusion seems to me to be serious and weighty. Christians participate truly in the world's preservation not by acting like others and laboring at the world's tasks but by fulfilling their particular role, [which is] not to formulate the problems as others do, not to attempt futile technical and moral solutions, but to succeed in

---

26. Greenman, *Understanding Jacques Ellul*, 36.

27. Ellul, *Presence in the Modern World*, 6. See Jacobs, *Year of Our Lord*, 199, for helpful reflections on Ellul's view of the church's presence in the world.

28. Ellul, *Presence in the Modern World*, 3.

discovering the actual spiritual difficulties that any . . . situation involves.²⁹

Our role as pastor theologians is to "succeed in discovering the actual spiritual difficulties" of the world. In my view, the dominance of the technological ideology that has come to govern our world reveals a deep spiritual urge, an eschatological longing in the human heart. However, this longing has become a project of rebellion as humans have sought to shape the world for our own ends through our own power. Rejecting the Lordship of Christ and asserting the lordship of the self, the world is seeking to solve the problems that hinder the self through the expansion and application of technology, creating the irony of the self that is seeking liberty but is being held captive by a system of technical necessity.

As the church, we must be present in the technological world, but we must not allow the world's self-evaluation of its problems—and its solutions to those problems—to determine the church's engagement with the world. The world doesn't grasp the true nature of her problems because the world doesn't know Christ and so seeks its own salvation through its own capacities, a process we could call "technological Pelagianism." As the church, we must be clear that we are not called to "labor at the world's tasks," but instead must be faithful to our role, which is to witness to the one who is Lord of the world, the one who makes visible the inner spiritual realities of the world. With this clarity of our mission, fully committed to being present in the world, the church can profane technology, thereby "deconstructing [technology's] soteriological myth and refusing to submit to technological necessity."³⁰ By deconstructing the soteriological myth through our proclamation and confidence in Christ's lordship, we can live in freedom from the messianic claims of technology that would take us away from Christ.

So how should we as pastor theologians guide our congregations in their relationship with technology? Allow me to make two suggestions.

First, we train our people to cherish the church through forming in them a robust ecclesial vision. On this, we can learn from the Amish. As we know, the Amish do not refuse all technology; attaching a buggy to a horse may not be a Ferrari, but it is a technology. So how do the Amish decide which technologies to adopt and which to reject? To evaluate technology, the Amish ask a simple question: "Will this or won't it help support the fabric of our community?"³¹ The reason the Amish reject much of modern technology is because they have come to the conviction that

---

29. Ellul, *Presence in the Modern World*, 6.
30. Ellul, *Presence in the Modern World*, 6.
31. Deneen, *Why Liberalism Failed*, 106.

the technological ideology fundamentally tears apart their community. What if we asked that question with our congregations? What would we say? How would that shape our relationship to the technological ideology? But we cannot even ask that question unless our congregations are deeply immersed in the church as their fundamental community. To profane technology is first to build the church.

Second, we must inculcate into our flocks a habit of theological reflection on technology. How many of our congregants, when they pick up their iPhones, think theologically about them? To profane technology means to create in the hearts of the people entrusted to our care the ability to analyze theologically the vision of humanity contained in the newest smartphone, in a hundred-inch HD television, or in Netflix. It means teaching our people regularly to ask, "What claim to lordship is being made on my life by this technology? What soteriological assertion is being made by this device? What vision of liberty is being promoted by this technology? What eschatological promise is being made by this advance?" Then, having eyes to see the broader technological ideology, they can walk through this world as those whose hearts are more fully committed to being present as witnesses to Christ's Lordship, confident in him as our Messiah, and putting our trust in no other.

By equipping our congregants to see the inner spiritual essence of technology, we are also equipping them to give themselves more fully to the Lord Jesus Christ.

Bibliography

Barrat, James. *Our Final Invention: Artificial Intelligence and the End of the Human Era.* New York: St. Martin's, 2013.
Deneen, Patrick. *Why Liberalism Failed.* New Haven: Yale University Press, 2019.
Ellul, Jacques. *Presence in the Modern World.* Eugene: Wipf and Stock, 2016.
———. *The Technological Society.* Toronto: Alfred Knopf, 1964.
Fukuyama, Francis. *The Origins of Political Order: From Prehuman Times to the French Revolution.* New York: Farrar, Straus and Giroux, 2011.
Gay, Craig M. *Modern Technology and the Human Future: A Christian Appraisal.* Downers Grove: InterVarsity, 2018.
Grayling, A.C. *Democracy and Its Crisis.* London: Oneworld, 2017.
Greenman, Jeffrey, Read Mercer Schuchardt, and Noah J. Toly. *Understanding Jacques Ellul.* Eugene, OR: Cascade, 2012.
Harari, Yuval Noah. *Homo Deus: A Brief History of Tomorrow.* New York: HarperCollins, 2018.
Hobson, George. *The Episcopal Church, Homosexuality, and the Context of Technology.* Eugene: Pickwick, 2013.

Jacobs, Alan. *The Year of Our Lord, 1943: Christian Humanism in an Age of Crisis.* Oxford: Oxford University Press, 2017.

Lawrence, Joel D. "After Sapiens: Preparing the Church for the Evolutionary Future of Humanity." *Bulletin of Ecclesial Theology* 6.2 (2019) 13–24.

Madison, James, Alexander Hamilton, and John Jay. *The Federalist Papers.* London: Penguin, 1987.

Mishra, Pankaj. *Age of Anger: A History of the Present.* London: Picador, 2018.

Pagden, Anthony. *The Enlightenment: And Why It Still Matters.* New York: Random House, 2013.

Siedentop, Larry. *Inventing the Individual: The Origins of Western Liberalism.* London: Allen Lane, 2017.

Topol, Eric. *Deep Medicine: How Artificial Intelligence Can Make Healthcare Human Again.* New York: Basic, 2019.

2

The Path More Traveled

The Place of the (Missing) Church in Christian Engagement of Technology

DANIEL J. BRENDSEL

> She had chosen to attend, at first from politeness but later because this daily ritual, the beautiful, half-forgotten cadences, seducing her into belief, gave a welcome shape to the day.
>
> —P. D. JAMES, *Devices and Desires*[1]

1. Lacuna Matata: Where Is the Church?

IN THE WIDE, WILD, and unwieldy world which is contemporary Christian discourse on the question of technology, one can find all manner of treatments: from how-to manuals for wise "use" of technology, to dense philosophical treatments of new challenges in medical ethics; from lightly disguised dirges for the technological demise of society, to brave explorations of the inevitability of transhuman and post-human developments. One can find just about everything one might desire in the ongoing debate. *Just about* everything. For one searches largely in vain for substantive treatments of the place of the church of Christ in all of this, of the distinct and constructive role that the church *as* church might play in forming a Christian vision of technology and a corresponding wise practice.[2] By my

---

1. James, *Devices and Desires*, 398.
2. Thanks are owed to Dan Treier, who in personal communication several years

lights, this is a regrettable lacuna. This essay can offer only the most modest of beginnings toward filling it.

1.1. Mapping the Terrain

We can start by mapping the terrain of contemporary Christian treatments of technology. Much literature focuses on how an individual or society "uses" technology. Such approaches may be called instrumentalist.[3] Here, technology (from the Greek *technē*, "craft," "method of making") is the stuff we make. A technology is "just a tool." It is hammers, DVD players, bulldozers, bubble chambers, smartphones. Often finer distinctions are drawn: "tools" on one side (e.g., hammers) are distinguished from "technology" or devices on the other (e.g., smartphones, pacemakers, birth control pills, the internet, anything else that glows or wows). However one identifies what counts as technology, on the instrumentalist approach it is still stuff we manipulate. So, we ask after "responsible" making and using. How might we make a well-crafted bulldozer? What does proper use of a smartphone look like? What is "the proper place for technology in our particular family"?[4] What Christian principles and ends guide good making and using of technology? How can we control technology rather than allowing it to control us? This literature mainly addresses *individual* decisions. If the church has any role to play in such treatments, it is not considered at length, nor does the church appear as a constructive shaper of a Christian vision of technology. Rather, it appears as a discerning institutional "user," asking, "What are 'best practices' in providing biblical instruction on websites, or in using audiovisual resources for corporate worship or promotions?"

Differently, Nicholas Carr made waves about a decade ago by asking, "Is Google making us stupid?" and, "What is the internet doing to our brains?"[5] This comes at things from the angle not of instrumental use of technology, but of how technological realities impact us. Various Christian

---

ago first planted the seed about the (missing) church that has grown into this paper. He has published similar observations in Treier, "Modernity's Machine," 91–111, at 91.

3. Brian Brock distinguishes *instrumentalist* from *humanist* accounts; in the latter, technology goes awry when we are unclear about proper ends (Brock, *Christian Ethics*, 31–33). As I see things, humanist identification of proper ends typically serves the discerning *use* of technological means to achieve those ends. Thus, I conflate these two categories under a single instrumentalist banner. Generally, neo-Calvinistic approaches may be understood in finally instrumentalist terms (e.g., Monsma, *Responsible Technology*).

4. Crouch, *Tech-Wise Family*, 19. Crouch is one who differentiates "tools" from "technologies/devices" (see *Tech-Wise Family*, 47–51).

5. Carr, "Is Google Making Us Stupid?," 56–63; Carr, *Shallows*.

thinkers have followed Carr in commenting on the effects of digital technologies and social media on personal consciousness, reading habits, and family and social life.[6] Ecclesiological scrutiny appears more often in this mode of reflection, with the church examined as something of a passive sufferer of technological use and dispositions. Marshall McLuhan was a leading prophet in this direction, arguing that late-modern media and technology has refashioned the church and its experience of authority.[7] Others have provided helpful clarifications and extensions of McLuhan's approach.[8] But in these writings, again, the church *as* church offers little by way of a constructive contribution to a Christian vision of technology.

Sometimes the church may lurk behind generic references to "community." In *Shaping a Digital World: Faith, Culture and Computer Technology*, Derek Schuurman calls "individuals, together with the wider Christian community" to develop a "responsible computer technology." Perhaps the church is included in "the wider Christian community," but Schuurman seems mainly to mean the collective force and resources of Christians banded together in any way.[9] Other Christian writers call for practices of resistance to the harshest effects of technological culture for individuals or "intentional communities" to take up. The church may be one of the communities in view, but (1) it is rarely named expressly, and more importantly, (2) its importance seems to be as one of a number of possible communities.[10] Again, the church hardly has a distinct and constructive role to play *as* church. In fact, there seems, at times, to be a principled *avoidance* of referring to the church in favor of more generic "religious communities." Albert Borgmann is worth lingering with for a while as an interesting case in point of lauding Christian "community" while being apparently reticent to focalize the church per se. I believe Borgmann gets us a good deal closer to addressing the church's role in shaping a Christian vision of technology, though he pulls up short, which can be instructive for us.

---

6. See, e.g., Challies, *Next Story*; Reinke, *12 Ways*, 84–85.

7. For a collection of essays introducing these considerations, see McLuhan, *Medium and the Light*.

8. E.g., Hipps, *Hidden Power*.

9. Schuurman, *Shaping a Digital World*, 26–27. See similarly Campbell and Garner, *Networked Theology*, 97–114.

10. See, e.g., Crouch, *Tech-Wise Family*; cf. also Boers, *Living into Focus*, seeking to popularize Albert Borgmann (on Borgmann, see below).

1.2. Albert Borgmann as Trailhead

Of particular significance are Borgmann's notions of "focal things" and "focal practices."[11] A focal thing is something sturdy, commanding attention; and, like a lens, a focal thing sharpens our vision. A focal thing illumines reality around it. One looks at a dollop of Cool Whip, and what does one see? Hydrogenated coconut, xanthum gum, sodium caseinate, polysorbate 60.[12] Most of us have no idea what all that is—which is to say, when we look at Cool Whip, we cannot "see through" it to anything else; we see only the Cool Whip. Not so with homemade whipped cream. Many are able to "see through" a dollop of whipped cream to the cows who donated milk. Or we "see through" it to the mother who can whip up such wonders and whose love lets us lick clean the whisk when she is done. Cool Whip is an "opaque article," but whipped cream is a focal thing. A focal thing commands attention in such a way that it "gathers the relations of its context and radiates into its surroundings and informs them."[13] And a focal practice, then, is "the decided, regular, and normally *communal* devotion to a focal thing."[14] It is the meal at which the family gathers to celebrate with the whipped-cream-topped pie, to feast on it together, to give thanks for the maker of the cream and other goodnesses, to contribute in all sorts of other ways—large and small—to bringing the meal about.

For our purposes, Borgmann is important in three respects. First, he recognizes that what we have to deal with is a *culture* of technology. The chief challenge of technology is not devices per se (their manufacture, use, formative power), but worldview and orientation, about which we will have more to say below. Here it suffices to note that technological worldview is given form as, rendered plausible through, and further advanced by way of a material culture. A material culture is never the sum of individual neutral artifacts. George Grant gives an example: to think of a computer as a neutral tool, which users determine the meaning of through intentional use, is to turn a blind eye to the societies and corporations, the political and economic matrices, and the material structures and infrastructure without which no computer-building takes place.[15] If our reflection on tools/devices

---

11. Borgmann, *Technology and the Character of Contemporary Life*, 196–210; Borgmann, *Power Failure*, 22.

12. Borgmann, *Power Failure*, 15–17. See also 86–87 on the challenge of living in a world of opaque surfaces.

13. Borgmann, *Technology and the Character of Contemporary Life*, 197.

14. Borgmann, *Power Failure*, 22; emphasis added.

15. Grant, *Technology and Justice*, 19–32; cf. Borgmann, *Power Failure*, 82; Brock, *Christian Ethics*, 20.

only addresses our "making" and "using" of them, our reflection starts too late (and ends too early).[16] In Brian Brock's words, "The problem of conceiving technology as neutral is that the true magnitude of the decision to build or use individual technologies like computers is hidden."[17] Responsible understanding of our technological moment must attend to technological orientation *and* material culture. Borgmann's invitation to focal things and practices is important because it has this larger cultural challenge of technology squarely in view: "Focal things and practices are the crucial counterforces to technology understood as a form of culture."[18]

When Borgmann speaks of *counterforces*, he is liable to being misunderstood. So we must clarify, second, that Borgmann neither rejects the culture of technology entirely, nor encourages retreat into "pretechnological enclaves."[19] Rather, he promotes focal things and practices to strengthen us to resist the deforming powers of our technological age: "The moral limitation and desiccation of technology do not come fully into view until they are seen against the vitality and humor of a focal practice."[20] Focal things and practices thus play a hermeneutical role for those attending to them. But what is more, as forms of inevitably "patterned and social commitment,"[21] focal practices also shape and cultivate. Borgmann rightly identifies a "mistaken assumption that the shaping of our lives can be left to a series of individual decisions."[22] So he champions focal things and practices, as Brent Waters explains, because they "embody a formative tradition against which the character and virtues of its adherents are conformed."[23] Borgmann fights fire with fire. Or to use a better, less conflict-oriented description: Borgmann *engages* technological culture with a differing material culture and tradition.

Third, Borgmann clearly views Christian faithfulness in a technological age as inseparable from rootedness in an ordered community, a formative tradition, a contrast culture. He describes it in several places as a "culture of the word" and a "culture of the table." Bread and wine appear often in his writing as examples of focal things and icons of his larger proposal. He encourages Christians to pursue embodied celebratory gatherings. But he

---

16. "Unintended consequences" of technological developments are also crucial facets of the "meaning" of technology and media. For a fascinating account of unintended consequences, see Cowan, *More Work for Mother*.
17. Brock, *Christian Ethics*, 92, summarizing Grant.
18. Borgmann, *Power Failure*, 22.
19. See Borgmann, *Technology and the Character of Contemporary Life*, 200.
20. Borgmann, *Power Failure*, 23.
21. Borgmann, *Technology and the Character of Contemporary Life*, 208.
22. Borgmann, *Technology and the Character of Contemporary Life*, 206.
23. Waters, *From Human to Posthuman*, 147.

avoids naming the Christian culture of the word and table as the church. In one place, he addresses the focal practice of gathering for Lord's Day worship, but it is to call out the *insufficiency* of this practice alone for shaping Christian sensibilities in our technological age.[24] He seems hesitant to call the Eucharist and the church, as such, central and indispensable.

Borgmann takes us a long way toward understanding the cultivation of Christian faithfulness and wisdom in a technological age. But in the end, he leaves us, as does most of the literature on the matter, with what we might call a church-less Christian practice, or a Christian engagement with the technological age in which the church is only a hint, an intimation, an optional aid for those seeking additional resources or encouragement. This is both ironic and unfortunate. For Borgmann himself claims that "it is but a short step from the culture of the word to the Word of God and from the culture of the table to the Breaking of Bread."[25]

In the final paragraphs of *From Human to Posthuman*, Brent Waters takes that "short step," singling out the Eucharist as a "focal thing and practice to form and sustain a counter theological discourse to that offered by posthuman discourse."[26] I am persuaded that we must follow him. Brian Brock has made a similar point in his remarkable *Christian Ethics in a Technological Age*: "One social space," Brock observes, "is divinely designated as a place for orienting us for life in all other places." It is the place of the church gathered for and enacting worship.[27] Waters has planted a seed, and Brock has offered a very important preliminary treatment. But there is much more work to be done. For the church is not just a maker and user of technological artifacts. It is not just a passive sufferer of the impacts of technological society. The church is not just one among many voluntary communities, which may be a supplier or encourager of individuals. Rather, the church *as church*—the visible, gathered body of Christ enacting worship in word and sacrament—has a central, active, and constructive role to play in the cultivation of wisdom for, and redemptive life in, our technological age.

---

24. Borgmann, *Power Failure*, 107–8.
25. Borgmann, *Power Failure*, 125.
26. Waters, *From Human to Posthuman*, 149.
27. Brock, *Christian Ethics*, 239; see also 291, 299. While I am sympathetic with Brock's reticence to speak of an "ethic" springing from "the church," favoring instead an "ethic springing from worship" (see *Christian Ethics*, 252; here Brock is citing Bernd Wannenwetsch), I will continue to highlight the *church* as a crucial birthing place of Christian ethics in our present cultural moment, if for no other reason than that there is warrant for such discourse in the discourse of Scripture. Nevertheless, when I refer to "the church," I mean especially the church *as revealed and engaged in (and sent out from) the event of covenantal worship in the power of the Spirit*.

2. The Path More Traveled: The Church at Worship

To provide an image of what I am suggesting, I will steal from Wendell Berry. In a 1969 essay, entitled "A Native Hill," Berry compares and contrasts a forest path and a paved road. "The difference between a path and a road," says Berry, "is not only the obvious one."

> A path is little more than a habit that comes with knowledge of a place. It is a sort of ritual of familiarity. As a form, it is a form of contact with the known landscape. It is not destructive. It is the perfect adaptation, through experience and familiarity, of movement to place; it obeys the natural contours; such obstacles as it meets it goes around. A road, on the other hand, even the most primitive road, embodies a resistance against the landscape. Its reason is not simply the necessity for movement, but haste. Its wish is to *avoid* contact with the landscape . . . its tendency is to translate place into space in order to traverse it with the least effort. It is destructive, seeking to remove or destroy all obstacles in its way.[28]

According to Matthew Dickerson, Berry contrasts worldviews.[29] The road symbolizes what Dickerson calls a "technological mindset."[30] The word "technology" is not only from *technē*, and thus a simple reference to the stuff of our making. Rather, as George Grant observes, "technology" unites *technē* and *logos*, both craft and reason. Technology is the "co-penetration of knowing and making."[31] To be technological is to know all things as problems to overcome by making—or as what Heidegger called "standing reserve"—neutral raw material at our beck and call to be wielded and controlled in our agendas of making.[32] To be technological is less having tools to make roads and having many roads, and more a default knowing of the trees and streams between points A and B as "standing reserve" or obstacles. By contrast, the path illustrates a humble orientation, a receptivity and responsiveness to given reality.

Dickerson's treatment of the above-quoted passage from Berry is helpful, but in choosing the word *mindset*, he fails to take paths and roads seriously enough. What if we thought of paths and roads not as thin symbols for mindsets, but *as physical forms and instances of material culture*? When

---

28. Berry, "Native Hill," 611–12.
29. Dickerson, "Wendell Berry."
30. Dickerson, "Wendell Berry."
31. Grant, *Technology and Justice*, 12.
32. For a trenchant treatment of Heidegger, see Brock, *Christian Ethics*, 31–65.

we understand Berry to be referring not to mere illustrations of thought patterns but irreducibly to dirt and gravel and asphalt, some important avenues open up to us.[33] For material paths and roads are never simply neutral artifacts but are always meaning-full. And their meaning is never wholly determined by the intentions of their makers/users. Rather, their meaning is bound up in a large and often unwieldy historical-cultural matrix.[34] Paths and roads are always parts of a material culture, embodiments of cultural sensibilities, reinforcers of cultural commitments. On the flip side, a culture is never just material things, but the tradition and system of commitments, interdictions, and authority which give rise to such things, and which material artifacts and practices extend and strengthen. A worldview and its embodiment are inseparable. So, it will do little good to present the road as only a cipher for a worldview without also realizing the cultivating power of the material road. The same is true of the path. To traverse on and in and with and along a path is to be cultivated in an *ethos*.

When we ask where the church might be in the contrast of path and road, I suggest that it is not primarily as a maker or user of a path or a road, and not as a thinker whose thought life is *represented* by a path or a road, but the church (specifically, the church engaged in worship) is to *be* a path—an instance of material culture—that is in important ways distinguishable from the road, which instantiates the material culture of technological society. In fact, it is quite fitting to speak of the church gathered for and enacting worship in word and sacrament as itself a path-like instance of a material culture, and this for at least two reasons.

The first has to do with the dynamics of path-formation. Scott Aniol invites us to "imagine a dense forest separating two cities."

> In order to engage in commerce between these cities, merchants must pass through the forest. For the earliest of these merchants, this was a very difficult task . . . Eventually, though, over time and with experience, the merchants discovered the safest, quickest route through the forest. Once they did, they began to carefully mark the path so that they would remember the best way to go . . . Their regular trips along that same route began to form a much more visible path to the degree that years later merchants hardly pay attention; they doze peacefully as their

---

33. In fact, Berry himself invites us to read his images in this way. See Berry, "Men and Women," 9, commenting on the significance of "common ground."

34. As Peter Galison demonstrates in his magisterial study *Image and Logic*, machines are misrepresented on the one hand as neutral objects, and on the other hand as simply "reified theories"; rather, they are only rightly understood as "*sited* instruments" within and part of a complex material culture (quotations at 52).

horses casually follow the heavily trod road. Here now is a well-worn path cut through the wood... This path may seem mundane, but in reality, it is embedded with values such as desire for safety, protection from the dangers of the forest, and conviction that this is the quickest way through. The snoozing merchants do not give thought to these values any longer, but the values are there nonetheless, and whether they know it or not, their journey has been shaped by those values. Those values are, as it were, worn into the shape of the path itself.[35]

A path *just is* cultural sensibilities and commitments etched into the dirt of the earth. To walk it is to submit to being shaped by a culture and formative tradition and already to begin being so shaped. To walk it is to be discipled by the *long* line of wayfarers who have gone before us contributing to its formation. Taking account of Chesterton's democracy of the dead, despite the congestion of contemporary highways, the path may prove to be the way more traveled by. Let us think of the church's gathered practices and order of worship as a well-traveled path that disciples us in Christian wisdom and cultural sensibility, crucial for analyzing the dynamics—the problems and possibilities—of technological culture.

This leads to a second reason why the path is a fitting metaphor for the Lord's Day assembly. As Berry's reflections attest, the formation of a path typically occurs with submissiveness and responsiveness to "given" reality. No forest path is a straight and uniform-in-width line, but here broadens out with an opening in the trees, there goes around a boulder, then meanders with a creek for some distance. Of course, forming a path requires some alteration of the terrain. Patches of grass will be worn and pressed down; fallen brush or low-hanging limbs are cut and cleared away. Paths exist as a form of working-in-concert with a given reality. But importantly, it is working *in concert*, working that is at the same time irreducibly *responsive*. Paths are training in the healthy receiving of gifts.

What happens when the church gathers for worship? For one thing, it *is* gathered. In properly theological terms, the church does not gather itself. It is *God* who gathers the church in covenant assembly, forming the church by his creative word in the call to worship, to which we respond with songs of praise. God declares his law, to which we respond with contrition in the confession of sin. God comforts us in the absolution, proclaiming forgiveness as our confession is barely off our lips, to which we respond with renewed joy. At its best, the worship of the church is a rhythm of God graciously, lovingly initiating, and the church, by the power of the Spirit,

---

35. Aniol, "Practice Makes Perfect," 99–100.

humbly, gladly, gratefully replying to the word of Christ. The church gathered in worship is confronted with a word it did not speak from a God it did not make, a God who cannot be co-opted as an instrument for our agendas. The church at worship has only to receive and respond. This is a second reason why it is fitting to identify the event of liturgical worship as a path-like instance of the church's material culture. Worship at its best involves the church traversing through the service with the grace and wisdom of responsiveness to given reality.

3. The View from the Path: Ecclesial-Liturgical Formation in a Technological Age

I submit that a necessary stage in the formation of a Christian vision and practice of technology is traveling the path which is the liturgical assembly—both theoretically by allowing the elements and ordering of Christian liturgy to order our deliberations on technology[36] and practically by enacting corporate worship Sunday after Sunday as the church of God. I will suggest three reasons why this is so. To continue our path and road metaphor, there are three things that we can "see" with respect to technology from a vantage point on, along, and at the end of the path which is the church at worship.

3.1. Contrast

The first thing that we can "see" more clearly from the path of the church at worship is the road "over yonder," which is technological culture. We fail to notice technological orientation precisely for its pervasiveness. The advantage of the formative tradition and material culture entailed in the church's liturgical practice is that it affords us opportunity to gain critical distance. The church at worship is something of a contrast culture that provides us with greater analytical purchase on the shape and patterns and logic of the wider cultures and orientations in which we all are (otherwise obliviously) embedded.[37]

The church's worship-as-contrast culture is particularly important vis-à-vis technological culture. Some may wonder if my title, "The Path More Traveled," is an ironic allusion to Robert Frost's famous poem. It is indeed, but the allusion is doubly ironic. Contrary to popular assumptions,

---

36. My inspiration here is Hauerwas, "Liturgical Shape," 153–68.

37. See further Brendsel, "Tale of Two Calendars," 15–42, esp. 30–33; also Gay, *Modern Technology*, 11–13.

the title of Frost's poem is not "The Road Less Traveled," but "The Road Not Taken." In earlier stanzas, as David Orr notes, we read that the two roads "equally lay / In leaves," and that "the passing there / Had worn them really about the same." In the final stanza, the speaker *frames* himself as a brave trailblazer whose decision to take the road "less traveled by" is what "made all the difference." But the title of the poem, "The Road *Not* Taken," is nearer the mark. Could it be, then, that "the poem isn't a salute to can-do individualism," but "a commentary on the self-deception we practice when constructing the story of our own lives"?[38]

However one reads Frost's poem, "the self-deception we practice when constructing the story of our own lives" is an apt description of modern technological society. To view all of life as a matter of self-construction, of using, of strategizing, is self-deception, if only because reality is *much more* than making. But technological culture treats all things in terms of technique and method. The technological mindset encounters, wherever it turns, obstacles to overcome or raw material to functionally ignore for now (but which may prove "useful" later on). Our agendas and techniques for making are determinative of our action and being in the world. The matter is stated clearly by Oliver O'Donovan in a slim volume on reproductive techniques.

> What marks this culture out most importantly, is not anything that it does, but what it thinks. It is not "technological" because its instruments of making are extraordinarily sophisticated (though that is evidently the case), but because it thinks of everything it does as a form of instrumental making. Politics (which should surely be the most non-instrumental of activities) is talked of as "making a better world"; love is "building a successful relationship." There is no place for simply *doing*. The fate of a society which sees, wherever it looks, nothing but the products of human will, is that it fails, when it does see some aspect of human activity which is not a matter of construction, to recognize the significance of what it sees and to think about it appropriately.[39]

I believe that O'Donovan is on target in his articulation of the present cultural moment. But the church at worship is a path of contrast, a focal practice that exposes our orientations toward technique and making, a place that trains us in *receiving* and *doing* and *responsiveness*. At its best, the church at

---

38. Orr, *Road Not Taken*, 9. Orr suggests that the "meaning" of the poem may be more ambiguous still.

39. O'Donovan, *Begotten or Made*, 2–3.

worship is a pattern of *receiving* the gifts of God's initiating grace, a culture of *doing* in remembrance, a practice and place the inner logic of which is *receptivity* to the wisdom of our forebears and especially to the God who is never an instrument for our wielding. On the path of the church at worship, we can see better the deformities taking place along "the road over yonder" and perhaps, by the Spirit's power, begin to be formed otherwise.

3.2. Construction

But the church is not *only* a contrast culture. The church at worship is also, more basically, a revelation of what ordered life as God's created world could be, an invitation to aim in hope toward what it will be, a beginning on that way. Walking the path of the church at worship is not only contrastive to other cultures, but also and especially constructive as we "see" the glorious end of the path—namely, eucharistic celebration.

Reformed liturgical theologian J.J. von Allmen has called the liturgical enactment "the epiphany of the church."[40] It is where our true identity as the covenant people of God in Christ is revealed and renewed with covenantal word and signs. This explains, in part, why I focalize worship in word and sacrament in my proposal about the constructive role of the church in forming a Christian vision of technology. Are there not many other engagements, "locations," and aspects about being the church of Christ that contribute to our maturation to live wisely in our technological age? There are. But I am persuaded that other contributions *originate* biblically, theologically, and historically in the liturgical assembly. Ecclesiology and liturgy are bound together. Indeed, the New Testament word *ekklēsia*, typically translated as "church," arguably has roots in the Old Testament concept of the *qahal* of Yahweh, the solemn assembly, the gathering of Israel to meet with their covenant Lord. In that assembly, Israel's identity and status as God's covenant people was marked out and confirmed, as at Sinai and the dedication of the Temple and the reforms of Hezekiah.[41] In this light, we can agree with Allmen in identifying "church," *ekklēsia*, as "not in the first place, or merely, a

---

40. Allmen, *Worship*, 42–56; cf. Schmemann, *Introduction to Liturgical Theology*, 12.

41. See להק in, e.g., Deut 4:10; 1 Kgs 8:14; 2 Chr 29:28, and note the LXX's use of ἐκκλησία/ἐκκλησιάζω in these passages. For discussion, see K.L. Schmidt, "καλέω, κλῆσις, κτλ," *TDNT* 3:487–536, esp. 527–31; cf. J. Roloff, "ἐκκλησία, ας, ἡ," *EDNT* 1:410–15, at 411–12, who thinks the roots (at least of *ekklēsia theou*) are more likely in apocalyptic Judaism's notion of the eschatological *qahal ' el*.

sociological or juridical term, but very definitely a liturgical term."[42] It is in worship that ecclesiology comes into its own.

By "worship," I do not mean only the Godward feelings and thoughts of an individual. And by saying that worship "reveals" the church's identity, I do not mean that the *idea* of our identity as God's church is taught to us through one means (the worship service) among many. Rather, I mean that in gathering for Lord's Day covenant-renewal-worship, the church *enacts* its identity. It has its covenant status confirmed through covenant ceremony. It covenantally *becomes* the people of God, in much the same way that a man and a woman publicly *become* husband and wife not by thinking about the union or being taught about the union, but by enacting the covenantal ceremony called a wedding. Importantly, when the church enacts its covenantal identity, this always occurs *through a set time* and *in a particular place of gathering*. This means that time and place are irreducibly part of how we know ourselves in relation to God and how we receive our identity from him. More than that, what we do in that time and place necessarily involves water and bread and wine, at least. So, in Alexander Schmemann's provocative words, "We *need* water and oil, bread and wine in order to be in communion with God and to know Him. Yet conversely . . . it is this communion with God by means of 'matter' that reveals the true meaning of 'matter,' i.e., of the world itself." Worship proves to be not only the epiphany of the church, but also "the epiphany of the world"[43]—the world of time and place and bodies and light and water and bread and wine.

We can go still further. What are bread and wine? They are not the kinds of things one finds on a walk through the wilderness. One does not pluck a loaf of bread from a tree or scoop a handful of wine from a stream. If we would eat bread together at the Lord's table,[44] there must have already taken place a gathering and a crushing of grain, as well as a mixing, a kneading, a baking, a slicing, a setting down on the table. There must have already occurred a long history of culinary science and discovery and apprenticing, as well as the development of agricultural know-how and skill in tilling and sowing, in threshing, in understanding the differences between crops. Additionally, there must have been countless scientific and manufacturing discoveries leading to the construction of useful equipment (e.g., plows, ovens, tables). If we would break bread at the Eucharist, then we must rely on agricultural realities, culinary understandings, social and economic arrangements, apprenticing, and

---

42. Allmen, *Worship*, 43.

43. Schmemann, *For the Life of the World*, 121.

44. The following passage leans heavily on Kass, *Hungry Soul*, 121–22; and Leithart, "Way Things Really Ought to Be," 159–76, who applies Kass's reflections to the Eucharist.

the passing on of traditional knowledge. Bread is the result of much and great cultural and *technological* labor, generations and generations of it. The same points must also be made about wine.

Bread and wine are the "stuff" of cultural and technological labor, which means that the "stuff" of cultural and technological labor is brought into the sanctuary and appears in its true place at the end of the liturgy. Worship is the epiphany of the world, including the cultural and technological development of it. The liturgical event climaxing in the covenant meal reveals, in Peter Leithart's words, that "the kingdom does not involve a cancellation of this-worldly concerns; it is not a wholly other world but rather *this* world transformed and transfigured."[45] Technological developments—even those arising from the line of Cain, as it were—are not off-limits. But this is not because they are "neutral," able to be used for good or bad ends entirely determined by individual "users." Rather, it is because technological developments and cultural artifacts and practices "fit" into a larger whole. Or they *may*, with discernment, be found to "fit" in the drama of God's mission. The church at worship is an enactment revealing the larger shape and logic of that drama,[46] and especially its proper end: a many-colored kingdom of eucharistic renewal and rejoicing. Do our technological pursuits point us toward that end? Or do they point us to other ends, or to means masquerading as ends (e.g., getting the word out, grabbing attention, maximizing conveniences, educating, increasing efficiency, connecting with others "like us," stirring up excitement, fundraising)? Realizing the end of the path ought to frame, guide, and hold accountable all our necessary endeavors in making and in developing the world, to which we are sent on mission from the sanctuary.[47]

At its best, the church at worship is the beginning and foretaste of true society, true culture, standing as an invitation to a better way for us and all nations of the world. At its best, the church at worship is not a pre-technological enclave, but a molding and directing of technological labor toward its proper eucharistic ends.

---

45. Leithart, "Way Things Really Ought to Be," 166; cf. Brock, *Christian Ethics*, 203–4, 243.

46. Here I meld two categories from Allmen: worship as "the recapitulation of the history of salvation," and as "the end and future of the world" (see *Worship*, 21–41, 57–79).

47. See Brock, *Christian Ethics*, 150, 229.

3.3. Crisis

"At its best"—I have used that little qualifier consistently, and needfully so. For, of course, the church at worship is often *not* at its best. There is likely a widespread need for liturgical reformation. The visible, on-the-ground church is *never* at its best. There is an ever-present need in this age for repentance. At the end of the path of the church at worship, we eat and drink "until the Lord comes." His return has not yet happened, which means our lives are still plagued by sin and disorder. Not only "the world," but also the church is infected by the idolatrous deformations characteristic of technological culture.

It is no use ignoring this or trying to establish "pure" places that the defiling power of "the world" does not touch. What other alternative is there? Let us think liturgically—that is, let us engage in the full movement of the path. We have noted that the church at worship offers a foretaste of the incorporation of all things, including our technological labors, into the festal praise of God. But that foretaste comes at the *end* of the path, only arrived at by walking the way that precedes it. Importantly, what we must pass *through* to get there is confession and absolution.[48] The renewal of all things into eucharistic joy only comes about through crisis, through fire, through death and resurrection. We are made new through the crisis which is confession of sins and baptism into the glorious grace of God's redeeming love. Our cultural and technological labors can and must be brought with us along that path. For they, too, require not just refurbishing or refilling or rebranding, but redemption. This means that a properly Christian vision of technology does not simply treat the stuff of technological culture as though it is empty "form" to be loaded as is with purportedly Christian "meaning" and "content." Rather, it all must go with us and Christ "through death and resurrection."[49] This happens experientially in the liturgical acts of confession and absolution.

So here is my modest practical proposal: if we would become wise, redemptive agents in our challenging technological society, we must become well-practiced in naming in corporate confession of sin, and, in lamentation, our various technological disorders and sins. The point is not judgmentalism or self-pity, but firm faith in God's promise that salvation *from*

---

48. Though he does not expand on it, I take Waters's choice of preposition to be of utmost importance: "*Through* the requisite practices of confession, repentance and amendment of life, the Lord's Table becomes the centerpiece of celebrative community" (*From Human to Posthuman*, 149; emphasis added). Waters's failure to include *God's word of forgiveness* is unfortunate (see below).

49. See further Schmemann, *For the Life of the World*, 53–55, 88–91.

our technological selves meets us where we are—namely, *in* our technological selves. I close with one example of something the church might need to confess and repent of; something which is, at least, aided by the technological patterns of our lives. It has to do with attention.

Once upon time, I would call people on strange objects called landline telephones. If I wanted to call my friend John, I would pick up the receiver, depress the right combination of physical nodules, then wait to the sound of ringing on the other end. What happened next? Abbie, John's sister, would answer. Or maybe Bill or Kathy, John's parents. Sometimes David, John's brother. And horror of horrors, I would have to talk to, to pay conscious attention to, someone I had not intended to pay attention to. That, I am convinced, played no small part in my developing relationships with them, in my growing to care for them as a kind of second family. The technological form of my life, as it were, required that I attend not only to my friend, but to the others around him. Thankfully, we have come to a point of technological development where I no longer have to expose myself to such traumas.

Now if I want to communicate with friends, I can rest assured that I will only ever have to interact with them, because their smartphones are directly on their person. Now if I want to get "the news," I can ensure that it will only come from a source that will promote my takes on things because of easy access to a smorgasbord of media outlets. Now if I want to "find a new church," I need only perform a Google search of the top three qualities *I* value most to find one that checks the boxes, circumventing many hard but important questions of unity-in-diversity as a local congregation.[50] Or if we are a church seeking "the right kind of churchgoer," we can publish what "we stand for" with images and links to "resources" and "vision" and "mission" statements on our website in order to "reach" the right market share—a market share likely to be people of a certain socioeconomic status, who can afford access to internet-connected devices and reliable means of transportation to get to our church.[51] It is increasingly easy to pay attention only or chiefly to the people we know, to people we have chosen ahead of time, to people we like, to people who are like us. Our technological rituals and material culture have not forced us to live in this way. But they have rendered such a life more plausible and convenient. And they have not called any of these curved-in patterns to account.

One of the most damning criticisms I have received in my pastoral ministry was from a gentleman who said that those in leadership at my

---

50. Cf. Brock, *Christian Ethics*, 282–83, on "lifestyle enclaves."

51. For a brief consideration of the latter, see Kallenberg, *God and Gadgets*, 17–20; for the former, see Campbell and Garner, *Networked Theology*, 128–29.

church were well-practiced in ignoring people. As I reflected on the matter, the Spirit moved in my heart in such a way that I had to agree with him. But I am persuaded that we are not peculiar in this. Large swaths of the church are well-practiced in ignoring people—or, to say it differently, well-practiced in paying attention to the people of our choosing instead of people normally on the margins of our attentiveness. We are well-*practiced* at this. We are cultivated in it. It is less a matter of making, moment by moment, conscious decisions to ignore our closest neighbors. It is more a systemic curving of all things inward to our personal desires and agendas, a curating of our days to our individual tastes and natural proclivities in attentiveness.[52] Technological culture, with its tools and practices, sustains oblivion to neighbor and immunity to surprise.

So, what is a faithful response for the church of God? I do not believe it is forswearing the use of smartphones and shutting down church websites. In many ways, that is far too easy, making it seem as if the problem were somehow only external to us.[53] Rather, the way forward is to walk the path of the church at worship. Particularly, we must identify and name our technological disorders and idolatries in corporate confession of sin and lamentation. We might confess, guided by Psalm 15's description of the one who may dwell on God's holy hill,

> Holy Lord, have mercy on us.
> We have done evil to our neighbors,
> not only intentionally and maliciously,
> but also by ignoring them
> and building up technological walls that contribute to our oblivion.

Or, adapting a prayer from the *Worship Sourcebook*, we might lament,

> Lord, we are afraid of people who are different from us:
> those more powerful than us, those poorer than us,
> those not of our color or tradition, those younger or older than us.
> How do we talk with these people, O God?
> How do we make peace with them?
> We are ill-practiced at this.
> In fact, we have practiced just the opposite,

---

52. That is to say, the church by method may unwittingly subvert stated confession (see Treier, "Modernity's Machine," 106; Brock, *Christian Ethics*, 208).

53. We need, instead, to do the hard work of deconstructing and demythologizing the promises and narratives of technological society so that we might rightly name what is sin, idolatry, and disorder (cf. Brock, *Christian Ethics*, 225, 242, 385).

> choosing, with phone and car and media,
> only to attend to people like ourselves.[54]

In more ways than one, we have need to plead God's mercy concerning our devices and desires. Yet we do so in hope, trusting the word of the gospel that Christ died and rose again for sinners, for those enmeshed in idolatrous culture, for us. And he did so in order to make us and all things new. Rising from confession of sin, we hear the absolution marking today as the day of salvation. And if today is the day of salvation, then now by the Spirit's power new creational possibilities are open to us, even with the very devices of our prior deformation: "If anyone is in Christ, then new creation has come!"[55] None of us can predict just how, by the Spirit's leading, that will play out in redeemed cultural and technological lives.[56] But we can be confident that the life that walks the path of confession and forgiveness and finds itself on the other side will be *new* life.

The matter of (in)attentiveness is just one example among many of technological disorder and sin that we might confess to the Lord in the hope of forgiveness and renewal. And what more shall I say? For time would fail me to tell of those who sought to conquer geographic limitation as if it were evil, catered to privately curated "entertainment experiences" in fashioning liturgical gatherings, wielded the "gospel" as if it were simply a tool for improving "quality of life" or a way of distinguishing "us" from other sectors of the religious marketplace. Women received back their dead by maintaining Facebook shrines to the deceased. Some submitted to what can only be called bodily torture, refusing to accept the givenness of their bodily makeup in the hopes of attaining by "medical" technique a better, more beautiful life. Others suffered no exposure to different opinions. They were protected by technological walls, sawn off from anyone unlike themselves. They went about in practices and postures and pursuits and paradigms of which the world *was* worthy. But God has provided something better for us. There is a path that helps us discover it. It is the church gathered into the presence of its covenant-making God, confessing its sins, receiving forgiveness in Christ, and finding itself ultimately at a banquet of joy.

---

54. Steenwyk and Witvliet, *Worship*, 233 (§4.5.29).

55. This is the best way to translate 2 Cor 5:17, which has no express verb in the protasis (see rightly NIV).

56. Arguably, what will materialize will be something of a creole, developed as the "tongue" of the city of God is enabled through the gospel to communicate more responsibly with the "tongues" of the nations (on the notion of a creole in cultural development and change, see Galison, *Image and Logic*, 46–47).

Bibliography

Allmen, J.J. von. *Worship: Its Theology and Practice.* New York: Oxford University Press, 1965.

Aniol, Scott. "Practice Makes Perfect: Corporate Worship and the Formation of Spiritual Virtue." *Journal of Spiritual Formation & Soul Care* 10 (2017) 93–104.

Balz, Horst, and Gerhard Schneider, eds. *Exegetical Dictionary of the New Testament.* Translated by Virgil P. Howard et al. 3 vols. Grand Rapids: Eerdmans, 1990–1993.

Berry, Wendell. "Men and Women in Search of Common Ground." *Sunstone* (July 1987) 8–12.

———. "A Native Hill." *Hudson Review* 21 (1968–1969) 601–34.

Boers, Arthur. *Living into Focus: Choosing What Matters in an Age of Distractions.* Grand Rapids: Brazos, 2012.

Borgmann, Albert. *Technology and the Character of Contemporary Life: A Philosophical Inquiry.* Chicago: University of Chicago Press, 1984.

———. *Power Failure: Christianity in the Culture of Technology.* Grand Rapids: Brazos, 2003.

Brendsel, Daniel J. "A Tale of Two Calendars: Calendars, Compassion, Liturgical Formation, and the Presence of the Spirit." *Bulletin of Ecclesial Theology* 3 (2016) 15–42.

Brock, Brian. *Christian Ethics in a Technological Age.* Grand Rapids: Eerdmans, 2010.

Campbell, Heidi A., and Stephen Garner. *Networked Theology: Negotiating Faith in a Digital Culture.* Grand Rapids: Baker, 2016.

Carr, Nicholas. "Is Google Making Us Stupid?" *Atlantic* 302.1 (July/August 2008) 56–63.

———. *The Shallows: What the Internet Is Doing to Our Brains.* New York: Norton, 2010.

Challies, Tim. *The Next Story: Faith, Friends, Family, and the Digital World.* Exp. ed. Grand Rapids: Zondervan, 2011.

Cowan, Ruth Schwartz. *More Work for Mother: The Ironies of Household Technology from the Open Hearth to the Microwave.* New York: Basic, 1983.

Crouch, Andy. *The Tech-Wise Family: Everyday Steps for Putting Technology in Its Proper Place.* Grand Rapids: Baker, 2017.

Dickerson, Matthew. "Wendell Berry, C.S. Lewis, J.R.R. Tolkien and the Dangers of a Technological Mindset." *Flourish Magazine* (Fall 2010). http://www.flourishonline.org/2010/12/wendell-berry-cs-lewis-jrr-tolkien-and-the-dangers-of-a-technological-mindset/.

Galison, Peter. *Image and Logic: A Material Culture of Microphysics.* Chicago: University of Chicago Press, 1997.

Garner, Stephen. *Networked Theology: Negotiating Faith in a Digital Culture.* Grand Rapids: Baker, 2016.

Gay, Craig M. *Modern Technology and the Human Future: A Christian Appraisal.* Downers Grove: InterVarsity Academic, 2018.

Grant, George Parkin. *Technology and Justice.* Notre Dame: University of Notre Dame Press, 1986.

Hauerwas, Stanley. "The Liturgical Shape of the Christian Life: Teaching Christian Ethics as Worship." In *In Good Company: The Church as Polis*, 153–68. Notre Dame: University of Notre Dame Press, 1995.

Hipps, Shane. *The Hidden Power of Electronic Culture: How Media Shapes Faith, the Gospel, and Church*. Grand Rapids: Zondervan, 2005.
James, P.D. *Devices and Desires*. New York: Knopf, 1989.
Kallenberg, Brad J. *God and Gadgets: Following Jesus in a Technological Age*. Eugene, OR: Cascade, 2011.
Kass, Leon R., Jr. *The Hungry Soul: Eating and the Perfecting of Our Nature*. New York: Free Press, 1994.
Kittel, Gerhard, and Gerhard Friedrich, eds. *Theological Dictionary of the New Testament*. Translated by Geoffrey W. Bromiley. 10 vols. Grand Rapids: Eerdmans, 1964–1976.
Leithart, Peter J. "The Way Things Really Ought to Be: Eucharist, Eschatology, and Culture." *Westminster Theological Journal* 59 (1997) 159–76.
McLuhan, Marshall. *The Medium and the Light: Reflections on Religion*. Edited by E. McLuhan and J. Szklarek. Toronto: Stoddart, 1999.
Monsma, Stephen V., ed. *Responsible Technology: A Christian Perspective*. Grand Rapids: Eerdmans, 1986.
O'Donovan, Oliver. *Begotten or Made?* Oxford: Clarendon, 1984.
Orr, David. *The Road Not Taken: Finding America in the Poem Everyone Loves and Almost Everyone Gets Wrong*. New York: Penguin, 2015.
Reinke, Tony. *12 Ways Your Phone Is Changing You*. Wheaton: Crossway, 2017.
Schmemann, Alexander. *For the Life of the World: Sacraments and Orthodoxy*. 2nd ed. Crestwood: St. Vladimir's Seminary Press, 1973.
———. *Introduction to Liturgical Theology*. Crestwood: St. Vladimir's Seminary Press, 1966.
Schuurman, Derek C. *Shaping a Digital World: Faith, Culture and Computer Technology*. Downers Grove: InterVarsity, 2013.
Steenwyk, Carrie Titcombe, and John D. Witvliet, eds. *The Worship Sourcebook*. Grand Rapids: Calvin Institute of Christian Worship, 2004.
Treier, Daniel J. "Modernity's Machine: Technology Coming of Age in Bonhoeffer's Apocalyptic Proverbs." In *Bonhoeffer, Christ and Culture*, edited by K.L. Johnson and T. Larsen, 91–111. Downers Grove: InterVarsity Academic, 2013.
Waters, Brent. *From Human to Posthuman: Christian Theology in a Postmodern World*. Ashgate Science and Religion Series. Hampshire: Ashgate, 2006.

3

The Alchemists' Dream

Three Judgments about Technology

ANDY CROUCH

THE BRITISH ETHICIST OLIVER O'Donovan offered this lapidary definition of *judgment* in his 2003 Bampton Lectures: "A judgment is an act of moral discrimination that pronounces upon a preceding act or existing state of affairs to establish a new public context."[1]

I want to offer three judgments about technology here. Almost everyone senses that we need a new public context for the discussion of technology: a framing of reality that will allow us to make some sense, including some moral sense, of the way of life that has overtaken our world in the span of a single lifetime—the lifetime, in my case, of my own parents.

My mother turned eighty years old in 2019. When I think about what life was like at the beginning of her life compared to her eightieth year, so much of the difference comes down to what we call technology. To be sure, technology has a more than eighty-year-long history. Yet in the span of fourscore years, it has come to define our world in a way that was certainly not true when my mother was born. This sudden change in human affairs leaves all of us, whether inside or outside the church, looking for the right public context. Judgment at its best can establish a healthy public context for living faithfully with new realities. And judgment does so by pronouncing on past acts, or on existing states of affairs, with moral seriousness.

---

1. O'Donovan, *Ways of Judgment*, 7. Thanks to my Praxis colleague, Philip Lorish, for calling my attention to this definition.

That is what I shall attempt here. The three judgments I have to offer may not initially seem especially moral in their tone. The first will seem primarily linguistic, the second perhaps more empirical, and the third perhaps alarmingly spiritual. But in fact, they culminate in a set of moral claims, and above all in the urgent need for a new kind of moral community.

With each of these judgments, I wade into a contested area in the philosophizing and theologizing of technology, and I take a side. In each case, I believe the side I am taking is the one that is less popular and less commonly argued. In doing so, I will inevitably disagree to some extent with the explicit and implicit statements of some of the other contributors to this discussion and this volume, who seem to me to argue, or assume, the more common way of thinking. I feel no little trepidation at diverging from the thinking of people I respect so much, not to mention the current consensus. But such is the risk of making judgments.

Judgment 1: Tools and Technology

My first judgment is about language and history, and it is this: there is a fundamental discontinuity, evident in the recent history of humanity, between *technē* and *technology*. This fundamental discontinuity is reflected in the shift in our vocabulary. Technology is a word that acquired its distinctive meaning quite recently. Befitting its *-ology* suffix, it simply meant *the study of* the "practical arts" for more than two centuries, and only began to be applied to those arts directly in 1859, according to the Oxford English Dictionary. We already had words like *technē* in Greek and, more narrowly, *tool* in English. Why did we reach for a new word? Because something really did change, dramatically and decisively, that made a difference.

It is commonplace to assert not discontinuity, but continuity in this context: no matter how novel a device may seem, and no matter the uneasiness it provokes in some quarters, someone will say, "Well, human beings have always had tools." What we call technology, this argument goes, is actually just more tools—just more *technē*.

But I think this judgment of continuity does not do justice to the difference between what we call technology and the tools that human beings have had literally all the way back to the dawn of their presence on this planet. There are two essential differences, the first having to do with power—especially the quantity of power and the source of power—and the second having to do with complex control systems that culminate in automaticity and autonomy. Technology is a name for automatic, autonomous things that depend on a qualitatively and quantitatively different source of power.

The dawn of the modern era involved a massive explosion of the power available to the human race. Not only did we tame and harness steam to vastly increase the power available to be applied to physical work, we also uncovered vast new sources of energy: hydrocarbons first, then nuclear power, and more recently, forms of environmentally available energy like hydro and solar. This is a truly new thing in human history. Of course, there were partial precedents—Rome had gravity-driven waterworks, and premodern people had windmills and waterwheels—but modern power is many orders of magnitude more abundant and efficient.

Modern power marked a fundamental discontinuity from the era of tools. All tools are force multipliers. They multiply human effort in the world. In a way, this is true of all culture—all culture requires physical making, which means it requires physical effort. Even when I am merely speaking, I am expelling air up through my vocal cords. When I type, I have to move my fingers. And I have tools that multiply that force—microphones that are used in amplifying speech, keyboards that channel and direct the act of writing.

All tools multiply force. And the force that almost all tools multiplied, until just a moment ago in human history, came from bodies: either the bodies of domesticated animals or the bodies of human beings. Premodern human beings, everywhere in the world at all times in human history, developed myriad ingenious ways to multiply and focus the organic power available from living bodies.

But in the modern era, we found new sources of power—all of which trace back, ultimately, to either combustion (in most engines and power plants), fission (in terrestrial nuclear power), or fusion (in the sun). All the power available to us traces its way back, you might say only slightly hyperbolically, to explosions—events of massive, concentrated force somewhere beyond the horizon of our awareness. Sitting in a comfortable, well-lit sanctuary, or in our living rooms on a December evening, it is hard to be aware of this, because the power has been stepped down multiple times through multiple transformers, all the way down to the minute amounts of direct current that power our electronics. Yet if we were to be transported suddenly to the places that generate all the power available to us—coal- or gas-fired plants, nuclear reactors, let alone the surface of the sun—we might readily think we had stumbled upon the fires of hell.

In addition to harnessing power in a truly novel way, at the dawn of the technological era we created what came to be called cybernetic systems: systems that create control loops that allow eventually for autonomous and automatic operation. With these two interdependent developments, we were able to finally realize the dream of the Sorcerer's Apprentice: things that work on their own, no bodies or minds directly required for their operation.

In Goethe's poem *Der Zauberlehrling* and in Disney's 1940 version in the film *Fantasia*, the sorcerer's apprentice succeeds in getting a broom to work autonomously—too autonomously, as it turns out. And in my own home, I have something very close to the magical broom that Goethe envisioned: the robotic vacuum sold under the brand name Roomba. This autonomous broom careens around my house in quite entertaining ways, doing an imperfect but real job of cleaning the floors.

This is new. This is technology. The Roomba is not just a tool—it is something categorically different, for which we have instinctively reached for a new word. This is why it is not really correct to say that the Amish, famously reluctant to embrace modern technology in the form of motor vehicles, still use *technology* in the form of their horses and buggies. For all its sophistication in the history of human tool-making (for example, its superiority in materials and craftsmanship to the ancient chariot), the Amish buggy still operates at the scale of animal bodies, harnessed and cared for by human beings. In my judgment, calling this technology simply muddles the issue.[2]

In one of the rare moments that Steve Jobs allowed himself to be captured on video in a non-promotional context, we see him in a classroom, in front of a whiteboard. The roughly one-minute clip (from a 1991 documentary commissioned by the Library of Congress) is worth quoting in full because of how directly it connects to this first judgment about tools and technology.

> I think one of the things that really separates us from the high primates is that we're tool builders. I read a study that measured the efficiency of locomotion for various species on the planet. The condor used the least energy to move a kilometer. And humans came in with a rather unimpressive showing about a third of the way down the list . . . not too proud of a showing for the crown of creation. . . . But then somebody at Scientific American had the insight to test the efficiency of locomotion for a man on a bicycle. And a man on a bicycle, or a human on a bicycle, blew the condor away—completely off the top of the charts.

---

2. Not all Amish communities make the exact same decisions about which tools—or technologies—to embrace. For example, many do use gas-powered stationary engines, which would plausibly qualify as technology by the rubric I am offering here.

> And that's what a computer is to me... It's the most remarkable tool we've ever come up with.... It's the equivalent of a bicycle for our minds.[3]

Jobs explicitly invokes the language of tools and their ability to multiply human bodies' power. Human beings—"the crown of creation," in Jobs's words, reminding us that though he did not profess Christian faith as an adult, he grew up in a Lutheran church—are not that impressive on their own. But aided by tools like the bicycle, we far outstrip the capabilities of other creatures.

The "bicycle for the mind" is a justly famous metaphor and an artfully chosen one. A bicycle is a human-scale, body-powered *tool*, in the sense that I have defined the word. Though it is in certain ways quite sophisticated in its materials and its harnessing of the laws of physics, it has the pre-technological quality of being intimately linked to human energy and will.

But, of course, Jobs was using this metaphor to talk about the computer, which we think of as almost the paradigmatic example of *technology*. And this suggests that other metaphors might actually have been more apt—successors to the bicycle that reflect technology's signature themes of vastly expanded power, automaticity, and autonomy. What if Jobs had said that a computer is a *motorcycle* for the mind? What if he said a computer is an *automobile* for the mind? Perhaps these still seem like appealing metaphors, but when we extend the metaphor to an *airplane* for the mind, let alone, say, *a Saturn V rocket* for the mind, we are in the realm of power that so outstrips human capabilities that it is necessarily harnessed to and controlled by cybernetic systems. Riding in an airplane—even more so, being an astronaut atop a rocket—is a strangely passive experience, because at some point these transportation technologies transcend human agency and control.

Returning to terrestrial transport, what if Jobs had compared a computer to *a self-driving car* for the mind, however anachronistic that might have been in 1991? Yet this is much closer to what computers actually are, at least for the great majority of lay, non-computer-science-literate users. They seem to have a logic of their own. When I ride a bicycle, my inputs as the human operator (pedaling, steering, shifts in weight) have a fairly clear relation to the tool's behavior. But anyone who has helped a less computer-literate relative operate a computer, even through a highly user-oriented interface like Apple's iOS, knows that this is not at all how it feels to operate a computer. It is often extremely difficult to know what it's doing, where it's going, or where it's taking us.

3. Jobs, "Computers are like a bicycle."

Jobs's metaphor, then, turns out to be both beautiful and profoundly misleading. He chose a *tool* to analogize something that is much closer to *technology*. If he had chosen a more accurate metaphor, we might have had more mixed feelings about where computers were taking us. This was not the first or last time that Jobs would perform an act of rhetorical sleight of hand on behalf of technology's uniquely powerful form of magic.

The writer Kevin Kelly titled one of his books *What Technology Wants*. The anthropomorphism is both obviously inappropriate and strangely plausible. It *does* feel like our devices have their own locus of power and desire—in a way that tools do not—because in fact they do harness impersonal sources of power and do operate with a kind of autonomy from us.

Of course, this is just a projection—we have granted them this power and autonomy because there is something *we* want very much. The philosopher Albert Borgmann, whose work lies underneath so much of what I am presenting here, sums it up as the "device paradigm."[4] I have found it useful, as a journalist, to decode that phrase with a simpler one: *easy everywhere*. What technology wants and what technology's makers want—very much unlike what tools and toolmakers want—is not to *extend* human engagement with the world the way the tools do, but to *replace* human engagements. We want the world to take over for us. The bicycle does not ride itself. It has a rider. But the bicycle is not actually our dream—the self-driving car, which "drives" of its own accord, both in the sense of being self-powered and self-directing, is.

We have been taught to want this, over and over, by the two fundamental promises that are made on behalf of every device. The first is (1) *now you'll be able to* [. . .], and the other is (2) *you'll no longer have to* [. . .]. To some extent, these are the promises that have accompanied every "technical" innovation (using *technē* in its broadest sense), including tools. But the difference in the technological era is that the balance has shifted in our time from *now you can*—the enhancement and extension of human capacities— to *you no longer have to*. Our main fascination with technology is not the things it enables us to do, but the things we no longer have to do.

This is clear for my Roomba vacuum. The *now you'll be able to* extension of my Roomba is actually quite minimal. What can I do with my Roomba that I could not do before? Watch with amusement as it careens around the house? Put my cat on top of it and make a funny video? The Roomba doesn't add much to my capacities, and that certainly is not the reason I purchased it. I purchased it for the negation: *you'll no longer have to vacuum* (which turns out not to be quite true, but true enough).

---

4. Borgmann, *Technology*, 40.

Even the truly astonishing deliverances of technology, the *now you'll be able to* moments it has delivered, come with a surprisingly large helping of *you'll no longer have to*. Technology has enabled not just air travel, but space travel. But the greater the power put at the disposal of human beings, the closer we become to, in the mordant phrase of the Apollo-era astronauts, "Spam in a can." Notwithstanding the genuine heroism of astronauts (and the scientific expertise they bring to their work, especially in the age of the International Space Station), there is a great deal of human agency that is subtracted when you are perched on top of a massive rocket. The scope of human activity allowed to astronauts is in some real respects considerably less than was available, say, to Lewis, Clark, and their companions as they explored westward across North America.

And this reflects two more realities of technology which are less often mentioned, because they are not drivers of sales and marketing. The inevitable correlates of *now you'll be able to* and *you'll no longer have to* are (3) *you'll no longer be able to* [. . .], and (4) *now you'll have to* [. . .]. Technology does not just expand what "we" (our devices acting on our behalf) can do—it also removes capacity and enforces new behaviors.

This observation is obviously not new. It goes back to Plato's *Phaedrus*, in which Socrates retells the story of Theuth inventing writing and presenting his invention to King Thamus. Thamus acknowledges that Theuth has done something very clever and that his invention will seem to give human beings more capacities.[5] But, Thamus observes, Theuth's gift takes away capacities as well. (1) *Now you'll be able to* write down stories and information, meaning (2) *you'll no longer have to* remember them—true, but (3) *you'll no longer be able to* exercise the human capacity for oral memory, and indeed (4) *now you'll have to* write something down in order to remember it.

It's amazing how often the *Phaedrus* is cited by the advocates of information technology as a way of dismissing current critiques of technology, as if the fact that worries about the direction of *technē* go back for thousands of years means that those worries are silly. In fact, it is clear that Socrates was exactly right about the trade-offs inherent in the widespread adoption of writing. Richard Bauckham's fascinating book *Jesus and the Eyewitnesses* marshals a wide range of evidence to remind us how extraordinary (from our perspective) are the abilities of members of oral cultures to commit oral traditions, verbatim, to memory. We cannot imagine being able to hear a discourse once and then repeat it word-for-word with extremely high fidelity. But such memorization was routine in Jesus's world and is still routine in oral cultures around the world today. For those of

---

5. Plato, *Phaedrus*, 274c–275b.

us embedded in a literate (or, increasingly, post-literate and image-based) culture, it is effectively inconceivable.

Now you'll be able to is always accompanied by *you'll no longer be able to*. To be sure, in any given case we may judge that this trade-off is beneficial, or fairly benign. A modern piano is tuned according to the principles of equal temperament, a system which allows a musician to play in any key without it sounding too dissonant. The promise of "tempering" (famously explored by J.S. Bach in his work *The Well-Tempered Clavier*) is, *now you'll be able to* play in any key, and *you'll no longer have to* retune your instrument to play in a different key.

But equal temperament comes with its own *you'll no longer be able to*. Tempering involves slightly altering the perfect harmonies that are available in any given key. Musicians who play stringed instruments like the violin, or highly trained vocalists, know that there are pure harmonies available that a pianist will never be able to play—and indeed, that most pianists are almost unable to hear. To a violinist who has learned to play perfectly in tune, even a tuned piano always sounds slightly out of tune. After the adoption of equal temperament, pianists *no longer are able to* play truly in tune, and violinists (to their frequent annoyance) *now have to* play slightly out of tune when they play with a piano!

If such trade-offs have been part of the story of *technē*, in the broadest sense of the word, since the beginning of the human story, why worry about them now? Because technology, in the narrow sense that I am using it, involves a much less favorable set of trade-offs. In Albert Borgmann's terms, what technology provides us is *commodities*—single, simple things.[6] They may be good things, but they are single, simple things nonetheless. And the trade-off required to access these commodities—to access the promise of *now you'll be able to*—involves giving up a very great deal in terms of *you'll no longer be able to*, and increasingly accepting a great deal of coerced behavior in the form of *now you'll have to*.

Borgmann's central image for this trade-off is the hearth—literally, his "central" image, since the Latin word for hearth, *focus*, has come down to us in the cognate English word thanks to the central role the hearth played in every Roman home.[7] In the modern era, in Borgmann's account, we replace the hearth, the source of warmth and light that was at the center of human domiciles for thousands of years, with the furnace, controlled by a thermostat. *Now you'll be able to* ensure that the temperature in your home is always seventy-two degrees Fahrenheit. And *you'll no longer have to* go out

6. Borgmann, *Technology*, 42.
7. Borgmann, *Technology*, 41.

and get wood to warm yourself and your family. But what *you'll no longer be able to do* is gather around a fire that illuminates the home, that brings warmth into the middle of the home, that gathers people from the edges of the home. You will no longer have a center to your home. The trade of the hearth for the furnace was one large step toward the reality of modern middle-class American home life, where many members of the household much of the time are alone in their bedrooms, engaged with glowing rectangles, rather than gathered at the center in community around the primal, mysterious (and for the Romans, religious) glow of the fire. What we have traded away for our devices is "focal things," in Borgmann's terms.[8] For the sake of a commodified *now you'll be able to,* we have forsaken the focal, the multi-dimensional, the religious and relational.

There have always been trade-offs in the story of *technē*, from writing to equal temperament, but they used to involve substantial gains as well as real losses—as the nearly divine fecundity of Bach's *Well-Tempered Clavier* makes clear. When what is lost is so much richer than what is gained, we are truly in the world of technology.

This is one of the meanings of Wendell Berry's parable of the path and the road.[9] The path adds *now you'll be able to* (travel more easily from this place to this other place) while doing minimal damage in the form of *you'll no longer be able to.* It is not hard to go off a path. But a road enforces a new kind of behavior. Driving on the road (even in a theoretically four-wheel-drive SUV), you'll no longer be able to leave the road; you are forced to travel along a single fixed route.

The path modestly expands what is possible, while foreclosing very little. It imposes almost nothing in the realms of *you'll no longer be able to* or *now you'll have to.* But the road—in precise proportion, note well, to how impressively technological it becomes—imposes severe costs of *you'll no longer be able to.* In some rural parts of the United States, on the entrance ramp to interstate highways, you will see a picture of a horse behind the international diagonal-in-a-circle that indicates exclusion. You are no longer able to ride a horse here, the sign says. A whole rich dimension of human culture and history is excluded by the road—which we can multiply countless times by the places and people whose cultural life withered when the interstates were routed far from them or the places and people whose cultural life was upended and replaced with something else of dubious value when an interstate exit reshaped its landscape.

---

8. Borgmann, *Technology*, 196.
9. Berry, "Native Hill," 601–34.

Jesus asked whether it was worth gaining the whole world at the cost of losing one's soul. But in the technological world, we have lost a great deal of our souls—the sense of our selves both at home and at risk in the vast mysterious cosmos, the experiences that anchored us in a rich reality beyond ourselves—and what we have gained is mere commodities. We have lost our souls without even gaining the world.

From Devices to Instruments

There is an alternative way to use technology. Though "what technology wants" is easy everywhere, we might have chosen, and still could choose, to redirect technology in a different path—using all our power and cybernetic control not to replace people, but to further involve them in creative work in the world. This kind of technology would not vastly expand the realm of *you no longer can* for a little bit of *you no longer have to*. Instead, it would open up new paths, to borrow Berry's words, for human flourishing. And the word for this kind of technology is *instruments*.

My wife is an experimental physicist who in her postdoctoral work used lasers, among other scientific instruments, to restructure materials at the nano scale, the scale where quantum mechanical effects become salient, in ways that have real-world application at our macro scale. The instruments my wife builds and uses certainly are high technology, but they are not devices, in the sense that they in no way replace human beings. They require a scientist to operate them, bringing the fullness of heart, soul, mind, and strength (because science, if done well, requires all these things) to the work of uncovering the beautiful regularity, predictability, and abundance of the created world.

Likewise, doctors use medical instruments to allow them to act with greater precision to bring more effective healing. But even the most sophisticated, so-called "robotic" instruments, such as the Da Vinci machine that assists in laparoscopic surgeries, are not in fact robots at all. They merely assist a human surgeon, not at all displacing the human judgment and dexterity that is so unique to us as human beings.

And, of course, there are musical instruments, some of them very high tech. Even a "classical" instrument like the grand piano only became possible with nineteenth-century advances in materials science. Perhaps the most fertile musical invention of the twentieth century was the two-turntable arrangement used by hip-hop DJs—two identical devices which, placed side by side and manipulated in ways unforeseen by their original designers, became an instrument that allowed human beings to unlock an entire new world of musical expression.

At the dawn of the technological era, when we started to discover how the electromagnetic spectrum works, how cybernetic systems work, we could have decided that what was wanted was more instruments—more ways for human beings to fully engage with the world. We could have decided we would only accept technological directions that significantly expanded the *now you'll be able to* dimension of human life without requiring drastic foreclosures in the form of *you'll no longer be able to*. An astronomer using a modern radiotelescope is giving up very little previous possibility, even if astronomers rarely look through optical lenses at the sky anymore. This is entirely unlike a "music lover" who only ever enjoys music played by a device, who cannot even make music in the most rudimentary way.

But we largely took the road of easy everywhere, not the path of instruments. Yet even now, to a great extent, each of us can still decide whether to build our lives around devices or instruments. We do not have to flee backwards to an imagined pre-technological past. We can seek out new kinds of instruments that will extend and develop our heart, soul, mind, and strength.

Judgment 2: The Singularity Will Not Arrive

My first judgment was about the past. There is a discontinuity in our history, which we named with the word *technology*. We could have passed through this discontinuity and continued the human story of tools and toolmaking through instruments and instrument-making. We overwhelmingly chose devices instead.

Judgment number 2 is about the future, and it is this: *there is no discontinuity on the horizon ahead for the human condition.*

To put it in more vivid terms, the singularity will not arrive. As with my first judgment, this could well seem like a minority view. Many thoughtful observers believe a moment is coming where human beings will be eclipsed by our own creations. Perhaps, as the idea is framed in the provocative work of Yuval Harari, this will even take the form of a successor species, a new kind of human being, who will achieve, or at least ascribe to themselves, the title *homo deus*, a being to whom mere *homo sapiens* will be as domesticated animals are to us.[10]

---

10. Harari, *Homo Deus*.

My judgment is that this is not in fact going to happen. The future of humanity is continuous in fundamental ways with our present reality. And the easiest way to see this is to look at our past.

Imagine describing my way of life to my great-grandmother—or perhaps my great-great-grandmother, who would have lived all her life in the nineteenth century. Not only do I have a robot that cleans the floors, but I have a robot that washes my dishes. Of course, we don't call it a robot, because "robot" is largely a mythical name for things that do not yet exist—so I do not refer to my autonomous vacuum as a robot, just a Roomba. For all its clever design, it is nothing like the robot of science fiction dreams. Likewise, the robot that washes the dishes in my home—using the automatic cybernetic systems that are the hallmark of robotics—is simply called a dishwasher.

The dishwasher is mundane to us, just as the Roomba already is and certainly will be to our grandchildren. But if you had described these devices to my great-grandmother, she would have been awestruck. What kind of human beings would have such power at their disposal? Not just apprentices, but sorcerers. Surely her great-grandson must have a life of untold leisure. Surely I must be like one of the philosopher-kings of whom Plato spoke, with all the labor in my life taken care of?

It would be so deflating to tell my ancestor the obvious truth: the future has arrived, and it is pretty ordinary. I am quite happy to have a dishwasher, but having one has not changed me or the human condition. I hear and read the stories of human beings from the past and instantly recognize myself in their stories. Far from being discontinuous with them, I can even read truly ancient works like the *Iliad* or the Hebrew Scriptures and see, for all the differences in our circumstances, a very fundamental human continuity.

Indeed, such discontinuity in human history as there has actually been, thanks to technology, has already happened. It happened when we made the shift to the device paradigm. But though the device paradigm fundamentally changed the *conditions of human life*, it did not fundamentally change *the human condition*. We have already traversed whatever discontinuity technology might have supplied us. We are already on the other side, where things start operating by themselves like magic, like a dream, like the myth of the Sorcerer's Apprentice. And on this side of that magical dream, being human is essentially the same as it was before.

To be sure, we are different from our ancestors in some ways—we are taller, as any visit to an old homestead will make clear, and generally heavier. Without a doubt, our epigenetic expression of the DNA that we inherited from them is different because of our vastly different environment. Even cognitively, there is no reason to doubt that for all the capacities we have lost along the way, like verbatim oral memory, we have gained many as well. But there has been no singularity, notwithstanding our astonishing technological "progress." My judgment is there never will be.

We can supplement this fundamental argument in other ways. The 2010s brought a surge of what you might called alarmist optimism about artificial intelligence (AI). But the results have been deflating. Benedict Evans, a technology analyst for the venture capital firm Andreessen Horowitz, is a thoughtful commentator with, as far as I know, no particular dog in the singularity fight. He observed on Twitter in September 2019: "With most new tech, the people closest to it are the most excited and people further away are skeptical. Machine learning/AI is the opposite. People who aren't close say 'OMG this is Skynet/singularity!' but the people who are deep into it say 'well, it works OK, I guess.'"[11]

Evans's phrase, "Machine learning/AI," reminds us that the nomenclature of the field has already shifted. Few serious computer scientists talk about AI—except possibly when raising capital from naïve investors. Like "robots," AI turns into something much more mundane when it actually arrives, in this case, machine learning. Machine learning, like many previous technological developments, is indeed impressive and will unlock various new kinds of power and automaticity. But it also has increasingly well-documented limitations, and in any case is simply not related to the "singularity" of a general artificial intelligence which could operate in the world in a way analogous to the way human beings do.

The most notable proponent of the idea of the singularity has been the inventor Ray Kurzweil, a technologist with genuinely astonishing breakthroughs to his credit (including instruments—I played a Kurzweil keyboard for many years as a professional musician). But on the topic of the future of computation, Kurzweil has been spectacularly—one might say singularly—mistaken.

In an article called "The Coming Merging of Mind and Machine" in 2009, Kurzweil wrote, "The Law of Accelerating Returns shows that by around 2020 a $1,000 personal computer will have the processing power of the human brain—20 million billion calculations per second."[12] This article appeared in *Scientific American*, which many lay people would consider a reputable organ of science journalism. Yet not one phrase in it had, or has, any scientific basis. Scientists generally reserve the description "law" for regularities so basic that they are attested everywhere in nature. Kurzweil appropriated this ultimate standard of scientific authority for his own

---

11. Benedict Evans (@benedictevans), "With most new tech [...]," Twitter, September 21, 2019, 1:52 p.m., https://twitter.com/benedictevans/status/1175482842144366592.

12. Kurzweil, "Coming Merging," para. 15.

roughly empirical account of how computing power had decreased relative to price. The phrase "the processing power of the human brain" is vacuous, scientifically speaking. Indeed, the more we know about human cognition, the less "processing power," in computer-science terms, seems like an apt description of the astonishingly complex systems by which human beings make sense of and navigate the world.

And even if Kurzweil was in some sense right to peg the brain's "processing power" at 20 billion MIPS (million instructions per second, the standard measure of traditional microchip processing), how has his prediction fared now that we live "around 2020"? In fact, the fastest personal computer chip in commercial production as of October 2019, the intel Core i7 6950X, was capable of 317,900 MIPS. This is indeed an amazing development—when Kurzweil wrote his article, an earlier generation of the intel Core i7 had only achieved 82,300 MIPS—but as a roughly fourfold increase, it is insanely short of his prediction. For clarity, Kurzweil's prediction, 20 billion MIPS, if written in the same notation would be 20,000,000,000 MIPS. As for this processor being available in a "$1,000 personal computer," here, too, Kurzweil was off, though not by five orders of magnitude—the processor alone sold for $1,625 in March 2020.

So Kurzweil's putative "Law" has in fact failed to pan out. But his other predictions have fared even worse: "By around 2020 a $1,000 computer will at least match the processing power of the human brain. By 2029 the software for intelligence will have been largely mastered, and the average personal computer will be equivalent to 1,000 brains."[13] The idea that in less than ten years "the software for intelligence will have been largely mastered" would cause any working computer scientist in 2020 to break out in laughter (or hives). As for the idea of a computer being "equivalent to 1,000 brains," this is so conceptually confused as to be ludicrous, reminiscent of the economists' joke about the potential for making a human baby in a single month if nine women would just share the work. Needless to say, we are nowhere near to having such a computer—except in the utterly banal sense that all computers, even the earliest ones, long ago outstripped human speed and precision *when performing certain kinds of very circumscribed operations.*

What would we do with this thousand-brain power? Kurzweil thought he knew: "You will be able to have any type of experience—business, social, sexual—with anyone, real or simulated, regardless of physical proximity."[14]

Every word in that sentence is disturbing, beginning with the very first one. Who is "you"? Who is this person who will have, or want, these

13. Kurzweil, "Coming Merger," para. 1.
14. Kurzweil, "Coming Merger," para. 5.

experiences? What does it even mean to have "any type of experience"? What in the world is going on with the three words, "business, social, sexual"? These are all interpersonal experiences. Will "you" be able to "have" them with other persons? Will those other persons need to consent? Will "you" just conjure up a simulation of whomever you like? And why in the world would anyone want a simulated *business* experience? If they had one, would they exclaim, "It's not a real balance sheet—but it feels so real"?

This is insanity—and it was insanity in 2009. Yet it was promulgated in a magazine called *Scientific American*. No, "you" will not be able to "have" any such "experiences" in 2020, or 2029, or ever, because Kurzweil fundamentally misunderstands what it means to be a person and how categorically different a person is from any computer we have ever invented or will ever invent.

We see these same dynamics in the hype about self-driving cars, even though we have had self-driving cars for years, and chances are that most readers of this essay have ridden in one. If you have ever been to the Orlando, Dallas-Fort Worth, or Atlanta airports (just to name a few), you have experienced autonomous transportation. Not only in the form of your airplane—which, thanks to autopilot technology, is much closer to self-driving than most airlines actually want their passengers to know—but in the form of the trains that shuttle passengers from one terminal to another. These trains have no human operator; they are self-driving.

Immediately someone will object that those trains are on a track, so they are not really the kind of self-driving technology we imagine. But this is actually the point: *when you put machines in machine-like environments*, they are able to operate autonomously. In the coming years, we will be able to extend the machine-like environments within which machines can operate. It is not inconceivable that there will be roads in the future, designed for autonomous passenger and cargo vehicles, that have the international diagonal-within-a-circle indicating that human-driven cars are not allowed. But the moment that you put any system currently in production, or even imagined, in an environment that is *actually designed for human beings*, those systems fail in all kinds of easily predicted, as well as maddeningly unpredictable, ways.

So in fact, autonomous technology will advance in the way all other technologies have: gradually, impressively, but without making any fundamental change in the human condition. Many conventional cars already have adaptive cruise control, which senses traffic in front of the vehicle and automatically adjusts the vehicle's speed. But no one who has driven a car with adaptive cruise control thinks the singularity has arrived. And in fact it only works in highly controlled conditions. We are not even close to building cars that can respond to the entire range of possible situations that an automobile can encounter in the real world.

The reason for this failure is subtle. As airplanes demonstrate, there are certain parts of the world (such as the fluid dynamics of flight through air) that operate with enough regularity that autonomous operation is possible within them. It is not impossible to imagine that autonomous vehicles could also one day master the much more complicated natural world on the ground. But the *natural* world is not the problem—it is the *cultural* world that, on the ground, is so real. Even in the air, the hardest problem to solve in aviation is not fluid dynamics but human ones—the intentions, choices, and mistakes of human pilots, as well as ill-intentioned or foolish actors like the operators of small drones.

The cultural world is the one that machines cannot master. The moment you introduce genuinely human actors into a system, machines—no matter the extent of their "learning"—will fail.

To give the two most obvious examples, "self-driving cars" will be utterly confounded by two very common human phenomena: humor and deception.

When these two quintessentially human phenomena are combined, we call them "tricks." Have you ever had someone play a trick on you? You are intelligent—genuinely so, not just artificially so—yet it may well have taken you quite a bit of time to figure out what was going on. Imagine a self-driving car having to respond, in real time, to all the various combinations of humor and deception of which human beings are capable—including the sinister one in which someone steps into the road, firearm in hand, to rob the occupants. We will never be able to give machine learning enough "training data" to accurately realize that the pedestrian seemingly in peril in the car's path, for whom the car would normally come to an abrupt halt, is in fact an armed robber—let alone to realize that that pedestrian is our nephew with a squirt gun faking a heist as we pull up to the curb.

We can actually take this insight further. The great urbanist Jane Jacobs masterfully outlined in her book, *The Death and Life of Great Cities*, the elements of an urban environment that make it a healthy place for human habitation: mixed-use buildings, plenty of chances for street-level interaction, limited traffic, priority for pedestrians.[15] It is not much exaggeration to say that these are *precisely* the conditions that are worst for autonomous vehicles. The closer an environment is to being genuinely good for human beings, the worse it is for a self-driving car.

15. Jacobs, *Death and Life*.

Fine, we might say. My self-driving car will never drive me through the West Village, let alone the streets of Bangalore, but it may be able to take over on the interstate. And yes it may—because *the interstate is already an inhumane environment.* No happy or sane person wants to stand near, let alone walk on, an interstate highway. For machine learning to work, we will have to create ever more machine-like environments. To generate useful data for a computer, you need to act like a computer.

For example, it would be very helpful for machine learning and the ad-targeting purposes of Facebook if you would kindly speak in binary—two states, on or off. And Facebook has kindly provided you a way to speak in this truncated machine language: the like button. The like button is a data scientist's dream data source: trainable, learnable data already in a form a computer understands. But it requires you to attenuate your complex reactions to a given Facebook post to a single, on-off state—and even this single state can be "tricked" by human deception or humor.

Add even a few more bits—say, the 280 English characters allowed in a single tweet by Twitter—and human creativity, and human tricks, will overwhelm any machine learning system. This sentence fits perfectly well in a single tweet: "It is a truth universally acknowledged that a single man in possession of a large fortune must be in want of a wife." It will never be possible to accumulate enough training data for a machine learning system to "know" what even novice readers of *Pride and Prejudice* immediately sense—that the sentence is ironic.

For the singularity to arrive, a computational alternative to human intelligence needs to arise. But such an alternative will never arise, because cognition, the way human beings do it, is embodied, emotional, and indeed spiritual as well. To sum up these qualities, we could say that human cognition is *relational.* What we call intelligence is the application of heart, soul, mind, and strength, all in the context of love, to the world in which we find ourselves. And it is almost certainly the case that there is actually no other way to make sense of the world. Mere computation, no matter how many millions of instructions per second, will never succeed in this task.

Here is perhaps the most striking way to put this: human intelligence requires a face. Robotics engineers can, of course, give their creations simulated faces, even very realistic ones (though no currently available robotic face comes close to passing the "Turing test" of fooling a human who interacts with it). But human beings do not only *have* faces—we *learn from* faces. In particular, at the very beginning of human learning are the intense, face-to-face interactions of caregiver and infant (interactions that non-sighted babies or caregivers ingeniously replicate through touch and other senses). The bond of love between infant and mother, or whoever plays the mother's role, is the foundation of all other human learning. Learning is not just intellectual (in fact, it is hardly "intellectual" at all at the beginning)—it is also emotional, social, and ultimately relational.

Could computers one day learn like babies, building up a relational account of the world through face-to-face interaction? Perhaps this is not entirely inconceivable, but what it would require is providing them with the several dozen muscle groups found in the human face, connecting those muscles to a sophisticated perceptual apparatus (not just visual or auditory, but olfactory and more), and hooking all of that, in turn, up to an embodied system of cognition (recognition, interpretation, and response) that literally goes all the way down to the human gut in the form of the vagus nerve. Furthermore, human babies accomplish all this cognition with a roughly twenty-watt power supply (the wattage consumed by the human brain). How would we ever engineer a silicon-based system to use this little power to mobilize curiosity, engage relationally, and infer effortlessly from a few examples the shape of the learner's world? Now we truly seem in the realm of the inconceivable.

This is why the singularity—non-human computers that can outperform us in the things that make us most human—is simply not going to arrive. But it does lead to a rather arresting thought. We do already, after all, have systems that accomplish exactly this task of acquiring human-level intelligence: human babies. Maybe instead of trying to re-engineer human cognition in silicon, long before any computational singularity, we will realize it is far more cost-effective, to achieve our desired end of increasing the supply of available intelligence, to simply make babies.

This sounds like a joke, but it is actually not funny at all.

Ordinary human babies, of course, have one problem as sources of raw computing power—surprisingly early on, they develop independence. They resist us. They grow up and develop their own ideas. The whole point of the quest for artificial intelligence is to give us access to intelligence that, like the Sorcerer's Apprentice, we can *command*. And as every parent and every society knows, it is awfully difficult to command other human beings, even when they are still small.

But we also observe that some people grow up to be more defiant, or more compliant, than others; more willing to resist orders, or take orders, than others; more disposed to creative work, or routine work, than others.

It is certainly possible that these differences in personality, mysteriously distributed among the general population, are mediated at least in part by specific genes, or expressed in reliable ways based on an interaction of genetics and environment. It is not at all out of the question that we might discover the locations of the genes for compliance, obedience, and tolerance for routine.

And then, of course, we could engineer human babies who would grow up to be our own apprentice's brooms—people willing to do what they are told, willing to do mental drudgery, willing to put the dexterity and contextual cognition that no computer will ever achieve to the service of their masters.

It is far more likely that we will master the rudiments of human genetics and epigenetics in the coming century, in ways that allow us to engineer human beings with particular "desirable" traits, than that we will develop computers that exceed our intelligence. The singularity is not going to arrive. But in the disappointment that we have not produced our computational equals, what will we be willing to do by way of substitute? The master race, the race that far outstrips human beings and puts them to work much as we did domesticated animals, may have already arrived—not at all different from us, because they will be us—once we learn to make babies.

Judgment 3: Magic and Mammon

How did we get things so wrong? Why did we displace the fullness of human engagement with the world with devices, and how did we come to have such a distorted vision of the technological future that we credited the fevered dreams of a Ray Kurzweil with bylines in scientific magazines? This leads to a third judgment, which is that in telling the story of technology, we have discounted the ongoing power of two realities. Or maybe that is not the right word, since what unites them is ultimately their false pretension to reality: magic and Mammon.

If Mammon's promise is *abundance without dependence* (a definition I owe to Praxis venture partner and pastor Jon Tyson), magic's promise is *power without relationship*. These are deep, enduring human dreams. The dream of Mammon is to have all that we want without any dependence on others or God. The dream of magic is to have the power we want without any need for relationship with others or God.

Indeed, one of the most celebrated things ever written about technology—almost always celebrated with no sense of irony or unease—is Arthur C. Clarke's aphorism, "Any sufficiently advanced technology is indistinguishable from magic."[16] What captivates us about our devices, with their effortless promises of *you will be able to* and *you'll no longer have to*, is how closely they realize the ancient human dream of magical powers.

---

16. Clarke, "Clarke's Third Law," 255.

Money, too, is at the heart of "what technology wants." As Craig Gay observes in his important 2018 book *Modern Technology and the Human Future*, the logic of technology is increasingly not intrinsically related to human flourishing or "ordinary, embodied human existence." Increasingly what drives technology is less what is good for people, but simply what is good for global capital.[17] The Facebook like button, after all, is demonstrably bad for human flourishing—some of its own inventors have publicly voiced their regret at having devised it—but it is very good for the engine of returns on invested capital that is Facebook, Inc.

The idea that capital plays a dominant role in the direction of Western culture is a truism, of course. But whence the importance of magic? And are these two in fact linked? I believe they are deeply linked. There is a location in Western cultural history where magic and Mammon come together in the clearest form, even though it has almost entirely been suppressed in our historical memory. The history of technology runs straight back to this fusion of magic and Mammon, which has been right under our noses all along: the practice of alchemy.

Alchemy is right there in the title of the best-selling book of the twenty-first century: *Harry Potter and the Philosopher's Stone*, a phrase that was changed for the US market to *the Sorcerer's Stone*. Presumably, Rowling's American publisher judged that few American readers would know the meaning of the Philosopher's Stone.

But J.K. Rowling meant what she originally wrote. The quest for the Philosopher's Stone was the heart of the practice of alchemy. Alchemists believed there was a substance that, if it could be isolated and produced, would allow the one who possessed it to turn all metals into gold and to achieve immortal life.[18] In this quest, Mammon and magic were perfectly intertwined.

Alchemists believed that there was a magical power locked within the natural world. If unlocked, it would transform human existence in the most fundamental way possible. The essential work of the alchemists was to purify and distill the elements of the world in such a way that they would be transformed into the most pure and powerful substance of all, gold. And this metallurgical transformation was just the beginning. What really was in view was the spiritual transformation of humanity. Just as metal was gradually freed of its impurities, so too the successful alchemists would be liberated

17. Gay, *Modern Technology*, 59.

18. Because there has been some Christian uneasiness about Rowling's celebration of magic in her books, it's worth emphasizing that in *Harry Potter and the Philosopher's Stone*, the stone is sought by the evil character Voldemort and rejected (and ultimately put beyond use) by the good character Professor Dumbledore.

from the impurity of an embodied existence, set free from toil and elevated to the status of a god, or perhaps, God with a capital G.

Having undergone this transformation, one would attain to immortal life, the kind of life available only to the purely spiritual. One of the aphorisms of Paracelsus, a key disseminator of the belief and practice of alchemy, was, "'I under [the Lord] outside my office, and he under me outside his office."[19] In God's world—in other words, the big picture of creation—the alchemist will admit that he is under God. But the alchemist's work, his *opus*, is able to supersede and even command God himself—to create a little world of power where even God must serve and obey the god-man.

It is no accident that Yuval Harari's book *Homo Deus*, which purports to be "a brief history of tomorrow," in fact draws its dream for tomorrow from the alchemical past. Having defeated our three ancient enemies of "famine, plague, and war," Harari says on the first page of the book, human beings are now on to a new agenda: immortality, happiness, and ultimately godlikeness.[20] You will not find the word *alchemy* in Harari's book. But the dream he describes is taken directly from the alchemical playbook.

There is an obvious reason that Harari does not cite the alchemical sources of the "new human agenda." Alchemy has been, we think, discredited. We no longer believe there is such a substance as the Philosopher's Stone, and when we attempt to read the cryptic texts of the alchemists, they are embarrassingly flimsy. To the extent that modern Westerners think about alchemy at all, we tend to suppose that its circular and confused investigations into nature led, in time, to the more rigorous disciplines of modern science—the path from alchemy to chemistry. And we tell ourselves that our modern technology is descended from chemistry, not alchemy. This story is half true, since it is indeed the case that the alchemists were deluded, while the chemists gradually, painstakingly built up an accurate picture of the world. It is chemistry, not alchemy, that accounts for the extraordinary achievements of technology.

But this story leaves out the other half—the imaginative half. Because in fact, the alchemist is fully alive in our technological imagination, as Harari's imaginative picture of "tomorrow" makes so clear. Science supplied the technique, but alchemy continues to supply the dream.

Indeed, even our popular picture of science is shaped more by alchemy than we realize. When we think of a scientist today, what we picture—at least in most of our popular culture—is actually an alchemist.

19. Jung, *Alchemical Studies*, 116.

20. Harari, *Homo Deus*, 1. This talk was given, and this paper from it drafted, before the novel coronavirus pandemic of 2019–20 rendered so evidently ludicrous Harari's (never plausible) claim that humanity had defeated its original three "ancient enemies."

Who, after all, embodies the public's imagination of a scientist? It is surely Albert Einstein—bushy brows, fuzzy hair, and all. But even more vivid in the imagination of recent generations is a fictional character—"Doc Brown," the almost-mad inventor from *Back to the Future* and its sequels.

And when we reflect on Doc Brown's signature characteristics, we realize that he is not a scientist at all. He is half-mad. He works all by himself, in a cluttered laboratory on the edge of town. He is feverishly pursuing his own secret knowledge because he knows that he is on the edge of discovering something that will revolutionize the world.

This is not an actual scientist. This is a *mad* scientist. I happen to be married to an actual scientist, the experimental physicist and educator Catherine Crouch, and I can tell you authoritatively she bears no resemblance to this picture. Like almost all her colleagues, she is deeply sane, works closely with other people, and has a deep humility in the face of the beauty and mystery that is the physical world.

It's so obvious, once you look for it: Doc Brown is not a scientist at all—he is an alchemist. So is Dr. Frankenstein, his nineteenth-century precursor. And they are in turn exact cultural descendants of the sorcerer in the Sorcerer's Apprentice myth—the magician who is, of course, also an alchemist. (It turns out that the alteration of Rowling's title was not such a misdirection after all.) All of them pursue, and perhaps claim to possess, the power to bring the dead to life, to prevent the living from ever seeing death, and the ultimate power over the world that is also the promise of Mammon—abundance without dependence, power without relationship.

The problem was it didn't work, of course. There is no such thing as the Philosopher's Stone. And the alchemists themselves sensed that what they sought was beyond their power to discover or create. This led them to the conclusion that they would need assistance. The sorcerer needs an apprentice. But since ordinary human apprentices (whether Mickey Mouse or Marty McFly) are not always reliable or helpful, the alchemists began to dream and experiment and write about actually creating one from scratch. They conceived of creating a *homunculus*, the "little man" they thought was present in male sperm. The Frankenstein legend draws directly on this part of the alchemical tradition—the quest to make from scratch a servant for the alchemist, who would help them accomplish their very difficult work.

Like all the alchemists' quests, the quest to make (rather than beget) a human being was doomed. And gradually the alchemists realized that they needed a different kind of help. Not another human, but a spirit—a "familiar spirit," a spiritual apprentice who would help the alchemist discover the spiritual secrets that were just out of reach.

At this moment, alchemy let into its workroom, into its laboratory, the demonic. The alchemists imagined they could find spirits sufficiently small and compliant that they could command their assistance (Prospero with his Ariel), but in the world as it actually is, there are no spirits we can safely commandeer for our purposes. No matter how friendly they may initially seem, demons are unreliable at best. They are like the genie in the lamp—which may seem to promise to help but never actually help the way you expected. To entangle yourself with a demon, especially one that will happily present itself to you as a friendly, familiar spirit, is to be drawn into more and more exploitation.

And so this is my final judgment: the rise of alchemy in the West, the dream of autonomous power and independent abundance, summoned the demonic into the history of Christendom. And to summon the demonic is to unleash the force of evil in history. Christianity had vanquished the old, exploitative pagan religions, and with it their most exploitative practices, up to and including the enslavement of persons. But roughly 450 years ago, slavery re-emerged in the allegedly Christian West.

Why and how did slavery—the most naked possible exploitation of human beings, one of the greatest recurring evils of human history—arise in Christendom after it had been eliminated by the spread of the gospel?

My judgment is that it began, in a meaningful sense, with the failure of the alchemists' dream. When the dreams of magic and Mammon begin to die—when the fantasy of being able to have all you want without relationship, without dependence, and without vulnerability fails—you go looking for someone who will nonetheless give these things to you. You reach out in any way you can, with whatever powers available to you, and begin to exploit and extract from others that which you thought was promised to you by the magical world, but which it will never deliver.

The alchemists' project failed, but their dream is alive in our technology—it is "what technology wants." Of course, most reasonable people will protest—the difference between us and the alchemists is that our technology works! It's not like the alchemists' dead-end experiments.

Two brief responses to this objection. First, all idols work at first—if they don't initially deliver, they don't become idols. They just don't keep working. Have we gone far enough, eighty or so years into the story of modern technology, to know that it actually works? Is it actually working? Is it delivering what we want? Are our lives fuller? Are we happier?

And the second thing to say is that *technē* works, but technology will not. *Technē*, the artful, cultural engagement with God's world, humbly uncovering its possibilities, has worked from the dawn of the human story. But *technology*, the alchemical dream, will not. Already it enslaves far more people than we are willing to admit—more people are enslaved today, according to the International Labor Organization, than were trafficked in all the years of the Atlantic slave trade. How many more human beings will we consent to enslave in order to realize our dream of easy everywhere?

And this is why the church must be—and is perhaps the only community that can truly be—the community that renounces magic and Mammon.

We have to become a community that in every part of our life rejects the idea that we can have power without relationship. We need to reject Mammon's deceptive promise of abundance without dependence—which will be very difficult, given how entangled we are in Mammon's empire. Then we need to build the household of God, which is a moral community, not just a liturgical community, that lives in conscious resistance to the promises of magic and Mammon alike. A community that will not exploit others in order to get what we thought we were promised. A community that recognizes the vulnerable as its most important members, because they are the ones who live in utter violation of the logic of the technological world. A community in which there is no one who is useless because there is no one who is merely useful.

It will be a long resistance. Mammon bestrides our world. We do not wrestle against flesh and blood. If God has not put the church here at this moment in history, amidst these shattered and shattering dreams, where in the world would he have put us? There is no greater calling we could aspire to than to bear witness to the way of Jesus Christ in our world of technology, our world of fevered and false dreams—the world the alchemists made.

Bibliography

Bauckham, Richard. *Jesus and the Eyewitnesses: The Gospels as Eyewitness Testimony.* Grand Rapids: Eerdmans, 2006.

Berry, Wendell. "A Native Hill." *Hudson Review* 21.4 (Winter 1968–69) 601–34.

Borgmann, Albert. *Technology and the Character of Contemporary Life: A Philosophical Inquiry.* Chicago: University of Chicago Press, 1984.

Clarke, Arthur C. "Clarke's Third Law on UFOs" (Letter to the Editor). *Science* 159.3812 (Jan. 19, 1968) 255.

Gay, Craig M. *Modern Technology and the Human Future.* Downers Grove: InterVarsity, 2018.

Harari, Yuval. *Homo Deus: A Brief History of Tomorrow.* New York: Harper Perennial, 2017.

Jacobs, Jane. *The Death and Life of Great American Cities.* New York: Random House, 1961.

Jobs, Steve. "Computers are like a bicycle for our minds." Michael Lawrence Films. YouTube video. https://www.youtube.com/watch?v=ob_GX50Za6c.

Jung, Carl G. *Alchemical Studies*. Translated by R. F. C. Hull. Collected Works 13. Princeton: Princeton University Press, 1967.

Kelly, Kevin. *What Technology Wants*. New York: Viking, 2010.

Kurzweil, Ray. "The Coming Merging of Mind and Machine." *Scientific American*, March 23, 2009. https://www.scientificamerican.com/article/merging-of-mind-and-machine/.

O'Donovan, Oliver. *The Ways of Judgment (Bampton Lectures)*. Grand Rapids: Eerdmans, 2005.

Plato. *Phaedrus*. In *The Collected Dialogues*, edited by Edith Hamilton and Huntington Cairns, 475–525. Translated by R. Hackforth. Princeton: Princeton University Press, 1989.

4

Why We Get Technology Wrong

DOUGLAS ESTES

> We live in an era of technology. The racing tempo of our century affects all areas of our life. There is scarcely an endeavor that can escape its powerful influence. Therefore, the danger unquestionably arises that modern technology will make men soulless.
>
> —JOSEPH GOEBBELS[1]

WE CANNOT TALK ABOUT technology today without talking about smartphones.[2] Based on the amount of hand-wringing that goes on in thoughtful Christian circles about smartphones, we can safely conclude it is currently the morass of all morasses, and it is made even more morassy once we mix in social media apps like Twitter, Facebook, Instagram, and Tinder. If we want to discuss the dangers of technology, we only need to lazily reach but a micron above our heads and take hold of the lowest of lowest hanging fruit of the discussion.

Trying to create a Christian vision for technology and using the smartphone as an example is something like trying to create a Christian vision for economics and using reverse mortgages or interest-only loans as an example. Yes, in many cases these types of loans and the companies that hawk them are an ethical morass, even as they are a seemingly unmovable part of our larger economic system. Because so many people use these financial

---

1. As cited in Zimmerman, *Heidegger's Confrontation with Modernity*, 65.
2. I would like to thank Chris Tenny and Adam Graber for their helpful comments on an earlier draft of this paper.

products, it affects almost everyone, directly or indirectly, in some way. Yet we would never use these products as a starting point for a Christian vision for economics. So, dear reader, please put away your smartphone now as you won't need to think about it for this essay. And if you are reading this on your smartphone, that's just fine; I promise I won't make you feel guilty for doing so. I'm just glad you're reading.[3]

From my vantage point, the negativity and confusion about technology among Christian thought leaders in North America is increasing.[4] Maybe that is due to our fractious socio-political climate, the sense that no matter how much things get better in some ways, injustice just increases; or to the destabilizing feeling that we experience today due to rapid changes in technology. If so, I am not sure our environment in the West for building the kingdom will get better before it gets worse.[5] This is exactly the reason why we need a helpful, hopeful, biblically and theologically robust Christian vision for technology.

A vision for technology, what is often called a philosophy of technology, is a relatively new field of study that has only truly come about in the last several decades. Prior to this, instances of thinking about technology by various thinkers tended to come from within these thinkers' fields of study (philosophy, politics, economics, and theology) rather than any attempt at a comprehensive philosophy. The good news for Christians: we are not yet too late to join the conversation. The bad news for Christians: we are heading in the wrong direction.

In fact, we have messed this up so much I believe we need to just stop and start all over. To be fair, it is not totally our fault. I believe a Christian vision for technology falls under a "grey area" of theology wherein two faithful Christians may come to different conclusions on the why and how of technology. In fact, philosophers of technology themselves often want to argue both

---

3. I believe the smartphone is a wonderful technology for adults. As I say when people ask me about this: "My thirteen-year-old son asked me for a smartphone. I said no. He also asked me for a chainsaw. I said no to that, too."

4. One reviewer noted that this confusion is a result of what is meant by the word *technology*. In English, technology is a concept term with quite a large scope—and with meanings that are more culturally malleable than exact. As a result, I use *technology* in this essay the same way that culture uses technology. For example, at time of writing, Wikipedia defines technology as "the sum of techniques, skills, methods, and processes used in the production of goods or services or in the accomplishment of objectives." Thus, ICBMs and gluten-free muffins are both forms of technology. However, it is quite common to encounter use of the term in thoughtful Christian circles with overtones added to the word that are not obvious to the general meaning of the word in culture.

5. I do not believe technology will lead to either a dystopia or a utopia; as past is prologue, our world will be the same as it ever was until the consummation of the ages.

sides of the why and how—intellectually honest, but not always very clear or helpful.[6] Though there are many mistakes we Christians are making that have led us to this point, I feel that there are three that rise above the "grey area"—three mistakes that all Christians, regardless of their nuanced view of technology, need to own. First, *we have not done our homework*; second, *we have rotten roots*; and third, *we have the wrong spirit*. If we want to have a Christian vision of technology that is both faithful to our faith *and* is helpful to our world (cf. Mark 12:30–31), we need to make a course correction, and soon, as the drone is quickly leaving the docking station.

We Have Not Done Our Homework

We get technology wrong because we have not done our homework. Are we not people of the Word? Then I ask, where is the Bible in this discussion? Where is theology in this discussion? Where is the *ressourcement* of the fathers in this discussion? Far too often when we discuss technology, even in Christian environments, our primary appeals are to modern philosophy, social science, anthropology, personal observations, and similar humanistic studies. Far too often I am left uneasy as there is little appeal to Scripture beyond broad references to biblical anthropology.[7]

On this, we cannot back down: if we want a Christian vision of technology, it must start with the difficult task of engaging the biblical texts.[8] Yes, I know what many readers are thinking—the Bible doesn't really talk about technology. Does it?

Of course it does! Technology abounds in the Bible. According to biblical accounts, some of the earliest patriarchs were known by their technological prowess (Gen 4:20–22). God saved Noah and his family through divinely inspired nautical technology (Gen 6:14–16). By special revelation, God taught the Israelites how to design the tabernacle according to his expectations (Exod 25:9). God interacted directly with human technology when the need arose (Exod 14:25). People were blessed with technological ability (1 Kgs 7:14). Apparently, technological precision was important enough to God that it was inspired and included in his word with extensive

---

6. The most prominent example of this is the tendency to take both an *instrumental* and a *determinist* position in arguments, without strong consistency; see Borgmann, *Technology and the Character of Contemporary Life*, 40.

7. There are rare exceptions that try to engage Scripture directly, such as Dyer's *From the Garden to the City* and Ellul's *The Meaning of the City*, but far more is needed. I make this observation based on (a) material in print and (b) anecdotal observations at public forums/conferences on technology.

8. Contra Honecker, "Folgen der Technik," 473.

detail (1 Kgs 7:13–45). God himself chose to inhabit a piece of finely crafted human technology—the Holy of Holies in the midst of the temple (2 Chr 3:8; though cf. Acts 17:24). God represented his divinity using an image of human technology: the merciless and devastating king of the ancient battlefield, the chariot (2 Kgs 2:11–12). God allows technology to be incorporated into his plan for judgment against sinful people (Ezek 23:24). Yet there are times when in our ministry we are to avoid technology (Luke 9:3). Jesus bodied advanced technology with his seamless tunic that was likely created on the latest and greatest loom (thus its desirability; John 19:23–24).[9] In a small way, Jesus used technology to assist him to deliver his sermons—via a boat (Matt 13:2), akin to the way later engineers built rostra, cathedrals, or microphones to amplify line of sight and sound. In a great way, the early church employed technology to spread the gospel—via well-engineered Roman roads,[10] akin to the way later engineers built caravels, interstates, or internet chat rooms to accelerate the spread of the message.

Even more importantly, technology seems to be so woven into human existence that it will be with us in heaven (Rev 21:10–21). Also likely is that technology was with people in the Garden to "work" the land (עָבַד, difficult without basic agricultural tech) and possibly to discover useful metals (based on the awareness of gold, Gen 2:12). Both of these environments are without sin, which seems to suggest that both trees, axes, and chainsaws can exist in a sinless environment. What is more, when God makes it clear that after the consummation of the ages, the "first way" will have passed away (Rev 21:4), the renewal of all things will have occurred (Rev 21:5), yet technology will still be with us (Rev 21:10, 12–14), and so technology cannot be tied only to our groaning world. In fact, if we consider that the divine play has three acts—creation, redemption, and consummation—then technology stands in the chorus of all three acts.[11]

Our entire Christian faith hangs on technology—so much so that we suspend a depiction of technology in the most central place, in the most sacred space, in Christian churches. That technology is the cross. In at least one way, Jesus exemplifies our relationship to technology: he was blessed by technology—a seamless tunic. He was also cursed by technology—a cross.

In the Bible we see hundreds of technologies described, talked about, and put to use. Yet there is no explicit critique of technology in the Bible. Why? Let's put our hands in our laps for a moment and stop wringing them.

---

9. For further discussion, see Estes, *Braving the Future*, 178–80.

10. In comparison to the poor roads of other cultures, see Strabo, *Geography* 5.3.8; and cf. Suetonius, *Augustus*, 30.

11. Swain, *Trinity, Revelation, and Reading*, 18.

Let's take a deep breath and think through why, for example, Paul never seems to speak about technology (even as he used it daily). After all, if Paul found the time to discuss hair braiding (1 Tim 2:9), why couldn't he have discussed beer boilers and sewer ducts?

This is not to say there are no criticisms of technology in the Bible. One of the more instructive is the building of a city with a tower at Babel (Gen 11:1–9). In its day, the tower was a marvel that used new advances in brick-making technology (Gen 11:3). However, the people intended to use technology to impose on God's space and to proclaim the greatness of humanity.[12] God came down to consider the city and tower that these people built (Gen 11:5). Since these people cooperated to challenge God, God confused their language and scattered them across the earth, which resulted in the abandonment of the building project (Gen 11:7–8). If those people had elected to use the tower to worship God, would God still have responded the way he did? Based on our survey, the answer appears to be no, as it was not the technology itself but the evil intent for the technology that caused God to respond.

This brief survey barely strips the jacketing back from the thick cable of all the Bible has to say about technology. (And it doesn't even get us into the writings of early Christians such as Bishop Basil of Seleucia [435–468] who *praised* human technological innovation as a sign of the *imago Dei*.)[13] There are far more outstanding questions than satisfactory answers: since contentment comes from limited possessions (1 Tim 6:8), is the φιλαργυρία ("greed") of technology a root of all kinds of evil (1 Tim 6:10; cf. 1 John 2:15–16)? Does God ask his people today to engage technology (Exod 35:10)? Does God still use his Spirit to fill people today with technological ability (Exod 35:30–35)? Does the Lord still work through engineers (1 Chr 22:15)? In light of the many, many, many instances of technology in the Bible, broad and generic appeals to theological anthropology alone (in my experience, the most common appeal to the Bible to discuss technology) is woefully inadequate. But, because the roots of our arguments are rotten, and we are possessed of the wrong spirit, we are blinded to the need to really dig into Scripture to develop a *biblical theology of technology*. Sadly, there is no easy "thou shalt not use thy smartphone," which has led us to a place where we try to speak of a Christian vision of technology without beginning with a careful and considerate exegesis of the whole council of God.

---

12. Similarly, see Moltmann, *God in Creation*, 27.

13. Basil of Seleucia, *Oratio* 1 (*PG* 85:36). For the relevant passage in English, and further discussion, see Habas, "Donations and Donors," 87.

We Have Rotten Roots

We get technology wrong because the roots of our thoughts about technology are rotten. When the soil around a tree does not drain properly, the roots of the tree begin to decay and rot; even though the tree may seem healthy at first, it is only a matter of time before the tree eventually dies. The rot at the root of this tree is the uncritical acceptance and appropriation of Martin Heidegger's ideas about technology.

Martin Heidegger is the most influential figure in the discussion of technology in at least the last two centuries.[14] Whether we realize it or not, his arguments have influenced everyone's opinion about technology, including many (perhaps almost all) Christian thought leaders writing about technology today. For example, if we place Heidegger at the root of the tree, his thought spreads to his student Hannah Arendt, and then to Michel Foucault and Jean-François Lyotard. Next, moving quickly up the branches, his thought was picked up by Albert Borgmann and Marshall McLuhan, who spread these ideas to Protestant thinkers such as John Dyer and Andy Crouch and has become the *de facto* "Christian view" of technology.[15]

Let me prove it: whenever you hear a Christian thought leader talk about how technology "shapes us" or "changes us," they are speaking Heidegger, not the Bible. Where does the Bible tell us that technology shapes us? The Bible does tell us that God formed people (Gen 2:7), but that as a result of the rebellion of people, people are marred by their rebellion (Gen 3; Rom 5:12–14). No, we are not shaped by technology; we are shaped by the little bit of leaven that "leavens the whole lump" (1 Cor 5:6).[16] We are ὑφ' ἁμαρτίαν ("under sin," Rom 3:9; also Eph 2:2). Against this formation—seemingly no matter what technology we use and don't use—if we are in Christ, we are "predestined to be conformed to the image of his Son" (Rom 8:29). For those of us in Christ, that which shapes us is no longer sin but is now the Spirit of God.

In fact, when I hear Christians claim that "technology is changing us,"[17] I think of technologies such as antibiotics and the Apollo program,

---

14. For similar sentiments, see Ihde, *Heidegger's Technologies*, 12; Scharff, "Technology as 'Applied Science,'" 162; Pitt, "In Search of a New Prometheus," 4; Rojcewicz, *Gods and Technology*, 27; and Dyer, *From the Garden to the City*, 184.

15. Thomson, "Phenomenology and Technology," 201. For example, Dyer noted his influence from Heidegger on the dedication of his book; Crouch used several Heidegger-originated concepts such as the distinction between pre-modern and modern technology (also à la Borgmann) in his 2019 Center for Pastor Theologians plenary address.

16. All verses quoted in this chapter are from the ESV.

17. For example, Hipps, *Flickering Pixels*, 14, 26.

and I think, "If that's the case, I'm thankful that I'm being changed!" No one alive can imagine what it was like to suffer without modern medicine, and I consider it a great blessing from God to live in the age in which we live. Now, does technology *affect* the way we live? Yes—in the same way every other thing in this world affects the way we live. Because we live in this world, one that is wholly at odds with its Creator (John 7:7; 1 Cor 1:21), everything in this world affects the way we live—economics, politics, chemistry, biology, technology, media, injustice, gravity, marriage—the list is endless (2 Pet 1:4; cf. Gal 4:3; by way of example, 1 Cor 7:28–35). We are not to be conformed to those things (Rom 12:2; Jas 1:27). That is the challenge of living as people of faith in a world of so many negative effects.

Technology doesn't shape us. It has no inherent power over us. That's Heidegger. That's not the Bible.

Heidegger believed that technology was the great evil of the modern era.[18] In order to make his case, Heidegger starts with the claim that there is a distinct difference between pre-modern and modern technology—before the late-eighteenth century, people had *tools*, but afterward people have *technology*. He tries to create a foundation for this by appeal to the etymology of the ancient Greek word τέχνη. Unlike tools, which we can simply use, technology surrounds us and controls us; in ages past, people were in control of tools but "humans are not in control of technology."[19] To explain how trapped people are in technology, Heidegger fabricated the word *Gestell*, which is so convoluted in meaning as to be largely untranslatable into English. Most philosophers approximate it as "enframing." Thus, humanity is enframed by technology.

But there's more. Heidegger sees technology as the great antithesis to what he calls "Being" because of how he derives his definition of "Being."[20] Heidegger is not a theist, and thus the greatest ontological essence in the cosmos is humanity, not God.[21] From an atheistic perspective, could technology overwhelm humanity? Yes. In that scenario, technology could irrevocably damage or destroy our human nature that has evolved at the mercy of a purely naturalistic scenario. In simple terms, we can say that at the root of Heidegger's argument is his palpable fear that one day

$$\text{Technology} \geq \text{People}$$

---

18. Cf. Richardson, *Heidegger*, 324.

19. Dusek, *Philosophy of Technology*, 76.

20. Di Cesare, *Heidegger and the Jews*, 96. For this reason Heidegger rejects Christianity; see Heidegger, *Contributions to Philosophy*, 77.

21. Cf. Weber, *Überwindung der Metaphysik in der Theologie*, 80.

For Christians, the error in Heidegger's thought should be immediately apparent—there is no divine nature at work in his theory. Like Ivan in *The Brothers Karamazov*, Heidegger can find no means of satisfaction because there is no God to resolve the incongruity. Fortunately, for those of us in Christ, we know that no matter if

$$\text{Technology} \geq \text{People OR Technology} \leq \text{People}$$

that

$$\text{God} > \text{Technology AND God} > \text{People}$$

This should instill us with a spirit of hope and not a spirit of fear.

Here's what's both ironic and irrational about Heidegger's humanistic fear: Heidegger argued that there is a way that humanity can prevent itself from being enframed by technology. What is this *deus ex machina* in Heidegger's story? A god.[22] Not God, but a god. By which he means a spark of humanity that is attributed to some unknowable divinity. But if technology has humanity truly enframed, how can humanity suddenly become enlightened so as to step outside of the control of technology? From a biblical perspective, there is no suggestion we are "enframed" by technology (Acts 13:39; Rom 8:21; 2 Cor 3:17); and even if we were (cf. Gal 5:1), this enframing would not supersede God's ability to transform us and work in our world (Heb 11:32–34; cf. 1 Pet 2:16).

It gets worse. Heidegger's objection to technology is not just philosophical, it's *political*. Martin Heidegger was born in Meßkirch, Germany, 1889. After a brief stint studying theology, he switched to philosophy and, after the Great War, became professor of philosophy at the University of Marburg in 1923. Heidegger published his greatest work, *Sein und Zeit*, in 1927. This work prefigured some of his thought on technology (aka "the early Heidegger"). However, in the early 1930s, Heidegger moved to Freiburg where he soon began to embrace the ideology of the National Socialist German Worker's Party, even going so far as to sign the loyalty oath for professors and promoting himself as *the* philosopher of National Socialism.[23]

The problem with Heidegger is not merely that he was a National Socialist—he was also "an antitechnological romantic."[24] Heidegger believed that the golden age of the ancient Greeks had finally succumbed to the

---

22. Heidegger, *Question Concerning Technology*, 47.

23. This is also the time in which Heidegger completely abandons Christian thought for (his interpretation of) Greek thought; see Weber, *Überwindung der Metaphysik*, 79.

24. Dusek, *Philosophy of Technology*, 76.

advent of modern technology.²⁵ Heidegger's romanticizing tendencies led him to view Germany as the true state for an ideal people who were slowly being crushed "in the great pincers between Russia on the one side and America on the other," both of whom are driven by "the same hopeless frenzy of unchained technology."²⁶ Thus, technology was the vehicle by which Heidegger couched his anti-American and anti-Russian sentiments. Heidegger was not alone in this; it was essentially the same romanticizing sentiment of the Nazi Party.²⁷ In the epigraph to this chapter, I cited the words of Joseph Goebbels, Reich Minister of Propaganda for Nazi Germany, who stated "modern technology will make men soulless." This from the man who soullessly used technology for mass murder and genocide. But that's not what Goebbels meant. Goebbels and Heidegger mean that technology (as they define it, the types they are uncomfortable with) is a byproduct of the unrooted people in the world—people like the Americans, the Russians, and the Jews. In fact, to Heidegger, the Jews are a "rootless" people, exactly the type of people who encourage the acceleration of technology so as to claim victory over "rooted" (true) people—people who happen to be German.²⁸ "For Heidegger, [machine technology] was the embodiment of Judaism."²⁹ Heidegger never repented.³⁰

To understand the damage that Heidegger has done is to compare him to his philosophical foil, Plato. Plato was a brilliant philosopher, but also quite wrong in many areas. Yet the influence of his thought in philosophy in general is so great that in some areas of belief Christians are more Platonic than biblical (anthropology and eschatology, for example). Likewise, the influence of Heidegger's thought in the philosophy of technology is so great that many Christians are more Heideggerian than biblical.

Without hesitation, we must exorcise the spirit of Heidegger from any attempt at creating a Christian vision of technology. Heidegger believed Christianity was part of a conspiracy theory for world domination invented

---

25. Di Cesare, *Heidegger and the Jews*, 80; and Schmidt, "Monotheism as a Metapolitical Problem," 147.

26. Heidegger, *Introduction to Metaphysics*, 40. See also Di Cesare, *Heidegger and the Jews*, 81.

27. Zimmerman, *Heidegger's Confrontation*, 41.

28. Heidegger, *Ponderings* VII–XI, §4, 75–76; also, Di Cesare, *Heidegger and the Jews*, 84–85, 88; and Schmidt, "Monotheism as a Metapolitical Problem," 147.

29. Di Cesare, *Heidegger and the Jews*, 98.

30. Evans, *Coming of the Third Reich*, 422. Therefore, I reject arguments that Heidegger's later thought on technology has somehow eclipsed his earlier philosophical and political commitments.

by the Jews.³¹ Just as he argued that "Christian" and "philosophy" are completely incompatible ideas, so too do we need to accept that "Heidegger" and "Christian philosophy of tech" are also completely incompatible ideas.³² Worse, if we jump in our DeLoreans and skip ahead a couple hundred years, Heidegger's romanticized eighteenth-century line between pre-modern and modern technology will look naïve in retrospect. So will all of the Christians who today follow Heidegger, unwittingly or not.

We Have the Wrong Spirit

We get technology wrong because we have the wrong spirit. Instead of a spirit of fear, we need a spirit of hope—a spirit "of power and love and self-control" (2 Tim 1:7; also, Heb 13:6). Where does this fear come from? Let's go back to Heidegger.

If Heidegger is wrong, why do we still sometimes feel "enframed" or "ordered" by technology? If we take a step back from that question, we will realize that we don't feel shaped by most instances of technology. In fact, if we consider all of technology as a whole, almost all of it seems quite the opposite; it's more of a help than a hindrance, more of a sail than a drag.³³ The main reason we feel shaped by technology actually has nothing to do with technology itself. It has to do with *change*.³⁴

In forming his romanticized view of technology, Heidegger argued that pre-modern technology is ontologically different than modern technology. To build support for this claim, he reimagines the ancient Greek word τέχνη—he imbues it with a philosophical definition it probably never had (also contra biblical/Hellenistic Greek usage as in Acts 17:29, 18:3; Rev 18:22).³⁵ Thus, even though many echo Heidegger on this (notably Borgmann), the argument is largely without linguistic merit.³⁶ Not only is Hei-

---

31. Specifically, Bolshevism; see Heidegger, *Contributions to Philosophy*, 38.

32. Heidegger, *Introduction to Metaphysics*, 8. Weber notes that contemporary accounts of Heidegger's teaching from that time included "violent and polemical" attacks on Christianity; see *Überwindung der Metaphysik*, 80.

33. There are a few obvious examples of technology that we can't seem to escape; most of these are communication technologies (TVs, smartphones, internet). I suggest that the reason for this has more to do with the nature of *media* and *communication* than technology.

34. Or as Goebbels put it, the "racing tempo" of our age.

35. Inwood, *Heidegger Dictionary*, 209; and cf. Roochnik, *Of Art and Wisdom*, xi–xii, 19.

36. Ihde, *Heidegger's Technologies*, 76–78.

degger romanticizing technology,[37] he is romanticizing classical Greek, and he is doing so because he is a "reactionary modernist" toward technology.[38] As a young child, Heidegger's small village world had no electricity, automobiles, airplanes, or nuclear weapons. Yet, the rapid change in the early twentieth century driven by two world wars created an understandable existential crisis among much of the world's population.

This rapid evolution is what the sociologist and philosopher Zygmunt Bauman calls "liquid modernity."[39] The world of Heidegger's birth (a world that we in the beginning of the twenty-first century still get a glimpse of from time to time), was a world where change always included the expectation of a *telos*. However, the world that nineteenth-century people were thrust into was defined more by rapid change than any identifiable *telos*. And the same is true for twentieth-century people now thrust into the increasingly changing twenty-first century, one in which it feels as if the wheels of the bus have surely fallen off. Bauman uses the example of our physical health to show how the rapid change of a liquid modernity has affected us to our core: we go to the doctor to discover ailments that not only we didn't know we had, but in many cases we didn't even know existed.[40]

Here's the straight line: We are in a liquid world, experiencing rapid and unsettling change. That change makes us reach for the only safe ground we can find—the past, but romanticized. We allow ourselves to retreat into romanticism out of a fear for the future. We long for the simple church building with the one steeple, the feel of the hymnal in our hand, and the sturdy wooden pew to support us. If we close our eyes, we can see it just over the horizon. Let me offer two brief examples.

One

There is a great deal of handwringing in Christian circles about "screens"— specifically reading the Bible digitally or bringing digital-visual images into worship.[41] Inevitably someone trots out the old chestnut from Marshall McLuhan that the "medium is the message" (followed quickly by a bunch of quotes from Nicholas Carr). If this is true, that the medium is the message,

37. Hickman, "Technological Pragmatism," 176.
38. Ihde, *Heidegger's Technologies*, 12.
39. Bauman, *Liquid Modernity*.
40. Bauman, *Liquid Modernity*, 79.
41. For examples and discussion of this, see Prior, "Screens Are Changing the Way"; Raabe, "Why Churches Should Ditch the Projector Screens"; and cf. Dyer, *From the Garden to the City*, 23–24; Randall, "Digital Bibles."

then Christians of all people are totally in the soup. That's because our discussion of whether we should read our Bibles on our tablets or with our ESV TruTone Study Bible (with acid-free paper, machine sewn binding, and gilded edges) is moot. If the "medium is the message," we have no access today to the "medium" of God's word, because virtually all of the Bible was originally transmitted orally, in an open-air medium that we do not really experience today in the West. Later it was written down in various media that we no longer use, in languages that no one alive understands well.

Are we really so naïve to believe that early Christians "brought their Bibles" to church? Yet that is what our romantic yearnings want us to believe. This is what the discussion often descends into—a romanticizing that has no attachment to the actual past. Fortunately for the spread of the gospel, the medium did change rather rapidly in the first several centuries of the church from papyri to codices. Thank God that the early proponents of codex technology did not fret about the medium!

Because we live in a print-on-demand era, we have misunderstood the very basis of our faith. When John talks about Jesus as the "Word" of God, the word he uses—λόγος (instead of e.g., ῥῆμα)—had a wide semantic range in the vernacular of the day such that it could mean word, sentence, message, concept, or wisdom, all depending on the context. What he is not describing is an exclusively written word (especially not the printed word or the pixeled word). Most emphatically, the λόγος of God always transcends the medium. This is why if I encounter a person who cannot hear, I can learn sign language to speak to them the gospel; or a person who cannot see, I can give them the λόγος in Braille. Our romanticizing has introduced fear, and fear is not our faithful friend.

Of course, I am not suggesting that each medium—oral, papyri, codex, book, screen, ASL, Braille—doesn't have positives and negatives. I am in no way denying that there are not trade-offs between reading the Bible in modern print Bibles, on tablets, or from papyri. In fact, in some ways, reading the biblical text off a screen among a large group of people is *closer* to the earliest Christian experience of hearing the Bible read aloud in an HVAC-less building than the modern everybody-bring-their-Bibles-and-read-it-for-yourself Protestant model. Why we get technology wrong is that our romantic attachments are coloring our analysis of technology.

Two

At the annual Center for Pastor Theologians Conference in 2019 (to which this essay belongs, and exists in dialogue with), one of the plenary speakers showed an image on the projector screen (the irony) of two examples of the elements of Communion: on the left, there was an image of an artisanal loaf with a pottered clay chalice containing the wine. On the right, there was an image of something akin to the Fellowship Cup, a pre-filled sealed plastic Communion cup with embedded wafer. This depiction of the problems of technology elicited a great deal of laughs and jokes from the audience (and I admit, from our romanticized American Protestant Christian view of biblical faith, it is funny). Laughter aside, there is a *deeply* unbiblical argument here. As Paul writes to the church in Corinth:

> The cup of blessing that we bless, is it not a participation in the blood of Christ? The bread that we break, is it not a participation in the body of Christ? Because there is one bread, we who are many are one body, for we all partake of the one bread. (1 Cor 10:16–17)

If we are one body, then it does not matter whether we take the cup in a painted, glossed, and kiln-dried vessel made to look "vintage" and eat an artisanal loaf mass-produced at Whole Foods to look like something we could find at an Old World boulangerie in the south of France.

Are we really so naïve to believe that early Christians celebrated the Lord's supper with artisanal loaves (that contain both leaven and modern strains of wheat)? If we suggest that robot-made bread is somehow different from bakery bread is somehow different from handmade bread is somehow different from unleavened bread, how are we to be one body? We were never one body it seems, after all.[42]

This was brought home to me this week after Sunday service when my youngest daughter Violet took Communion for the first time after her baptism. While the rest of the church used the machined-bread squares but hand-poured cup, the pastor noted that for the first time they had Communion bread that was gluten-free. Violet, who is allergic to gluten, went in the back and got the gluten-free Fellowship Cup, so that she could take Communion without needing medicine afterward. Since it is unlikely that our church has the capacity for volunteer bakers to be back in the church kitchen crafting gluten-free artisanal loaves that affirms our romantic sensibilities, praise God for technology.

Why, then, when we show an image of a "hand-crafted" Communion kit and a "machine-made" Communion kit to pastors and theologians, do we all laugh? Because we cannot break free from our romanticizing tendencies.

---

42. It is interesting to note that the Didache, the earliest extant Christian text that addresses practical issues of discipleship, does talk about the mode of baptism but does not talk about the mode of Communion.

The world is so liquid; it feels as if everything is flowing away from us. But a romantic response to technology is neither biblical nor theological, it is Heideggerian. And for the good of the gospel, and our ability to communicate it well to future generations, we must abandon the spirit of romanticism and embrace a spirit of hope, basing that hope on our confidence that God will work in whatever way with whatever people he sees fit.

Can We Discover a Christian Vision for Technology?

To develop a Christian vision of technology, we need a redo. Let's agree to drop the smartphone routine. When we cherry-pick examples of technology that clearly have strong positives and negatives, we will never set a Christian vision for technology on slab footing. If we need to criticize an instance of technology, then by all means criticize the instance without lumping it in with technology in general.

To discover a Christian vision for technology, we must go at length to the Bible, the faithful extra-biblical literature, the writings of the early church, the longer tradition of the church, and only then bring in modern thoughts on the philosophy of technology. To discover a Christian vision for technology, we must exorcise Heidegger from our thoughts and our vocabulary. To discover a Christian vision for technology, we must be candid with ourselves about our romanticizing tendencies.

To discover a Christian vision for technology, we must work harder, stop the hand-wringing and the quasi-dystopian fears, and offer people a helpful, hopeful, Christian vision for technology.

Let us reason together: What exactly is a Christian vision of anything? For example, what is a Christian vision of money? What is a Christian vision of animals? We would never establish a Christian vision of those features of our world without serious biblical and theological study, without bracketing out philosophers who hold metaphysical positions anathema to the Christian faith, and without setting aside our romantic attachments to these features.

Even though technology is perhaps the fear *du jour*, I do not believe we Christians should respond to it differently than any other worldly features. Rather, we can look to the longer history with these features to inspire our thinking on creating a Christian vision of technology. We must put aside our fears and come to terms with the technological future if we will have any chance of speaking with wisdom from the past.[43] This, by the way, is not in any way suggesting that we should put our hopes in technology (cf. Rom

---

43. Cf. Simon, "History Begins in the Future," 193.

8:22–24).[44] Of course not: "Is not your fear of God your confidence, and the integrity of your ways your hope?" (Job 4:6).

Bibliography

Bauman, Zygmunt. *Liquid Modernity*. Cambridge: Polity, 2000.
Borgmann, Albert. *Technology and the Character of Contemporary Life: A Philosophical Inquiry*. Chicago: University of Chicago, 1984.
Di Cesare, Donatella. *Heidegger and the Jews: The Black Notebooks*. Cambridge: Polity, 2018.
Dusek, Val. *Philosophy of Technology: An Introduction*. Malden: Blackwell, 2006.
Dyer, John. *From the Garden to the City: The Redeeming and Corrupting Power of Technology*. Grand Rapids: Kregel, 2011.
Ellul, Jacques. *The Meaning of the City*. Grand Rapids: Eerdmans, 1977.
Estes, Douglas. *Braving the Future: Christian Faith in a World of Limitless Tech*. Harrisonburg: Herald, 2018.
———. *SimChurch: Being the Church in the Virtual World*. Grand Rapids: Zondervan, 2009.
———. "Sin and the Cyborg: On the (Im)Peccability of the Post-human." *Bulletin of Ecclesial Theology* 6 (2019) 69–79.
Evans, Richard J. *The Coming of the Third Reich*. New York: Penguin, 2005.
Habas, Lihi. "Donations and Donors as Reflected in the Mosaic Pavements of Transjordan's Churches in the Byzantine and Umayyad Periods." In *Between Judaism and Christianity: Art Historical Essays in Honor of Elisheva (Elisabeth) Revel-Neher*, edited by Katrin Kogman-Appel and Mati Meyer, 73–90. Medieval Mediterranean 81. Leiden: Brill, 2008.
Heidegger, Martin. *Contributions to Philosophy (From Enowning)*. Translated by Parvis Emad and Kenneth Maly. Studies in Continental Thought. Bloomington: Indiana University Press, 1999.
———. *Introduction to Metaphysics*. Translated by Gregory Fried and Richard Polt. Yale Nota Bene. New Haven: Yale University Press, 2000.
———. *Ponderings VII–XI: Black Notebooks 1938–1939*. Translated by Richard Rojcewicz. Studies in Continental Thought. Bloomington: Indiana University Press, 2017.
———. *The Question Concerning Technology: And Other Essays*. Translated by William Lovitt. New York: Garland, 1977.
Hickman, Larry. "Technological Pragmatism." In *A Companion to the Philosophy of Technology*, edited by Jan Kyrre Berg Olsen, Stig Andur Pedersen, and Vincent F. Hendricks, 175–79. Blackwell Companions to Philosophy 43. West Sussex: Wiley-Blackwell, 2009.
Hipps, Shane. *Flickering Pixels: How Technology Shapes Your Faith*. Grand Rapids: Zondervan, 2009.
Honecker, Martin. "Folgen der Technik." *Zeitschrift für Theologie und Kirche* 87 (1990) 471–86.
Ihde, Don. *Heidegger's Technologies: Postphenomenological Perspectives*. Perspectives in Continental Philosophy. New York: Fordham University Press, 2010.

---

44. There are plenty of problems akin to romanticism on the "tech will save us" side of the discussion, but since that position is less common in Christian circles, I do not address it in this essay (though the same concerns apply).

Inwood, Michael. *A Heidegger Dictionary*. Blackwell Philosopher Dictionaries. Oxford: Blackwell, 1999.

Moltmann, Jürgen. *God in Creation: An Ecological Doctrine of Creation*. Translated by Margaret Kohl. London: SCM, 1985.

Pitt, Joseph C. "In Search of a New Prometheus." In *Broad and Narrow Interpretations of Philosophy of Technology*, edited by Paul T. Durbin, 3–15. Philosophy and Technology 7. Dordrecht: Kluwer, 1990.

Prior, Karen Swallow. "Screens Are Changing the Way We Read Scripture." *Christianity Today*, Spring 2019.

Raabe, Tom. "Why Churches Should Ditch the Projector Screens and Bring Back Hymnals." *The Federalist*, June 18, 2019.

Randall, Rebecca. "Digital Bibles Help Men Read More but Retain Less." *Christianity Today*, September 23, 2019. https://www.christianitytoday.com/news/2019/september/digital-bibles-help-men-read-more-retain-less.html.

Richardson, John. *Heidegger*. Routledge Philosophers. London: Routledge, 2012.

Rojcewicz, Richard. *The Gods and Technology: A Reading of Heidegger*. SUNY Series in Theology and Continental Thought. Albany: State University of New York Press, 2006.

Roochnik, David. *Of Art and Wisdom: Plato's Understanding of Techne*. University Park: Pennsylvania State University Press, 1998.

Scharff, Robert C. "Technology as 'Applied Science.'" In *A Companion to the Philosophy of Technology*, edited by Jan Kyrre Berg Olsen, Stig Andur Pedersen, and Vincent F. Hendricks, 160–64. Blackwell Companions to Philosophy 43. West Sussex: Wiley-Blackwell, 2009.

Schmidt, Christoph. "Monotheism as a Metapolitical Problem: Heidegger's War Against Jewish Christian Monotheism." In *Heidegger's Black Notebooks and the Future of Theology*, edited by Mårten Björk and Jayne Svenungsson, 131–57. New York: Palgrave Macmillan, 2018.

Simon, Zoltán Boldizsár. "History Begins in the Future: On Historical Sensibility in the Age of Technology." In *The Ethos of History: Time and Responsibility*, edited by Stefan Helgesson and Jayne Svenungsson, 192–209. Making Sense of History 34. New York: Berghahn, 2018.

Strabo. *The Geography of Strabo*. Translated by Horace Leonard Jones. 8 vols. Loeb Classical Library. Cambridge: Harvard University Press, 1917–49.

Suetonius. *The Lives of the Caesars*. Translated by Catharine Edwards. Oxford World's Classics. Oxford: Oxford University Press, 2000.

Swain, Scott R. *Trinity, Revelation, and Reading: A Theological Introduction to the Bible and Its Interpretation*. London: T&T Clark, 2011.

Thomson, Iain. "Phenomenology and Technology." In *A Companion to the Philosophy of Technology*, edited by Jan Kyrre Berg Olsen, Stig Andur Pedersen, and Vincent F. Hendricks, 195–201. Blackwell Companions to Philosophy 43. West Sussex: Wiley-Blackwell, 2009.

Weber, Ludwig. *Überwindung der Metaphysik in der Theologie*. 2nd ed. Reihe Philosophie 19. Herbolzheim: Centaurus, 2005.

Zimmerman, Michael E. *Heidegger's Confrontation with Modernity: Technology, Politics, Art*. Indiana Series in the Philosophy of Technology. Bloomington: Indiana University Press, 1990.

5

Sacrament and Technology

CHRISTOPHER J. GANSKI

How do sacraments assist us in our engagement with technology? Sacraments and technology have many analogous functions in how they structure our experience of the world. Many have observed the ways in which modern technology functions powerfully in our life as a worldview or social imaginary.[1] As tools of human making of material reality, technology brings with it a distinct way of inhabiting the world that imposes upon us patterns of life, distinct values, and habits of thought. Sacraments also involve the use of material things, but for the sake of God-ordained ends. As spiritual tools, sacraments impose upon us a theological worldview with a distinctly Christ-centered way of *being-in-the-world*. Sacraments and technology both shape how we imagine ourselves in our environments. Both make use of and manipulate material stuff. Both are culture-making objects we invest with symbolic power and authority. Both generate patterns of meaning and systems of relationships that shape and direct human indwelling of the world. The difference is that sacraments are tools of grace. They are *instruments* by which God *cultivates* and *works* redemption within human nature. In other words, they are God's technology. Technology is a tool for our *making* of the world, but a sacrament is a tool of God's *(re) making* of us. However, as means of grace this does not mean sacraments are concerned merely with immaterial reality. As spiritual tools, sacraments sanctify human nature by forming us into the image of Christ, which ultimately transforms how we engage the world of stuff.

---

1. For a penetrating analysis of the worldview character of technology see Borgmann, *Technology*.

The relationship between technology and sacraments is more than incidental; it is primordial. They are connected to one another through our status as human beings created in the image of God. The use of technology and sacraments raises the same questions about the meaning of human nature in relationship to God and the rest of creation. In this essay, I argue that a Christian approach to the right use of technology depends upon cultivating a sacramental imagination, which is necessary for a proper understanding of human nature. To have a sacramental imagination is to recover the full sense of the human being as both a *worshipper* of God and a *worker* of creation. A sacrament is a kind of technology that holds together both aspects of our nature as worker and worshipper. I realize this might seem like an odd definition of sacramentality. The Christian tradition has tended to think about sacramentality as a metaphysical question that asks how the *presence* of God is related *to, with,* or *through* created realities. Sacramentality understood under these terms sees the sacraments as special rites and objects where God becomes graciously present and knowable within the material world. I would affirm this aspect of the function of sacraments, but I want to highlight the redemptive-historical dimension of sacramentality. Such an account emphasizes how the sacraments arise out of the real history of Jesus Christ, and how our use of them connects us with his living person. They are tools by which our fallen humanity is incorporated, nurtured, and ultimately conformed to his glorified humanity.

This historical dimension of the sacraments is important to consider in the light of the history of technological development. The narration of history since the Enlightenment is increasingly a story of technological development and innovation. New technological achievements augur new directions in what is possible for human nature.[2] Arguably, one could claim that technology has become the sacrament of our secular age. George Grant goes so far as to call technology "the ontology of our age."[3] We look to new technologies with a sense of hope and optimism about the future. We are ever more reliant on technology for the basic functioning of society. Increasingly, all our experiences of the world are mediated through digital screens and media platforms. We fuse technology to our bodies. For most of us, it is simply unimaginable to get along in the world without a smartphone. Technology has a sacred status in our modern world; we have invested it with salvific significance for the future.

---

2. Recent popular examples of this tech-optimistic historiography are Harrai, *Homo Deus*; and Pinker, *Enlightenment Now*.

3. Grant, *Technology and Justice*, 32.

Here we must recognize the negative conforming potential of modern technology in our secular age. Technology has never been a neutral medium. Even though tools are an extension of human nature, they in turn reshape our spiritual and moral character in unexpected ways. Alexander Schmemann insightfully describes life in a secular age as "the negation of man as a worshipping being, as *homo adorans*: the one for whom worship is the essential act which both posits his humanity and fulfills it."[4] While it is not necessarily the case that technology is "the negation of man as a worshipping being," the overall logic of living in a modern technological society is the reduction of worship, less need for God, the diminishment of a sense of divine presence and reality. For every human problem there now seems to be a technological answer or fix. Life in modern society is one in which a secular orientation to material reality is invisibly formed in us by our simple use of technology. This means that technology poses not only a moral and ethical dilemma for the Christian, but an apologetical one. In subtle and not so subtle ways, immersion in technological society is constantly negating our life as worshippers (*homo adorans*) of the true God.[5]

How are we to respond to this apologetical dilemma of social practices that inculcate in us a sense of divine absence within the cosmos? Learning to regulate our technological use is necessary, but we need more than that. We need counter-technologies that habituate us into an alternative imagination of our environments. We need practices centered around material things that re-introduce divine presence back into the world. We need sacraments. I propose that the sacramental life is a necessary Christian apologetic for resisting the inherent secularism of modern technological society and its drainage of divine presence from creation. The goal of this essay is not to depict sacraments as the antithesis of technology, but as the necessary spiritual tools we need to fulfill our vocation as *homo adorans* and *homo faber* (man the worker). To accomplish this task will first require us to a give an account of technology as grounded in a Christian anthropology, and second, to understand how sacraments function as spiritual technologies given for the sake of reshaping us into the image of Christ.

A Biblical Genealogy of Technology

What do we discern about the origins of technology in the Bible? Can we even ask this question? Here I am working with minimalist definition of

---

4. Schmemann, *For the Life of the World*, 118.

5. For critical analysis of technological society's secularizing impulses, see Ellul, *Technological Society*; Borgmann, *Power Failure*; and Gay, *Modern Technology*.

technology that would be inclusive even of tools from ancient societies. Craig M. Gay defines technology as *"the systematic application of knowledge, methods, and tools to various practical tasks."*[6] With such a definition, we see the Bible has quite a bit to say. From the outset, Scripture shows a certain *ambivalence* towards technology. The first explicit mention of tools suggests an inauspicious beginning. Technology starts in the city founded by Cain after he murdered his brother, Abel. We learn that Tubal-Cain became the "the forger of all instruments of bronze and iron" (Gen 4:22)[7]. The association of technology with the city of Cain should not be interpreted as the Bible's negative view of technology. However, it is testimony that technology, and all of human civilization, emerges within a fallen and sinful world which is a mixture of blessing and curse. In the city of Cain, we also find the origins of the arts, poetry, and musical instruments, but also bigamy, vain celebrity culture, and urban violence.

This brings us to an important point of contrast between the origin story the Bible tells about civilization and technology as compared with other Ancient Near East religions. In the Canaanite mythologies of the period, the arts of human civilization—such as metallurgy, animal domestication, and building houses—were attributed to gods and demigods. We see the same within Greek mythology with Prometheus and Athena handing gifts of technological arts to humans. But in the Torah, according to Umberto Cassuto, "We find only ordinary human beings, and there is no mythological element whatsoever. This is a great innovation introduced by the Torah: it discards the mythological tradition and opposes the blurring of the boundaries between the Godhead and mankind. It emphasizes that human civilization was of human origin."[8]

The Bible demythologizes technology. Technology does not have divine origin, but merely human origin, which means it is impacted by human sinfulness. The Bible never makes the mistake we are prone to today, which is to confuse technological advancement with spiritual achievement. The Bible's ambivalence towards technology is in recognizing that as a human invention, it can be used for good or for evil. This is what I mean by ambivalence. We need only read the story about the Tower of Babel for an explicit example of human technological ingenuity being used towards disobedient purposes (Gen 11). In an age of tech-optimism, it is important to remember the Bible's refusal to equate technological advancement with the moral and spiritual progress of the human race.

6. Gay, *Modern Technology*, 3.
7. All verses in this chapter are from the ESV.
8. Cassuto, *Commentary on the Book of Genesis*, 188.

Homo Faber

Technology is an expression and manifestation of human nature within creation. However, to recognize its human origins is not to cut God out of the picture. God may not have invented technology, but he did create human beings made in his image that do create technology. The development of technology is rooted in our nature as *homo faber*—"man the maker." As *homo faber*, the development and use of tools is central to our survival, work, and interaction with creation. This is not incidental to what it means to be created in the image of God. The antecedent of being *homo faber* of course is God the creator (or maker) of heaven and earth. After creating, God makes humans in his image and commands them to exercise "dominion" over all creation and to be fruitful and multiply. Then God blesses them for this activity (Gen 1:26–28). God places the first human couple in a garden with the job to "work it and keep it" (Gen 2:15).[9] This is called the cultural mandate.

However, we are not like God in that we cannot work and make something out of nothing. We need tools to engage creation, whereas God does not. It is hard to imagine how the first humans could have been obedient to their task without the development and use of tools. This assumption is further supported when we understand that the meaning of the cultural mandate was a call to civilization-building. The vocation of the first couple was not to tend and maintain a quaint English garden for the divine monarch to wander around. They were given a mandate to build out a city-garden within creation, which was meant to be the beginning of civilization (cf. Rev 21–22). Such an intention is suggested by the description of Eden as a place rich in natural resources such as gold, bdellium, and onyx. Also, remember that the Garden of Eden has a prime geographic location for civilizational development as it sits at the intersection of four great rivers (Pishon, Tigris, Gihon, Euphrates). The cultural mandate given to humans prior to the fall presumes a natural development of tools, instruments, and technologies to aid and assist in the task. Technology does not have a special mythological status and power that it does in other ANE cultures, but it is grounded in the goodness of human nature as created in God's image. This is an important Christian affirmation of the good of technology.

Technological development is a natural manifestation of human nature created in the image of God as it instinctually seeks to fulfill the primordial reality of the cultural mandate. Technology is not something outside of us in the world, that exists independently of us, but rather is a manifestation of human nature itself. *The Bible does not have a dystopian*

---

9. For exegetical support for this vocational interpretation of the image of God see, Middleton, *Liberating Image*.

view of technology; it has a dystopian view of human nature, which is responsible for technology. This dystopian take on human nature does not cancel out the goodness of the image of God in us, but it understands how greatly marred and distorted this nature is. To riff on Pascal, we could say that technology demonstrates simultaneously the *greatness* and *wretchedness* of humanity.[10] What makes an analysis of technology so complicated is that it involves a self-reflection upon our own *greatness* and *wretchedness* inextricably bound together. This means a Christian reflection on technology must be grounded in theological anthropology. Technology at its heart always raises questions of what it means to be a human being.

Homo Adorans

This forces us to return to the theme of what it means to be made in the image of God. To be image-bearers is to be *homo faber,* but it is also to be *homo adorans*—man the worshipper. Prior to the fall, the activity of *homo faber* and *homo adorans* were one and the same. To work was worship, and worship was work. We learn this by understanding that Genesis depicts creation as a cosmic temple of God's presence with the Garden as the Holy of Holies within creation.[11] The first human beings were set in the Garden not simply as *workers*, but as priests. God walked in the Garden in the cool of the day and had intimate fellowship with the man and the woman (Gen 3:8). The Lord God took the man and put him in the Garden of Eden to *"work it and keep it"* (Gen 2:15). The Hebrew for work (*avodah*) is the same word that in different contexts means worship (cf. Exod 8:1). We see the clearest commingling of meanings of work and worship in the description of the Levitical priests in the tabernacle who keep (*samar*) and work (*avodah*) it (Num 3:18–39). Work in Eden prior to the fall had a cultic meaning. It was *cultivation* of creation, the making of culture, which at the same time was an expression of worship of the Creator. It was a *guarding* and *service*. In the Garden, there was a seamless integration of our *worship* and our *work*. Humans did not work for the sake of food, shelter, or survival. We did not work because we *needed* to. God provided for all our basic needs through the Garden he planted. Work was simple obedience to God; it was our "reasonable act of worship," our way of relating to God as those who had been installed as priest-kings at the heart of creation. Given

---

10. Pascal, *Pensées*, 202. "The greatness of man is so evident, that it is even proved by his wretchedness" (97).

11. For an interpretation of Genesis along these lines see Beale, *Temple and the Church's Mission*; and Walton, *Genesis*.

this understanding of the image of God in man as both *homo faber* and *homo adorans,* the emergence of any technology prior to the fall would have been a tool of worship as much as it was a tool for work.

The Great Dissolution

After the fall, there is a great split and dissolution in our identity as *homo faber* and *homo adorans* that changes everything. Outside of the Garden, the meaning of work fundamentally changes on account of the curse. "Cursed is the ground because of you; in pain you shall eat of it all the days of your life; thorns and thistles it shall bring forth for you; and you shall eat the plants of the field. By the sweat of your face, you shall eat bread" (Gen 3:16–19). In the Garden, work was a joyful and pleasing obedience to the mandate of the Creator, but east of Eden, work becomes a burdensome necessity for the sake of human survival. And yet, despite our expulsion from the Garden, the *imago Dei* in us can still only be fulfilled in us as *homo adorans*. But sin complicates the relationship.

The story of Cain and Abel illustrates the profound tension in us between *homo adorans* and *homo faber*. Cain was a *worker* of the ground and Abel a *keeper* of sheep. In the course of time, Cain brought an offering of the fruit of the ground to the Lord, and Abel brought the firstborn of his flock. God had regard for Abel's offering, but he had no regard for Cain's offering (Gen 4:2–6). While we do not know what exactly was unacceptable about Cain's offering to God, the story underscores the fact that there is something about Cain's *work* of the ground that shows an off-kilter relationship to God. Something in his work is threatening alienation from God. "Sin is crouching at the door" (Gen 4:7). God holds out the possibility of Cain making it right, but Cain gives in to sin, and the story ends tragically with bloodshed. As a consequence, *homo faber*'s alienation with the material creation is further deepened. The ground cries out with Abel's blood, and Cain is cursed from the ground. His sin symbolizes the shattering of human community and violent alienation from the earth.

Cain represents the path of *homo faber* within a fallen world, alienated from the Creator. His story, however, has an unexpected outcome. He goes on to build a great city of renown that is the birthplace of civilization, culture, and technology. Abel represents *homo adorans* in a fallen world whose end is martyrdom. The way of *homo faber* is through the exercise of *power;* the way of *homo adorans* is that of *suffering*. Running through the very middle of human history is this archetypal antagonism in human nature between *homo adorans* and *homo faber.* It is from within this alienated relationship—an internal fracture in human nature—that technology emerges and develops within the world. And it is only through sacrament that they are reunited.

What does this archetypal history mean for our understanding of technology? First, it means that we understand technology as an expression of our nature as *homo faber*, created in the image of God, but perversely fallen. Prior to the fall, work and technology were straightforward expressions of worship and right relating to God. After the fall, technology in the line of Cain becomes a way of establishing our identity, legacy, dominance, and power in and over the world. *When technology is directed away from a God-glorifying understanding of the cultural mandate, it easily becomes about liberating human nature from the effects of the curse without the help of God.* The curse brought upon us physical pain and suffering, a hostile relationship to the environment, alienation from human community, and mortality. From the beginning, human technology has sought to mitigate and overcome the reality of the curse in life. This instinct is not wrong. The problem is that in a state of alienation and enmity towards God, our technologies easily take on salvific significance and import. Through the power of our own technological ingenuity, we are deluded into thinking we can deliver ourselves from the effects of the curse without God.

But even more, technological development cut free from a proper understanding of *homo adorans* becomes an expression of the idol of human ambition and conquest. It is the promise that the serpent made in the Garden, that to eat of the tree we will become like God, knowing good and evil (Gen 3:22). It is significant that the final story of the primeval history in Genesis epitomizes this thinking. The people of the earth gather in one place and say, "Come, let us make bricks, and burn them thoroughly." And they had brick for stone and bitumen for mortar. Then they said, "Come, let us build ourselves a city and a tower with its top in the heavens, and let us make a name for ourselves" (Gen 11:3–4). Babel is the archetypal story of how humans seek to exalt themselves and storm the doors of heaven by means of their own ingenuity and technology. Even God recognizes the dangerous potential of human technology uninhibited: "Behold, they are one people, and they have all one language, and this is only the beginning of what they will do. *And nothing that they propose to do will now be impossible for them*" (Gen 11:6). This story illustrates how closely aligned are our technological ambitions with our spiritual aspirations. They cannot be separated. Technology is bound up with the serpent's promise to Eve in the Garden that we could become like God and take to ourselves the knowledge of good and evil. At the heart of human sinfulness is the desire to overcome our creatureliness and to become like God. Technology is a powerful means by which we seek to actualize this perverse desire. At its heart, the question of *right use* of technology has to do with understanding and abiding by our God-ordained limits as creatures made in God's image. Central to being *homo adorans* is embracing our creaturehood and finitude.

A theological account of technology must be located within the full context of an understanding of human nature as created in the image of God, but fallen into sin. We must not separate our reflections on technology from a theological understanding of the human person. A right use of technology has to do with the healing of human nature. This healing presumes a proper understanding of the original meaning of our nature, but it also must include a proper grasp of the nature of salvation which restores it. This is where sacraments come into play. Sacraments are God's technology. They are the instruments God has ordained for the remaking of human nature in his image.

Sacrament of a New Humanity

A sacramental imagination is one that grounds our humanity in the humanity of Jesus Christ, the Incarnate, crucified, and now exalted Son of God. Jesus is the historical and personal link between our reflection on technology and sacraments. As the eternal Son, he is the one through whom all things were created (John 1:2), and as *homo faber*, he is the carpenter from Nazareth, the son of Joseph and Mary (Mark 6:3). As *homo adorans*, he is the Son of God, to whom the Father says from heaven at Jesus's baptism: "This is my beloved Son, in whom I am well pleased" (Matt 3:17). Jesus is the one true image-bearer, in whose humanity is accomplished the reconciliation and healing of *homo faber* and *homo adorans*. What is central about Christian sacraments is how they incorporate and unite our humanity with Jesus's humanity. Sacraments serve the God-ordained purpose of reuniting the cracked image of God in us, the division between *homo faber* and *homo adorans*. The relevance of them for thinking about technology is their *functional* capacity to incorporate and conform our humanity to Jesus's own. There is no right use of technology without a human nature that has been made righteous.

Here it is necessary to take a brief detour into sacramental theology. Understanding what sacraments are is essential for knowing how they connect and form our humanity to the person of Jesus. The most influential definition of a sacrament comes from Saint Augustine who describes it as a visible sign of an invisible grace. John Calvin follows Saint Augustine's definition, but he emphasizes how sacraments *signal* and *seal* faith in us.[12]

12. Calvin, *Institutes*. For Calvin's treatment of the nature of a sacrament, see *Institutes*, 4.14.1–24

The increase of faith in us bears fruit in holiness, but what is key for Calvin is how a sacrament focuses our spiritual attention outside of ourselves to the finished work of Christ. What gives a sacrament its meaning is how it puts us in touch with the saving person and work of Christ. There is a *doing* in which a sacrament involves us, but it is a *doing of faith* that makes us receptive to God's doing. From the perspective of the Reformation, there are two sacraments instituted by the Lord: baptism and the Lord's Supper. Baptism is the sacrament of initiation and the Supper the sacrament of nurture. As Rowan Williams observes: "What makes Christian sacraments unique is not so much something inherent in the doing of them, some 'specialness' in the action, but the uniqueness of Jesus Christ in his dying and rising."[13] Sacraments connect us to this unique work of God in the world.

They cannot be separated from the word of God. This is important to observe because God's original work was one that took place through his spoken word. And God continues to work in creation through his word. As the Roman Catholic theologian Louis-Marie Chauvet says, the sacraments are "the Word of God at the mercy of the body."[14] This captures nicely Calvin's own view. According to Calvin, sacraments have the same office as the word of God, which is to "offer and set forth Christ to us, and in him the treasures of heavenly grace."[15] For Calvin and the other magisterial Reformers, preaching in addition to baptism and the table has a sacramental power to make Jesus Christ present and manifest. This means word and sacrament are both *instruments* of grace, by which Christ becomes present with the world. What distinguishes them from one another is not distinct qualities of grace they offer, but the different way each impacts our humanity. Sacraments become necessary because of our creatureliness. According to Calvin, sacraments are God's accommodation to the human body. They are necessary because we are not angels, but corporeal beings. The word preached communicates to one aspect of our humanity, while the sacraments address another. In his infinite kindness, God "condescends to lead us to himself even by these earthly elements, and to set before us in the flesh a mirror of spiritual blessings."[16] To make the point in technological terms, the sacraments make the person of Jesus and his dying and rising operational in our lives.

The necessity of sacraments for the Christian life is then rooted in our nature, not only as *homo adorans*, but also as *homo faber*. *Homo faber* is

---

13. Williams, *On Christian Theology*, 195.
14. Chauvet, *Sacraments*.
15. Calvin, *Institutes*, 4.14.17.
16. Calvin, *Institutes*, 4.14.3.

to be tool-making creature. She is not a spirit-being, but has a body made from the dust of the earth. Like the rest of animal life, her body is finite and subject to the conditions of mortality. Nevertheless, as *imago Dei* she is stationed in a place of transcendence in relation to creation as caretaker and cultivator. The innovation of tools and technologies is necessary for her to exercise dominion, to be fruitful and multiply, to cultivate and flourish within creation. To be *homo faber* is to need tools to be *functional* in the world. It is no different with spiritual realities. God gives us sacraments as tools to make the reality of the gospel *functional* in our lives. Sacraments are the way in which God exercises dominion over our lives and makes us fruitful and flourishing. Spiritual transformation cannot happen simply through thinking and feeling as separate from the body. For the gospel to work in us, it must impose new patterns of life upon our bodies, it must become embodied perception of the world.[17]

This requires spiritual tools and technologies. Sacraments are the God-ordained instruments through which the gospel becomes fully functional in our life. And here it must be noted that we should be careful not to think too narrowly about sacraments. They are a complex set of practices that have the capacity to organize and order the lived existence of a whole community. When "rightly administered," they generate their own cultural and social ecosystem. As a complex set of practices, they are inclusive of prayer, preaching, reading Scripture, confession, singing, the exercise of the keys, and the development of liturgies. The purpose of all these things is to conform our nature to the renewed humanity of Jesus Christ in his dying and rising. In Jesus Christ, the split between *homo faber* and *homo adorans* has been healed, and sacraments are the God-ordained *instruments* that effect that healing in our lives.

Sacraments in an Age of Technique

Many will wonder whether I have made too much of the sacraments. And some will doubt that a sacrament could ever play as formative a role in a person's life as their technology. These are understandable concerns, but I want to note that our skepticism towards the sacraments is a sign of how much of our imaginations have been domesticated by life in a technological society. There is a profound tension between the kind of sacramental imagination I am advocating for and our immersion in a technological

---

17. For a good reflection on how the Supper makes the gospel *functional* and *embodied perception* in the Christian life, see Billings, *Remembrance, Communion and Hope*.

life. At its core, the social imaginary of modern technological society is secular and anti-sacramental.

Here Jacques Ellul is particularly helpful for diagnosing the spiritual character of technology, which he describes through the concept of *technique*. According to Ellul, *technique* "does not mean machines, technology, or this or that procedure for attaining an end. In our technological society, *technique* is the totality of methods rationally arrived at and having absolute efficiency in every field of human activity."[18] *Technique* is a way of inhabiting the world that tends to mechanize all of life for maximum control for the sake of the most efficient and productive outcomes. *Technique*, says Ellul, "transforms everything into a machine," by which he means that every aspect of human existence, whether it is social, political, or religious, can be comprehended and treated in mechanical categories. Everything can be constructed, deconstructed, and then reconstructed to be more productive and efficient. This mechanized approach is the triumph of *means* over *ends*. Everything in life is instrumentalized and so must be evaluated according to how well it works. The problem is that in an age dominated by *technique*, the *ends* of things become swallowed up by our obsession with *means*. A civilization built around *technique* is "committed to the quest for continually improved means to carelessly examined ends. Indeed, *technique transforms ends into means*."[19] Technology is not value neutral, but always has embedded within it a set of values that deeply shapes us and the world. Unfortunately, the church's embrace of *technique* thinking has at the same time meant the embrace of a functional secularism within its life and practice.

We see the triumph of *technique* illustrated in conversations around church growth. In a technological society, church itself is transformed into a *technique*. It becomes a tool and instrument in the hands of visionary pastors and church planters who reimagine and innovate new ways of "doing" church. Any reflection on what the church *is* theologically becomes upended by conversations about the effectiveness of the church's doing. *Technique* mechanizes the church, and successful church leaders are those that have cracked the code of church growth and social impact. Rarely, however, is there any serious conversation about the theological meaning of the church and her God-ordained *ends*. The ends of the church as bride, body, household, temple, or people are never given serious thought. All is subjugated to new and better means of doing church.

When we treat the church as a *technique*, we embrace an ecclesiology of disenchantment. Living in an age of *technique* is to indwell a disenchanted

---

18. Ellul, *Technological Society*, xxv.
19. Ellul, *Technological Society*, vi.

universe. Disenchantment is not necessarily disbelief in God's existence, but it is an incapacity to imagine how divine presence practically impacts and functions within ordinary existence. Divine causality and natural causality are regarded as a zero-sum equation. The more we scientifically grasp and technically master the natural order, the less we need theological explanations. Disenchantment, says Max Weber, means that "principally there are no mysterious incalculable forces that come into play, but rather that one can, in principle, master all things by calculation . . . One need no longer have recourse to magical means in order to master or implore the spirits, as did the savage, for whom such mysterious powers existed."[20] This means that life in the age of *technique* is functionally atheistic. We don't have much need for God to explain the world, nor to effect change we desire. All will eventually be within our understanding, power, and grasp. While Christians may publicly disavow this mentality, they functionally embrace it through an uncritical embrace of *technique* thinking. The danger of *technique* is that it mediates creation to us devoid of the presence of God. Such a mediation is alien to the biblical view of cosmos, which everywhere declares the glory of God and proclaims his handiwork (Ps 19:1).

Sacraments cannot be assimilated to a disenchanted universe. And that is why they have increasingly dropped out of the life of churches that have embraced *technique*. However, a sacramental imagination empowers the church to resist conformity to *technique* through a different approach to mediation. *Technique* mediates the world to us as an object to be known and mastered for our purposes. Sacrament mediates a world to us that is a good creation of God, in which we belong as creatures; a creation that finds its fullest flourishing and purpose as a temple of God's presence. *Technique* relegates the mediation of God's presence into the interior and private experience of the human subject, while sacrament promises that God's presence is publicly communicated through outward and ordinary means.

Sacraments defy an approach to the world as technical mastery. They remain a "mysterious and incalculable force" that defies manipulation, mechanization, and routinization. They are a place where God promises to be at work in the material world by ordinary means. They are not magical in the sense that Weber speaks, but neither can they be naturalized. They mark a supernatural intervention within human nature that does not overturn the order of natural causes. To have a sacramental imagination does not require us to suspend our scientific understanding of the world nor cut off technological pursuits. But sacraments do impose upon us an alternative value system of what it means to indwell the world. Technology

---

20. Weber, *Science as Vocation*, 139.

tends to liberate us from the need for community, while sacraments bind our lives to community. Technology liberates us from the constraints of the body, while sacraments affirm the goodness and necessary finitude of the body. Technology frees us from dependence on authority, while sacraments place us under God's authority through the church. Technology trains us to trust in our own inherent capacities, while sacraments teach us about our constant need for God's grace. Technology seeks to spare us from pain and suffering at all costs, while sacraments show us how the suffering of Christ was the only path for true human flourishing.

Technology of the Lord's Supper

Sacraments are the tools God innovated to accomplish his work in the world. In 2011, I accepted a call to plant a Reformed church in city-center Milwaukee. We started as a group of less than twenty, most of whom had little in the way of a sacramental imagination or formation. My one condition for accepting the call to plant the church was that we would be a church that celebrated the Lord's Supper weekly in worship. I made this a condition because I knew that if I could get the Lord's Supper at the center of the church's worship life, I could keep *technique* thinking out of the church. I knew that if a healthy Lord's Supper piety formed the heart of our community, we would have the spiritual tools to shepherd people in the right *functional* culture and sets of practices needed for their true Christian growth. After eight years, I can attest that our commitment to the Supper has born incredible fruitfulness in the church. We are not a large and impressive congregation, but we are a healthy, spiritually deep, missionally active church which the Lord has blessed. The Supper is not a church-growth technique, as that category is understood, but God uses his ordained means of grace to grow churches for the purposes and ends he has set. Sacraments are God's technologies given to accomplish his own gracious promises in us as his image-bearers. When we understand and embrace God's *ends,* the sacraments are then truly the *effective* means for accomplishing his work of new creation.

Bibliography

Augustine of Hippo. *Instructing Beginners in Faith.* Translated by Raymond Canning. Augustine Series. Hyde Park: New City, 2006.
Beale, G.K. *The Temple and the Church's Mission: A Biblical Theology of the Dwelling Place of God.* Downers Grove: InterVarsity, 2004.
Billings, Todd. *Remembrance, Communion and Hope: Rediscovering the Gospel at the Lord's Table.* Grand Rapids: Eerdmans, 2018.

Borgmann, Albert. *Technology and the Character of Contemporary Life*. Chicago: University of Chicago Press, 1984.
———. *Power Failure: Christianity in the Culture of Technology*. Grand Rapids: Brazos, 2003.
Calvin, John. *Institutes of the Christian Religion*. Translated by Ford Lewis Battles. Louisville: Westminster John Knox, 1960.
Cassuto, Umberto. *A Commentary on the Book of Genesis: From Adam to Noah*. Jerusalem: Magnes, 1989.
Chauvet, Louis-Marie. *The Sacraments: The Word of God at the Mercy of the Body*. Collegeville: Liturgical, 2001.
Ellul, Jacques. *The Technological Society*. New York: Random House, 1964.
Gay, Craig M. *Modern Technology and the Human Future: A Christian Appraisal*. Downers Grove: InterVarsity, 2018.
Grant, George. *Technology and Justice*. Toronto: Anasi, 1986.
Harari, Yuval Noah. *Homo Deus: A Brief History of Tomorrow*. London: Vintage, 2015
Middleton, J. Richard. *The Liberating Image: The Imago Dei in Genesis 1*. Grand Rapids: Brazos, 2005.
Pascal, Blaise. *Pensées*. New York: Modern Library, 1947.
Pinker, Steven. *Enlightenment Now: The Case for Reason, Science, Humanism, and Progress*. New York: Penguin, 2018.
Schmemann, Alexander. *For the Life of the World: Sacraments and Orthodoxy*. New York: St. Vladimir's, 1963.
Walton, John H. *Genesis: The NIV Application Commentary*. Grand Rapids: Zondervan, 2001.
Weber, Max. *Science as Vocation*. In *From Max Weber: Essays in Sociology*, translated and edited by H.H. Gerth and C. Wright Mills, 129–57. New York: Oxford University Press, 1946.
Williams, Rowan. *On Christian Theology*. Oxford: Blackwell, 2000.

6

Proceed with Caution

Lessons from Saint Augustine, Jonathan Edwards, and Miroslav Volf

JONATHAN HUGGINS

Can the past guide the present in dealing with technological advancement?

Introduction

TECHNOLOGY IS ALL AROUND us. New gadgets, tablets, phones, tracking devices, and apps are appearing every few months. Medical and engineering technologies are also advancing, often improving the lives of countless people in need. Personal technologies, like tablets, phones, trackers, and personal computers, are consuming more and more of our time, energy, and attention. We use these for both work and leisure. We get excited about all the new advancements, and our brains literally ignite over the pleasure they bring. And it all keeps updating and advancing, often at baffling speed. How are we to evaluate whether or not various technologies are good for us? Should we trust that the companies that produce these items know what they are doing? That, surely, they would never harm us? Is it all good, or at least benign? Where can we find wisdom?

In this chapter, we will look to the past for Christian wisdom concerning human flourishing and consider how this might inform our use of technology. The Christian theological tradition is a rich resource for wisdom from which we may find help in living a godly and flourishing life in any age.[1] There are many places one could look. Here we will focus on Saint Augustine and Jonathan Edwards, because their insights are especially prescient. Fair warning: these are mostly cautionary tales. But perhaps that is exactly what we need, given how fast and furious personal technologies enter our lives.[2]

There's a growing body of studies that demonstrate a connection between personal digital technology (especially social media outlets) and depression, anxiety, and isolation.[3] Many of these devices are proving addictive and harmful to personal relationships. Much of our entertainment and relational communication is engaged via screen technology. This is not always negative, of course, but more and more studies are showing that screen engagement affects us in negative ways. The images or platforms we access via our devices are sometimes referred to as "hyper-real," because they are perfected and crafted to illicit certain mental/emotional responses. They often go beyond what is "real," or natural, in terms of the images or the experience they provide. The platform determines, in part, our experience in such a way that our personal agency is diminished once we have surrendered to the medium. We are able to do all sorts of things that we cannot do in the real world, or without technology. But the experience is mediated and determined by forces outside ourselves (such as computer programmers, etc). This should at the least cause us to pause and consider our ways. Are these developments actually good for us? Do they serve our well-being? And if not, how can we break our addictive tendencies? How can we make better decisions and lead more practically wise lives? These studies, and perhaps our own personal experience, reveal the need to reconsider our technological habits. Perhaps looking to the wisdom of the past, honoring the insights of our ecclesial parents, can help us find a way forward today.

I do not intend to argue that we should abandon all technological advancement. I do not even intend to argue that we should never use personal

---

1. Though always subject to Holy Scripture, the Christian tradition is a treasure store of the Holy Spirit's guidance in the past. I do not intend to critique the tradition here, though that may be appropriate at times. One might disagree with Saint Augustine or Jonathan Edwards on the points we will examine below. However, here I seek only to consider their insights in light of our current situation with technology. I will regard them as established authorities within our Protestant-evangelical theological tradition.

2. For a more positive account of the possibilities provided through digital technology, see Estes, *Braving the Future*.

3. For some general reflections on the effects of technological use upon our brains see Reinke, *12 Ways*; Carr, *Shallows*; Alter, *Irresistible*; Turkle, *Alone Together*. For more formal psychological studies see De-Sola Gutiérrez, "Cell-Phone Addiction: A Review"; Hunt et al., "No More FOMO."

technology like tablets, smartphones, the internet, or fitness trackers. I will focus my analysis on how certain technologies might impact our souls.[4] More specifically, I will argue that the wisdom of Saint Augustine and Edwards suggest that we should be careful with how these technologies affect our minds and hearts, with how they shape or misshape our loves, with how they help or hinder our capacity to see that which is truly good, true, beautiful, and just. Saint Augustine and Edwards suggest that we should pause, reflect, and consider the effect of technology on our ability to think, feel, act, and (especially) love well.

I will conclude by consulting Miroslav Volf's work on joy and human flourishing. His work provides us with a working definition of flourishing which has been developed through several large-scale studies at Yale Divinity School's Center for Faith and Culture.[5] Volf's taxonomy helps us to apply the insights of Saint Augustine and Edwards, and to think about human flourishing today.

Lessons from Saint Augustine

Confessions

We begin with Saint Augustine (AD 354–430), the bishop of Hippo and great theologian of the Latin West. He is arguably the most influential theologian in Western Christianity and claimed by both Protestants and Roman Catholics as an authoritative resource. There are three sections in the *Confessions* I will examine that have the potential to offer us insight as we reflect on them in relation to technology and the soul.

The first section is found in book III. Saint Augustine is recounting his time as a student in Carthage. He begins by stating that there "all around me hissed a cauldron of illicit loves."[6] And since his "soul was in rotten health,"[7] he was often wrestling deeply with disordered loves. He notes especially his attraction to theatrical shows. His experience at such shows, which he regards as common to most spectators, revealed a sordid

---

4. By "soul," I mean our inner lives. I'm concerned with how we think, feel, will, determine, and love. I do not intend a Platonic dualism by this term. I affirm that humans are something like a psychosomatic unity of body and soul and that our embodiment matters. To address issues related to the body and technology goes outside the intentions of this particular study.

5. See Volf's profile page at https://faith.yale.edu/people/miroslav-volf for more on this.

6. Augustine, *Confessions*, III.i.

7. Augustine, *Confessions*, III.i.

shallowness of heart. He would derive pleasure from the joys and pains of the actors and shed tears over their tragedies. He sensed that this led him to feel, *artificially*, a lot of emotion over things that were not real. He would seek out the opportunity to feel these emotions, not because he wanted to experience such suffering in real life, but because he *wanted to derive pleasure from the pain* in a way that would only touch him at a surface level. However, he writes, "Like the scratches of fingernails, they produced inflamed spots, pus, and repulsive sores."[8] He later recognized that a life committed to such triviality "was no real life at all."[9] Saint Augustine recognized that his desire to find pleasure in the emotions of a theatrical play were "but amazing folly,"[10] and that "the more anyone is moved by these scenes, the less free he is from similar passions."[11] The passions they encouraged were by no means virtuous. He notes, "At the theatres I shared the joy of lovers when they wickedly found delight in each other, even though their actions in the spectacle on the stage were imaginary; when, moreover, they lost each other, I shared their sadness."[12] Theologian Matthew Levering comments on this section, "Lacking real compassion and charity for others, he would take pleasure in weeping and rejoicing with fictional characters on the stage. His love was not real."[13]

Saint Augustine was, at least later in life, aware of the effects such spectacles were having upon his soul. He recognized that his sense of virtue was not real. Feeling compassion for a character on stage (or screen) is not the same as having it for your neighbor. He might have thought of himself as a decent person because he felt all the right things in an artificial setting. But as he notes, this did not carry over into real life situations. Saint Augustine's reflections on things like the theatre cannot be reduced to a mere Platonic suspicion of the arts. His reasoning in these passages is not built upon Platonic ideas. Rather, he reflects on what he sees in his own heart and mind. He recognizes, in biblical terms, vices that are present in his passions and virtues that are absent in his life. If it had any effect on his real-world life, it was not a positive effect. He recognizes that his imagined virtue did not lead him to follow the commands of Christ.

Do we think well about how our various forms of entertainment might likewise affect our souls? What guides what we consider to be good or

---

8. Augustine, *Confessions*, III.ii.
9. Augustine, *Confessions*, III.ii.
10. Augustine, *Confessions*, III.ii.
11. Augustine, *Confessions*, III.ii.
12. Augustine, *Confessions*, III.ii.
13. Levering, *Theology of Augustine*, 94.

acceptable entertainment? Do we simply indulge the same entertainments as everyone else? Or should our Christian faith give some shape to how we determine what content is good or acceptable? Many of us access our entertainment through technological devices. Whether it is sports, TV shows, games, news, or communication, technology is involved. And we have so many options when it comes to entertainment. We find access through these technologies to forms of entertainment we would never have otherwise if we lived in a different time. We can see things from all around the world. Some of it is wonderful and good. Some of it is evil and corrupting. Sometimes it's hard to tell what it is. But it's possible that the many entertainment opportunities we can access through technology are not all good for us, and may corrupt our minds, hearts, and souls more than we would expect. There are some things, such as explicit portrayals of sex and violence, that we would never have access to apart from technology. Since they are easy to access, and can have a negative effect on us, we should be cautious. Saint Augustine recognized the power of the theatre to awaken thoughts and feelings in himself that he might not have, or even desire, otherwise. We should also be so aware and vigilant in discerning and choosing the virtuous and godly path—the path that leads to life and flourishing.

One vivid example of how exposure to evil can awaken evil in the human heart is found in book VI of the *Confessions*. Here Saint Augustine recounts an incident involving his friend, Alypius. He had been Saint Augustine's student and had embraced Manichæan thought alongside his teacher. He had made some progress in a Manichæan view of continence and virtue, though Saint Augustine states that it was a surface-level deception and "only a shadow and simulation of virtue."[14] When Alypius came to Rome, he found the gladiatorial games detestable and gruesome. He thought himself immune to their attraction and strong enough to resist any pull towards such wicked pleasure. However, Alypius happened upon some friends who pressured him to go to the amphitheater with them to watch the games. Saint Augustine's account of what happened next is worth quoting in full.

> He said: "If you drag my body to that place and sit me down there, do not imagine you can turn my mind and my eyes to those spectacles. I shall be as one not there, and so I shall overcome both you and the games." They heard him, but nonetheless took him with them, wanting perhaps to discover whether he could actually carry it off. When they arrived and had found seats where they could, the entire place seethed with the most

14. Augustine, *Confessions*, VI.vii.

monstrous delight in the cruelty. He kept his eyes shut and forbade his mind to think about such fearful evils. Would that he had blocked his ears as well! A man fell in combat. A great roar from the entire crowd struck him with such vehemence that he was overcome by curiosity. Supposing himself strong enough to despise whatever he saw and to conquer it, he opened his eyes. He was struck in the soul by a wound graver than the gladiator in his body, whose fall had caused the roar. The shouting entered by his ears and forced open his eyes. Thereby it was the means of wounding and striking to the ground a mind still presumed on himself when he ought to have relied on you. As soon as he saw the blood, he at once drank in savagery and did not turn away. His eyes were riveted. He imbibed madness. Without any awareness of what was happening to him, he found delight in the murderous contest and was inebriated by bloodthirsty pleasure. He was not now the person who had come in, but just one of the crowd which he had joined and a true member of the group which had brought him. What should I add? He looked, he yelled, he was on fire, he took the madness home with him so that it urged him to return not only with those by whom he had originally been drawn there, but even more than them, taking others with him.[15]

The story is still gripping—and relatable—even 1600 years later. Consider this story in light of our questions about modern technology and the access it provides to multiple forms of entertainment. Perhaps we can relate to the idea that there is some form of entertainment we find repulsive. Something in which we think we would never become interested. Then, perhaps at the suggestion of a friend, we find ourselves hooked on something we once thought objectionable. Or, because much of this can be accessed privately, without anyone else knowing, we too are "overcome by curiosity," thinking ourselves "strong enough to despise whatever (we) saw," only to find ourselves "struck in the soul" by a grave wound. Perhaps we found pleasure in that which is vicious and became "inebriated" or taken over by "madness." Alypius found himself in a situation that was too powerful for his self-control or his character. Is it possible that certain technologies give us access to things too powerful for our character? Or perhaps we think ourselves strong enough to avoid corruption. *This story reminds us to be cautious. It reminds us not to trust ourselves.* Alypius needed better friends in this moment. We certainly should not engage such risky environments or media without a good and virtuous community around us. When it comes to evaluating whether or not some

---

15. Augustine, *Confessions*, VI.viii.

use of technology is good for us, we would do well to consider the power of unknown, even unwanted, vices, and how they can bypass or subvert our good intentions and capture the heart and mind with their dark power. This may be done in obvious ways that we are aware of and that others can see. Perhaps more insidiously is when we are captured in secret ways, unrecognized by us and invisible to others.

Saint Augustine also provides us with insight on the negative effects of *distraction*. In book X of the *Confessions*, he writes about how various human creations in fashion, art, and crafts have been made "to entrap the eyes . . . pictures, images of various kinds, and things which go far beyond necessary and moderate requirements and pious symbols. Outwardly they follow what they make. Inwardly they abandon God by whom they were made, destroying what they were created to be."[16] The same might be said of technologies designed to capture our eyes. They capture the heart as well. This is a problem because they can keep a Christian from contemplating God or the things of God. Saint Augustine says that we live in an "immense jungle full of traps and dangers . . . (that) surround our daily life on every side with a buzz of distraction."[17] These things pull at our attention and call us to give our minds to "vain concern(s)." He writes about how hard this can be (even in the late-fourth century), and how it can keep us from our prayers or from "thinking out some weighty matter," as we turn aside to watch something "like an empty headed fool."[18] He laments, "When my heart becomes the receptacle of distractions . . . and the container for a mass of empty thoughts . . . frivolous thoughts somehow rush in and cut short an aspiration of the deepest importance."[19] This sounds like normal life in the twenty-first century. How often are we kept from what is most important because of a distraction? Often the distraction is pleasurable. Some technologies are designed to give us a pleasure boost, even if they are trivial. Saint Augustine helps us to be aware of this possibility and thus to be vigilant in avoiding it.

On Christian Teaching

Another place in Saint Augustine's work where we find some valuable insight for these issues is in book I of *On Christian Teaching*. Here Saint Augustine develops a helpful distinction between *enjoyment* and *use*.[20] Some

---

16. Augustine, *Confessions*, X.xxxiv.
17. Augustine, *Confessions*, X.xxxv.
18. Augustine, *Confessions*, X.xxxv.
19. Augustine, *Confessions*, X.xxxv.
20. Latin: *frui* (enjoyment), *uti* (use). Augustine doesn't mean "use" in the

things are meant to be enjoyed, and some things are meant to be used (but not enjoyed). Still others may be both enjoyed and used. The purpose of enjoying something is that it might make us happy (in the sense of well-being, blessedness, or flourishing). To use something is to employ it toward the enjoyment of something else (something higher), to assist us in fully enjoying and holding fast to the higher thing. Saint Augustine writes, "To enjoy something is to hold fast to it in love for its own sake. To use something is to apply whatever it may be to the purpose of obtaining what you love—if indeed it is something that ought to be loved. (The improper use of something should be termed abuse.)"[21] His explanation includes a warning about loving the wrong sorts of things. It is important both to know what is worthy of love, and therefore enjoyment, and not to mistake what should be enjoyed for what should be merely used. He argues, "If we choose to enjoy things that are to be used, our advance is impeded and sometimes even diverted, and we are held back, or even put off, from attaining things which are to be enjoyed, because we are hamstrung by our love of lower things."[22] Thus, it is very possible to be distracted by lesser things from the ultimate or higher goods that serve our ultimate happiness. This is detrimental because the things that are meant to be used do not make us truly happy or able to flourish. So, while the distraction may be pleasurable, it cannot produce long-term or deep happiness. That is because, for Saint Augustine, that happiness is only found in God. As he says a few paragraphs later, "The things which are to be enjoyed, then, are the Father and the Son, and the Holy Spirit, and the Trinity that consists of them."[23] He later discusses how one might rightly also love oneself and others. But the love or enjoyment we might find in those must be for God's sake, or on God's account. Only God is loved for his own sake.

Saint Augustine helps us here to think about how technology might assist us in, or keep us from, loving and enjoying God for his own sake, and loving ourselves and others for God's sake. We should also consider whether or not we are using technology to serve these greater loves or enjoying technology for its own sake. The end result of the latter, according to Saint Augustine, leads to unhappiness, or a lack of flourishing. It also means that we are not living in a righteous or holy manner. He writes, "The person who lives a just and holy life is one who is a sound judge of these things. He is also

---

contemporary sense of mere instrumentality, but rather relating to someone or something for the sake of another.

21. Augustine, *On Christian Teaching*, 1.8.
22. Augustine, *On Christian Teaching*, 1.7.
23. Augustine, *On Christian Teaching*, 1.10.

a person who has ordered his love, so that he does not love what it is wrong to love, or fail to love what should be loved, or love too much what should be loved less (or love too little what should be loved more)."[24]

From Saint Augustine we learn to love what is real and to enjoy what is ultimate—namely, God himself. He cautions us to consider whether or not our activities and interests lend themselves to true virtue. He reminds us to consider whether we are too distracted or whether our loves are so distorted that we cannot love and enjoy God (and other things in relation to God). By taking his insights seriously, we learn to ask ourselves certain questions. What is this doing to me inside? What is this leading me to love? What is this teaching me to want? Is this distracting me from something else more important? We learn to be more aware of what is going on within us. We learn to be more mindful concerning ourselves and our practices. If we are not aware of this, and cautious, we can easily be led astray from the path of discipleship and godliness, which for the Christian is the path of blessedness.[25]

Lessons from Jonathan Edwards

Jonathan Edwards (1703–1758) was an eighteenth-century pastor theologian in colonial New England. He is remembered for his contributions to the First Great Awakening and for weighty theological tomes. Edwards wrote a lot about God's beauty and excellence and the sweetness of love and joy associated with that beauty and excellence. "Edwards regarded beauty as fundamental to his understanding of God, as the first of God's perfections, as key to the doctrine of the Trinity, as a defining aspect of the natural world, as basic to the phenomenon of conversion, as visible in the lives of saints, and as marking the difference between the regenerate and the unregenerate mind."[26] For Edwards, a mind for God's truth could not be separated from a heart for God's beauty. To love God was to think deeply upon divine doctrine *and* to delight deeply in divine excellence.[27] One can see in Edwards's many works how much he desired to know and love God with true "religious affections." Consider these lines from his "Personal Narrative":

---

24. Augustine, *On Christian Teaching*, 1.59.

25. Blessedness (Greek, *makarios*) is related to happiness, well-being, and flourishing in Scripture.

26. McClymond and McDermott, *Theology of Jonathan Edwards*, 93.

27. "Beauty" and "excellence" are distinguishable but closely related divine attributes in Edwards's works. See Van Wyk, "Excellency," 208.

> Once, as I rid out into the woods for my health, *anno* 1737; and having lit from my horse in a retired place . . . to walk for divine contemplation and prayer; I had a view, that for me was extraordinary, of the glory of the Son of God; as mediator between God and man; and his wonderful, great, full, pure and sweet grace and love, and meek and gentle condescension. This grace, that appeared to me so calm and sweet, appeared great above the heavens. The person of Christ appeared ineffably excellent, with an *excellency great enough to swallow up all thought and conception*. Which continued, as near as I can judge, about an hour; which kept me, the bigger part of the time, in a flood of tears, and weeping aloud. I felt withal, an ardency of soul to be, what I know not otherwise how to express, than to be emptied and annihilated; to lie in the dust, and to be full of Christ alone; to love him with a holy and pure love; to trust in him; to live upon him; to serve and follow him, and *to be totally wrapt up in the fullness of Christ*; and to be perfectly sanctified and made pure, with a divine and heavenly purity.[28]

Edwards uses the word, "excellency" here, and at other times, as a close, if not exact, synonym for beauty. In the passage above, Edwards overflows with holy delight as he contemplates the glory of Christ in a place that is removed from distraction. He is alone in the woods. The natural world around him is not a distraction. In fact, it is a source of "secondary beauty" wherein God reveals his glory. God is the source of all beauty and is himself the supremely beautiful One. Edwards regarded the spiritual as "primary" and the natural world as "secondary." But that did not make the natural world less meaningful. In fact, he wrote that "the beauty of the world is a communication of God's beauty."[29] Thus, secondary beauties can lead us to honor and delight in the primary beauties. He writes,

> *God's excellency, his wisdom, his purity and love, seemed to appear in everything; in the sun, moon and stars; in the clouds, and blue sky; in the grass, flowers, trees; in the water, and all nature*; which used greatly to fix my mind. I often used to sit and view the moon, for a long time; and so in the daytime, spent much time in viewing the clouds and sky, to behold the sweet glory of God in these things: in the meantime, singing forth with a low voice, my contemplations of the Creator and Redeemer . . . I felt God at the first appearance of a thunderstorm. And used to take the opportunity at such times, to fix myself to view the

---

28. Edwards, "Personal Narrative," 802; emphasis added.
29. Edwards, *Miscellanies*, no. 293.

clouds, and see the lightnings play, and hear the majestic and awful voice of God's thunder: which often times was exceeding entertaining, leading me to sweet contemplations of my great and glorious God.[30]

And again,

And when the light of the morning came, and the beams of the sun came in at the windows, it refreshed my soul from one morning to another. It seemed to me to be some image of the sweet light of God's glory.[31]

Compare this with common habit in our society of looking at our phones first thing in the morning. Is there glory there? Edwards would not likely think so. While he loved natural beauty because of its power to point to the Creator, "beauties deriving from the artifice of human beings could be deceitful and misleading."[32] The Christian tradition has recognized that the time when we wake up in the morning and when we go to bed at night are particularly vulnerable times. That's one reason why morning and evening prayer liturgies have been written. But today's morning and evening liturgies often include checking the latest posts on our social media, or binge-watching the latest TV show, or reading the news. These things affect our souls—how we think and feel about ourselves, the world, and all things. Contrast that with turning our attention to God's word in Scripture, as Christian tradition has recommended that begin and end our days. Edwards sees beauty here as well, and invites us to delight in it when he writes,

I had then, and at other times, the greatest delight in the holy Scriptures, of any book whatsoever. Oftentimes in reading it, every word seemed to touch my heart. I felt an harmony between something in my heart, and those sweet and powerful words. I seemed often to see so much light, exhibited by every sentence, and such a refreshing ravishing food communicated, that I could not get along in reading. Used oftentimes to dwell long on one sentence, to see the wonders contained in it; and yet almost every sentence seemed to be full of wonders.[33]

Are our social media feeds full of wonders? How about the news? How often have we had our minds and hearts sent reeling, or angered, or made anxious because of what we read online just after waking up, or just before going

---

30. Edwards, "Personal Narrative," 16:795; emphasis mine.
31. Edwards, "Personal Narrative," 16:799–800.
32. McClymond and McDermott, *Theology of Jonathan Edwards*, 95.
33. Edwards, "Personal Narrative," 16:798.

to bed? Perhaps Edwards shows us what it could be like if we looked to Scripture at those times. But this will require us being more mindful of the effects of media technology upon us.

It should be noted that, for Edwards, only the truly converted could see and delight in God in these ways. It is a mark of the elect to have a "sense of the heart" or an ability to apprehend and appreciate spiritual truth and reality. In his *Treatise on Grace*, he writes, "The first effect of the power of God in the heart in regeneration, is to give the heart a divine taste or sense, to cause it to have relish of the loveliness and sweetness of the supreme excellency of the divine nature."[34] But once this sense is given, believers can *see the beauty of God in nature and in Scripture*. One can feel the sweetness of God's beauty in the heart. This is how the Holy Spirit transforms believers to share in God's moral beauty.[35] That is, as we behold and contemplate the beauty of God, it affects us. True virtue and moral goodness are kindled in the heart of one who delights in God's moral beauty. If this is so, it has important implications for the way technology might affect our ability to develop moral virtue and goodness. Does visual technology keep us from beholding the beauty of God?

Edwards regarded beauty as among the most fundamental of God's attributes. This beauty is seen in all that God created. As one contemplates creation in relation to the Creator, one could apprehend the excellency of God and of God's truth. In that sense, the natural world is like an *icon* of God. An icon is a sign or symbol that is used as an aid for worship. The icons themselves are not to be worshipped. Rather, they direct one's attention to God through their form. Can technology help us to see God, like an icon does? Or does it only hinder us from seeing?

We have likely all watched a film or read a book (maybe even on a tablet) and felt powerfully moved. Or, we've had our eyes opened to something true, good, and beautiful. Digital media can certainly be an avenue for art whereby we are transformed into wiser and more compassionate people. However, our attention moves quickly through images on a screen, even when they are reflective of natural beauty or divine truth. *Good attention requires slowness*. It requires intentional contemplation. Hyper-reality may actually make it more difficult to appreciate natural beauty. We sense this when we give our attention to our screens and feel delight for a few moments as we catch up on the latest posts. But then when we put the device

---

34. Edwards, "Treatise on Grace," 21:174.

35. See Edwards, *Religious Affections*, where he says, "As the beauty of the divine nature does primarily consist in God's holiness, so does the beauty of all divine things. Herein consists the beauty of the saints, that they are saints, or holy ones: 'tis the moral image of God in them, which is their beauty; and that is their holiness" (2:258).

away, we can feel sad or depressed with the world around us. The short (or long) trip into hyper-reality steals our ability to see the glory around us in our day-to-day lives. The quixotic becomes the enemy of the mundane. To truly appreciate what we see on a screen, we would have to slow down, pay attention, and give thanks. We would have to connect these images to God in such a way that we apprehend God's perfections. It is possible that technology is just too fast to encourage the virtues that come from a slow and contemplative worship of God.

Lessons from Miroslav Volf on Flourishing

What might all of this have to contribute to our view of flourishing, and technology's role within that? To answer that question, we need a good working understanding of what "flourishing" might mean. After all, we cannot take aim at something called "flourishing" or "happiness" or "well-being" if we do not know where the target is located. Otherwise, we'll shoot the arrows of our attempted happiness all over the place, but never hit our bullseye. For help at discerning a definition, we will look to the work of Miroslav Volf. He has written extensively on joy and human flourishing in recent years and has developed a threefold definition for a flourishing, joyful life. He calls it a "tripartite structure." The structure includes "life going well, life led well, and life feeling as it should." He explains,

> Life going well refers to the "circumstantial" dimension of the flourishing life, to the desirable circumstances of life—be they natural (like fertile, uncontaminated land), social (like a just political order or a good reputation), or personal (like health and longevity). Life led well refers to the "agential" dimension of the flourishing life, to the good conduct of life—from right thoughts of the heart and right acts to right habits and virtues. Life feeling as it should is about the "affective" dimension of the flourishing life, about states of "happiness" (contentment, joy) and empathy. Each of the three features has its own integrity, but each is not like a leg of some "good-life stool" bearing separately the weight. Instead, each is also tied to the others, both influencing them and being influenced by them.[36]

36. Volf and Croasmun, *For the Life of the World*. See also Volf and Crisp in *Joy and Human Flourishing*, 133–35; and Volf, *Flourishing*, ix–xi. Also of note, in Volf and Croasmun, *Joy and Human Flourishing*, 13n4, they point out that "as far as we can tell, the term 'human flourishing' was coined by Elizabeth Anscombe as something akin to the sense we use here in her landmark essay, 'Modern Moral Philosophy,' *Philosophy* 33, no. 124 (January 1958)."

Flourishing is when life goes well, is well led, and feels as it should. This definition might raise some questions or concerns. After all, can anyone ever flourish if *all* these things have to be in order? And where is God in this definition? If God is our highest good—as Christians believe—and communion or friendship with God is our highest goal, where does God fit in a flourishing life? For Volf, and for us, God is at the center of each of these. God exercises divine grace, sovereignty, and providence over the world. Thus, God can be looked to for mercy and blessing in our circumstances. God also addresses our ultimate circumstance in the gospel: rescuing us from the powers of sin and death, reconciling us to himself, forgiving our sin, declaring us righteous, and filling us with the Holy Spirit. God is also the source of true virtue. Abiding in Christ, the believer is filled with all strength and wisdom for good character and a fruitful life. The affective dimension is nourished by God, as the Holy Spirit creates holy affections in our hearts and fills us with internal peace (cf. John 16:33; Phil 4:7). Thus, if we take the definition in this God-centered way, it can work for our purposes here.

The "agential" aspect seems to most directly connect to our concern with engaging technology in ways that are good for the soul since it is about good habits (virtues). Of course, these directly impact the "affective" dimension, but we are concerned with our practices, not so much with how life feels. We are also concerned with how our practices affect our sense of well-being. But it may be the case that we cannot control how life is going or whether it feels right and good. We may, however, exercise responsibility for our own actions and practices. Since we can control these, to some extent, this is the principle place where we have some determinative power in whether or not our lives are flourishing.

Volf, and his co-author Croasmun, address technology's connection to flourishing throughout their work. He speaks directly to the potential harm at one point by noting, "Much of what passes for 'joy' is false or corrupt. Witness, for example, our lives on social media, where we regularly rejoice over those who mourn (Twitter's schadenfreude), and mourn over those who rejoice (Facebook's envy and 'fear of missing out,' or FOMO)."[37]

According to Volf, we cannot have a flourishing life if our lives are not well-led. That is, happiness involves virtue. Virtues are good habits of life. And those habits include how we use technology, especially personal technological devices. If we want to know true happiness, we need to consider our ways carefully. Combining the insights of Volf with those of Saint

---

37. Volf and Croasmun, *For the Life of the World*, 179.

Augustine and Edwards will help us proceed with wisdom (and caution) toward a more fully flourishing life.

Concluding Observations

It is possible that we, as Christians, have not fully considered whether our engagement with technology reflects wisdom and virtue. We may be going along with the culture, doing what everyone else seems to be doing, without much critical reflection. Perhaps we don't want to appear to be out of step with the world around us. Or we don't want to be perceived as backwards. We certainly don't want to deny that certain technologies do make people's lives better. Many medical and engineering advances make countless people's lives feel better and go better. But many other technologies are elective, in that we don't need them to survive or thrive. We make use of them for entertainment purposes. Here we have the opportunity and responsibility to handle them wisely. We should consider whether or not their use is good for us. Will they help us live virtuously?

It is important to remember that we are looking to the Christian theological tradition for wisdom, not necessarily for rules. Wisdom is a practical approach to everyday living. The Bible and the tradition do not address every possible circumstance or situation in our lives. Rather, they provide us with the needed roots or foundation for growing or building our lives according to righteousness and godliness. They help us think through our various situations with a view toward "the fear of the Lord"—the biblical definition of wisdom (see Prov 1:7, 9:10; Ps 111:10). They help us discern what it might mean in countless circumstances to "turn away from evil and do good"—a secondary definition of wisdom (see Pss 34:14, 37:27; Prov 3:7, 14:16). We don't always get a specific command to address every issue. But we do get the necessary principles by which we may choose wisely what to do or not to do. This is how wisdom works. The Scriptures and the tradition together provide powerful resources that are sufficient for training our senses in good discernment. They help us determine what is good, true, right, and beautiful in our own cultural-technological context.

Saint Augustine and Edwards give us, at the least, some things to consider as we evaluate and choose to, or not to, make use of some technological developments. This is especially the case for elective and entertainment-based technologies (including social media). With Saint Augustine, we are challenged to consider whether we care more for the real or the unreal. We are also challenged to make a distinction between what we love and enjoy on the one hand, and what we may use to further our love and enjoyment on the other. He presses us to consider whether the things we enjoy help us love God and neighbor, or whether they have replaced God and neighbor in our hearts. Saint Augustine also cautions us against distraction. Are we being led astray from that which is truly good and important by that which has become interesting and accessible (on my phone, for instance)?

Edwards challenges us to consider whether or not we love what is truly there, in the world around us. He leads us to look for God in the real and natural world, which acts as a kind of icon to the glory of God. Hyperreality might numb our senses to the beauty of the Creator manifested in his creation. Edwards believed that our hearts were shaped by deep contemplation of God and his divine beauty. Technology might actually keep us from seeing this. The collected wisdom of Saint Augustine and Edwards explored here may not lead us to forego technology altogether, but it does encourage caution. The kinds of technology we have mentioned need not be rejected, but perhaps their use must be channeled or chastened.

Volf's definition encourages us to consider whether or not our practices are contributing to a flourishing life. Life must be led well (good habits and character) to be experienced as good. Practical wisdom is necessary for a life well-led. That practical wisdom is what we are aiming to acquire in these studies. Our joy and well-being depend on making good and wise decisions. Flourishing depends on virtuous action. What's the point of a Christian view of technology if it does not serve the purpose of human flourishing and happiness—in the ultimate sense? Goodness and happiness cannot be separated. So, we must ask ourselves: Does technology help us to be good? Is it character-forming or deforming? Or better, does our use of technology help us know, love, and reflect God? If not, we must change the way we engage it if we wish to have a life that is happy in the Lord.

Bibliography

Alter, Adam. *Irresistible: Why We Can't Stop Checking, Scrolling, Clicking and Watching.* London: Bodley Head, 2017.
Augustine of Hippo. *Confessions.* Translated by Henry Chadwick. Oxford World's Classics. Oxford: Oxford University Press, 2008.
———. *On Christian Teaching.* Translated by R.P.H. Green. Oxford World's Classics. Oxford: Oxford University Press, 2008.
Carr, Nicholas G. *The Shallows: How the Internet Is Changing the Way We Think, Read and Remember.* London: Atlantic, 2011.
De-Sola Gutiérrez, José, et al. "Cell-Phone Addiction: A Review." *Frontiers in Psychiatry* 7 (October 24, 2016) 175.
Edwards, Jonathan. *Miscellanies*. In vol. 16, *The Works of Jonathan Edwards*, edited by George S. Claghorn. New Haven: Yale University Press, 1998.

———. "Personal Narrative." In vol. 16, *The Works of Jonathan Edwards*, edited by George S. Claghorn. New Haven: Yale University Press, 1998.

———. *Religious Affections*. In vol. 16, *The Works of Jonathan Edwards*, edited by George S. Claghorn. New Haven: Yale University Press, 1998.

———. "Treatise on Grace." In vol. 21, *The Works of Jonathan Edwards*, edited by Sang Hyun Lee, 149–97. New Haven: Yale University Press, 2008.

Estes, Douglas. *Braving the Future: Christian Faith in a World of Limitless Tech*. Harrisonburg, VA: Herald, 2018.

Hunt, Melissa G., Rachel Marx, Courtney Lipson, and Jordyn Young. "No More FOMO: Limiting Social Media Decreases Loneliness and Depression." *Journal of Social and Clinical Psychology* 37.10 (2018) 751–68.

Levering, Matthew. *The Theology of Augustine: An Introductory Guide to His Most Important Works*. Grand Rapids: Baker Academic, 2013.

McClymond, Michael J., and Gerald R. McDermott. *The Theology of Jonathan Edwards*. Oxford: Oxford University Press, 2012.

Reinke, Tony. *12 Ways Your Phone Is Changing You*. Wheaton: Crossway, 2017.

Turkle, Sherry. *Alone Together: Why We Expect More From Technology and Less from Each Other*. New York: Basic Books, 2012.

Van Wyk, John Ray. "Excellency." In *The Jonathan Edwards Encyclopedia*, edited by Harry S. Stout, 208. Grand Rapids: Eerdmans, 2017.

Volf, Miroslav. *Flourishing: Why We Need Religion in a Globalized World*. New Haven: Yale University Press, 2015.

Volf, Miroslav, and Matthew Croasmun, *For the Life of the World: Theology That Makes a Difference*. Grand Rapids: Brazos, 2019.

Volf, Miroslav, and Justin E. Crisp, eds. *Joy and Human Flourishing: Essays on Theology, Culture, and the Good Life*. Minneapolis: Fortress, 2015.

Part 2

TECHNOLOGICAL REFLECTIONS *on* THEOLOGY

7

A New Catechism for the Digital Age

Answering the Questions Posed by AI, Consciousness, and Transhumanism

BRUCE BAKER[1]

THE SEEMINGLY UNLIMITED POTENTIAL of artificial intelligence and robotics raises fascinating questions. Can an AI become conscious? Is there a difference between AI intelligence and human intelligence? Can a robot sin? Can we program morality? Can we upload our minds? Is transhumanism a technical possibility? Do we need to rethink eschatology? These questions call for sound theological responses.

In this paper, I hope to contribute to a constructive theological discussion of such questions. I suggest catechism as a helpful format to address these questions in the context of biblical teaching and preaching. By no means do I wish to imply that the catechism presented here is a definitive statement of any church tradition. Far from it, what we have here is a discussion starter. The catechism format has advantages and disadvantages. It can help clarify certain points of doctrine and bring theological wisdom into philosophical discourse. However, since the catechism presumes a posture of faith, it is aimed at use within a community of faith and may not be helpful as a presentation of apologetics for a secular audience.

---

1. Portions of this paper were presented at the Fifth Annual conference of the Center for Pastor Theologians, Chicago, IL, October 14, 2019.

Question 1: Why do we need a new catechism? Aren't the old ones good enough?

The old catechisms are as good as ever. They express timeless truths and remain relevant. However, creeds and catechisms are written for a particular time and place. From time to time, the church discerns a need to articulate fresh expressions of faith. In the face of disruptive technologies such as AI, we may now be living in such a time. We need new catechisms not because the old answers are wrong, but rather because the old questions are being asked in new ways.

Frank Wilczek, recipient of the 2004 Nobel Prize in physics, sums up the popular interest in, and anxious curiosity about, AI by asking three "contentious questions": Can an artificial intelligence be conscious? Can an artificial intelligence be creative? Can an artificial intelligence be evil?[2] Wilczek answers simply, "Based on physiological psychology, neurobiology, and physics, it would be very surprising if the answers were not Yes, Yes, and Yes."[3] Wilczek bases this simple reply on Francis Crick's "Astonishing Hypothesis":

> "You," your joys and your sorrows, your memories and your ambitions, your sense of personal identity and free will, are in fact no more than the behavior of a vast assembly of nerve cells and their associated molecules. As Lewis Carroll's Alice might've phrased it: "You're nothing but a pack of neurons."[4]

Based on this axiom, Crick concludes, "The idea that man has a disembodied soul is as unnecessary as the old idea that there was a life force. This is in head-on contradiction to the religious beliefs of billions of human beings alive today."[5] Crick's statement is indeed astonishing, but not for its scientific rigor; rather, the statement is astonishingly wrong in its distorted, even perverse idea that human persons can be divided into two separate parts—a material body and a "disembodied soul." What an erroneous and non-biblical description of a human person this is!

Crick seems to delight in the notion that his hypothesis offends religious faith, but in doing so he displays ignorance of the Bible, because his idea of a disembodied soul is not a biblical concept and does not represent Christian faith. He is merely picking apart a straw man that does not represent a biblical account of human nature. In doing so, Crick gives voice

---

2. Wilczek, "Unity of Intelligence," 66–75.
3. Wilczek, "Unity of Intelligence," 66–75.
4. Crick, *Astonishing Hypothesis*, 3.
5. Crick, *Astonishing Hypothesis*, 261.

to the popular idea that science and technology can teach us everything we need to know about what it means to be human. We need a new catechism to address these sorts of speculations head-on with clear theological thinking, because such misunderstandings are as likely to arise within the church as outside it.

That's the reason for offering this "new catechism": not to correct established catechisms or church traditions, but rather to provide a background for sound biblical teaching and preaching in light of the impact of technological advances upon popular cultural imagination.

Question 2: Can an AI become conscious?

The Bible does not contain the word "consciousness." The term consciousness needs to be placed in some sort of semantic framework in order to provide a satisfactory theological answer to the question. The first response to this question, therefore, is to ask the clarifying question: What do you mean by "conscious"?

AI experts Byron Reese and Max Tegmark each offer helpful guidelines in an effort to narrow down the meaning of the term conscious.[6] They pose questions about worldview and metaphysics. How you answer their surveys predicts to an extent how you would answer the question of whether an AI (or machine) can become conscious.

Here, for example are Reese's survey questions, based on the parable of the "Chinese room":[7]

- Does the Chinese room think?
- Does the Chinese room or the Librarian *understand* Chinese?
- Whatever you think "the juice" is, could the machine—get it? (If you don't think it exists at all, count that as a yes answer.)
- Do you answer the "What are we?" foundational question with "machines"?

---

6. Reese, *Fourth Age*; Tegmark, *Life 3.0*.

7. The Chinese room is a thought experiment credited to American philosopher John Searle. The basic idea is that a person who does not speak Chinese sits in a room with a library of Chinese texts. The person has a set of instructions for how to answer questions written in Chinese and slipped under the door. By following instructions, the person is able to retrieve the appropriate Chinese answers and slide them back under the door in response. To the person in the room these are meaningless symbols, but to someone outside the room reading the responses, they are apt and intelligent answers to the questions asked. See Cole, "Chinese Room Argument."

- Did you answer the "What is your 'self'?" question with either "a trick of the brain" or "emergent mind"?
- Did you answer the "What is the composition of the universe?" question with monist?[8]

Consciousness is generally used to describe a living being's sense of *self-awareness*. This entails a capacity to have feelings, sensations, and interior thoughts, which implies the existence of a mind that can originate ideas and take action. This presumably requires some degree of intelligence, as a prerequisite to being able to discern reality, to think, and to interact with the surrounding environment. Self-expression, imagination, and art are sophisticated marks of consciousness.

The question about AI consciousness thus needs to be broken down into constituent questions like these in order to make sense: Can a machine or AI be intelligent? Be a self? Become self-aware? Be imaginative? Have (or be) a soul?

In a biblical context, perhaps the most significant way to frame the question of consciousness is to step back and look at the underlying biblical meaning of *soul*. Both the Old and New Testaments are rich with nuance and implications for the meaning of soul. The English word "soul" is often used to translate two biblical words, but without capturing the broad, rich meaning and implications of their biblical usage—*nephesh* (נֶפֶשׁ) and *psychē* (ψυχή) are the Hebrew and Greek words most commonly translated as "soul."

The question of consciousness thus leads immediately to the next question (Q3) about soul.

> Gen 2:7: "Then the Lord God formed the man of dust from the ground and breathed into his nostrils the breath of life, and the man became a living creature (נֶפֶשׁ)."
>
> Deut 6:5: "You shall love the Lord your God with all your heart and with all your soul (נֶפֶשׁ) and with all your might."
>
> Ps 103:1: "Bless the Lord, O my soul (נֶפֶשׁ)."
>
> Matt 22:37: "You shall love the Lord your God with all your heart and with all your soul (ψυχή) and with all your mind."
>
> Matt 16:26: "For what will it profit a man if he gains the whole world and forfeits his soul (ψυχή)? Or what shall a man give in return for his soul?"

---

8. Reese, *Fourth Age*, 179.

John 12:27: "Now is my soul (ψυχή) troubled."

Question 3: Can an AI possess or become a soul?

As seen in the previous discussion, we need to attempt to define "soul" before we can answer this question. The creation story in Genesis introduces the concept of soul in the context of living, breathing creatures created by God. If Genesis is interpreted as making a definitive statement of what it means to be a *nephesh-haya* ("living creature/soul"), then the answer to the question is: no, machines and AIs are not souls. They are human-made artifacts, not living creatures, and thus are categorically different from the living beings created by God and described by the words *nephesh-haya*. Soul refers to the very life of the creature, sustained in some mysterious way by God's design, creativity, and active will.

It is worth noting that the term *nephesh-haya* (נֶפֶשׁ חַיָּה) is used broadly and with many poetic meanings to describe many aspects of both animals and humans. In the creation story, God brings forth many kinds of living creatures, all designated as *nephesh-haya*: sea-life and birds (Gen 1:20), livestock, creeping things, beasts of the earth (Gen 1:24), and ultimately humankind (Gen 2:7). The human soul is distinctly different from the other animal souls. Humans are made male and female in the image of God, and human persons are elevated to the status of children of God. These are not attributes transferrable to non-living machines made by humans.

These doctrines seem obvious from the biblical texts. Perhaps the more interesting question, in an effort to engage secular thinkers in constructive dialogue, is to ask whether an AI or machine can demonstrate levels of intelligence, creativity, artistry, emotion, and other traits generally assigned to humans.

> Gen 2:7: "Then the Lord God formed the man of dust from the ground and breathed into his nostrils the breath of life, and the man became a living creature."
>
> Rom 8:11: "If the Spirit of him who raised Jesus from the dead dwells in you, he who raised Christ Jesus from the dead will also give life to your mortal bodies through his Spirit who dwells in you."
>
> Rom 8:16: "The Spirit himself bears witness with our spirit that we are children of God."

Question 4: What do science and philosophy teach about consciousness?

Scientists and philosophers offer many different answers depending on their personal worldviews, faith, and theological perspectives. There is no one "scientific" answer any more than there is one theological answer, or one Christian answer.

Questions pertaining to spiritual reality demand consideration of spiritual modes of perception and the possibility of revealed truth. Any other approach to the subject matter will be inclined toward closed-mindedness regarding the possibility of a bigger reality than can be explained in mechanistic, materialistic terms, or it will proceed along non-scientific lines of thought by refusing to bring a rational approach to the study of revealed truth.

> You know something only in accordance with its nature, and you develop your knowledge of it as you allow its nature to prescribe for you the mode of rationality appropriate to it. That is the kind of objectivity we adopt in all rational behavior whatsoever.[9]

To keep in step with the burden of rational inquiry into consciousness—which requires knowledge to be pursued in accordance with the nature of its subject—demands that we not treat consciousness as though it were a mere biological artifact of deterministic materialism in a godless universe. That is not a rational argument, but rather an axiomatic *a priori* declaration of faith in a materialistic worldview. It begins in a false, unprovable premise, which it takes as a given, and ultimately the materialist argument offers no rational reason to place trust in its own conclusions (see Q7).

Byron Reese is right to point out that what you think of the prospects for AI consciousness will depend upon your belief system. The cause of failure in dialogue is often due to unspoken differences between competing belief systems.

In beginning of his book, Reese refers to the debate over ideas about living machines and computer consciousness.

> To those who follow all this debate, the net result is confusion and frustration. Many throw their hands up and surrender to the cacophony of competing viewpoints and conclude that if the people at the forefront of these technologies cannot agree on what will happen then what hope do the rest of us have?

---

9. Torrance, *God and Rationality*, 52.

> Is there a path out of this? I think so. It begins when we realize that these experts disagree not because they know different things, but because they *believe* different things.[10]

If consciousness is a quale or experience of a human person made in the image of God, then rational scientific inquiry will treat it as such. A biblical understanding of the created order gives scientists and philosophers good reason to study the biological, material, and metaphysical aspects of mindfulness, consciousness, and intelligence without blindly "defining away" the function of consciousness as a quale of the soul. This is why questions about the spiritual reality of life need to be answered within a belief system that bears witness to that reality.

> Col 2:8: "See to it that no one takes you captive by philosophy and empty deceit, according to human tradition, according to the elemental spirits of the world, and not according to Christ."

> 1 Cor 1:20: "Where is the one who is wise? Where is the scribe? Where is the debater of this age? Has not God made foolish the wisdom of the world?"

Question 5: Why does the question of AI consciousness get so much attention?

AI consciousness garners attention because it offers a tantalizingly plausible way to rationalize belief in nothingness—the belief that there cannot exist any real, spiritually transcendent point to human existence. As shown in the discussions above, such attempts falter and lack the cohesiveness that a wider perspective of spiritual reality provides. Nonetheless, the questions persist because many people desire to rationalize their belief in the antithesis of a universe created by God.

The desire to rationalize belief in a universe devoid of God is perfectly natural, and it has been with humankind throughout history. AI is simply the latest and greatest place to look for some counterexamples to the biblical affirmation that human identity entails the spiritual reality of a persistent, eternal quale to personhood.

The rapid advance of AI seems to continually push back the frontier of capabilities that are presumed to belong only to humans. In recent memory, Deep Blue defeated the world chess champion (1997), then

---

10. Reese, *Fourth Age*, x–xi.

Watson defeated the world's Jeopardy champion (2011), then AlphaGo defeated the world Go champion (2017).

AI has made great strides in the creative arts as well. One of the most interesting and telling demonstrations of the challenges in training AI to produce art is the case of the so-called "Next Rembrandt." Data scientists at Microsoft and Delft University teamed up to code a machine learning algorithm to paint like the master. Microsoft executive Ron Augustus described the goal of the project: "We are using technology and data like Rembrandt uses his paints and brushes to create something new."[11]

> After 18 months of data crunching and 500 hours of rendering, the team finally felt ready to reveal to the world its attempt to resurrect Rembrandt. The painting was unveiled on April 5, 2016, in Amsterdam and immediately caught the public's imagination, with over 10 million mentions on Twitter the first few days of it's [sic] going on display.[12]

The desire to shrink the gap between artificial and human intelligence is driven by more than the psychological desire to avoid cognitive dissonance in one's assent to belief in a godless universe. There are powerful financial incentives at work also, as du Sautoy notes well.

> The current drive by humans to create algorithmic creativity is not, for the most part, fueled by desires to extend artistic creation. Rather, the desire is to enlarge company bank balances. There is a huge amount of hype about AI, even as so many initiatives branded as AI offer little more than statistics or data science.
>
> Businesses have a large stake in convincing the world that AI is so great that it can now write incisive articles on its own, and compose lovely music, and paint Rembrandts. It is all fuel for convincing customers that the AI on offer will transform their businesses, too, if they invest. But look beyond the hype, and you see it is still the human code that is driving this revolution.[13]

So far, there remains a qualitative difference between humans and machines when it comes to creative arts, general intelligence, creative puzzle solving, moral deliberation, empathy, natural language, sports skills, and a host of other attributes. Nonetheless, the boundaries will continually move. The questions are here to stay.

---

11. Du Sautoy, *Creativity Code*, 118.
12. Du Sautoy, *Creativity Code*, 118.
13. Du Sautoy, *Creativity Code*, 282.

Rom 1:19–21: "For what can be known about God is plain to them, because God has shown it to them. For his invisible attributes, namely, his eternal power and divine nature, have been clearly perceived, ever since the creation of the world, in the things that have been made. So they are without excuse. For although they knew God, they did not honor him as God or give thanks to him, but they became futile in their thinking, and their foolish hearts were darkened."

1 Tim 6:20: "O Timothy, guard the deposit entrusted to you. Avoid the irreverent babble and contradictions of what is falsely called 'knowledge.'"

Question 6: Is there a plausible scenario for an AI or machine to achieve consciousness?

The basic argument in favor of machine consciousness goes like this: (1) Since human beings are material beings—i.e., our bodies and brains are entirely physical—(2) our minds, thoughts, feelings, and sense of self must be "emergent properties" of material existence. (3) We have no good reason to believe that our ability to build ever more complicated machines, computers, and code is limited by any physical impossibility. (4) Therefore, at some point in the future, we are likely to be able to build a "thinking machine" capable of consciousness, and (5) we will probably discover this new form of consciousness by surprise, without having realized what has happened, when the machine expresses itself in some manner we have not yet imagined.

This argument might sound plausible on the surface, but it begins with the false presumption that human consciousness is based in a purely "material" existence. This fails to acknowledge biblical teaching. Human beings are more than merely material substances. Humans bear the image of God (Gen 1:26). Humans are filled with the Spirit of God (Gen 6:3, 41:38; 1 Cor 3:16). Humans are both spirit and flesh (Rom 8:1–17; Gal 5:17), in relationship with God (John 17).

Thus, from a biblical perspective, the argument is simply fraudulent. In ascribing consciousness to a machine, the very notion of consciousness has been redefined as something different from what a human being would possess. But from a purely materialist perspective, it hangs together better (it has at least a modicum of coherence).

The second step in this argument is based in the premise of an "emergent phenomenon," a concept that "has a lot of cachet in science at the moment," as Marcus du Sautoy says.[14] The reason for the popularity of this concept is that it offers a way out of the conundrum of how transcendent, apparently inexplicable properties such as consciousness can exist if everything in the cosmos is purely material. Du Sautoy explains why this is a popular point of view.

> It is an antidote to the mechanistic view that everything can be boiled down to atoms and equations. The phenomena heralded as emergent range from the wetness of water to human consciousness. One molecule of H_2O is not wet, but at some point, a collection of molecules gains the property of wetness. One neuron is not conscious, yet a combination of many can become so.[15]

This is clearly a different understanding of consciousness and self-awareness from any portrait of human nature given in the Bible. Although we may not be able to give a precise, analytical, reductive definition of the meaning of the word "soul," theological anthropology readily affirms that there is more to human life than can be explained in material terms, and that human identity, life, and soul are more than merely emergent properties defined entirely in materialistic terms.

> 1 Cor 3:16: "Do you not know that you are God's temple and that God's Spirit dwells in you?"

Question 7: Is there a way to combine materialism with a biblical understanding of human nature?

In the strictest sense of materialism, the answer to this question is no, there is not. These are mutually exclusive ideas. "Eliminative materialism," as defined by Churchland, "denies the existence of immaterial thoughts and experiences."[16] Similarly, Dennett "denies the existence of ontologically distinct experiences, over and above bodily events."[17] These two philosophers base their arguments upon an axiomatic, *a priori*, and abject denial of anything that cannot be explained as strictly material. In other words, they say that nothing exists unless they say so, because they claim the prerogative to define what is material and what is not. According to their self-referential

---

14. Du Sautoy, *Creativity Code*, 281.
15. Du Sautoy, *Creativity Code*, 281.
16. Churchland, "Eliminative Materialism," 67–90.
17. Boden, *Artificial Intelligence*, 129.

definition of materialism, there is no such thing as consciousness, at least not as the word is commonly used—with reference to a transcendent sense of self. This is why they call their worldview *eliminative* materialism, because it eliminates the possibility of consciousness or anything else they cannot explain in their materialistic metaphysical concepts.

This is obviously circular logic, as can be seen by this simple outline of its rationale:

A. ("Eliminative") Materialism is the sum total of reality, by definition.

B. Consciousness, as popularly understood, implies a form of mindfulness (thoughts and experiences) that transcends materialism.

C. Therefore, consciousness (at least as popularly understood) does not exist, because that would violate the axiom (A).

We finish where we began, by denying the possibility of any reality other than that which can be explained by sheer (or "eliminative") materialism. Materialism is all there is, by definition. By this line of circular reasoning, there exists nothing which the materialistic philosophers cannot explain by dint of their materialism.

This rationale is patently incoherent. If materialism/naturalism is true, then we have no reason to trust our own powers of discernment, because naturalism argues that our minds are merely meaningless accidents of nature. The naturalist therefore has no rational reason to trust his or her cognitive faculties. As Plantinga explains, regarding the assumption "that our cognitive faculties are reliable . . . a naturalist who accepts evolution is rationally obliged to give up this assumption."[18]

You are forgiven if this seems confusing. People of different views on the meaning of the metaphysics often end up talking past one another, unable to mount any persuasive arguments. The problem usually boils down to a failure to clarify their differing axioms and presumptions of worldview and faith at the outset. Margaret Boden, a renowned philosopher, sums up aptly, "The topic is a philosophical morass."[19]

Other philosophers have made attempts to meld a softer sort of materialism with the experience of transcendent "spiritual" reality by painting fuzzier boundaries around materialism, essentially abandoning the strictures of "eliminative materialism." We might label these attempts as "soft" materialism, to distinguish them from Churchland's and Dennett's "strong" materialism.

---

18. Plantinga, *Where the Conflict Really Lies*, 326.
19. Boden, *Artificial Intelligence*, 122.

Warren Brown and Nancey Murphy are proponents of soft materialism. They try to avoid the self-defeating logic of eliminative materialism by allowing for the qualia of "soulishness" to emerge from within a materialistic framework.[20] Murphy and Brown propose a metaphysics in which "soulishness" is an emergent property of the organism that arises from the material substrate of biological existence. They label their approach "nonreductive physicalism" (NRP), because they are trying to hold in tension the paradox that the human person is alive as a physical/material entity, and yet at the same time possesses qualities that cannot be reduced to physical cause-and-effect explanations.

The approach of NRP is more promising than strict materialism or naturalism, but is not without its own problems. NRP at least acknowledges that "soulishness" (whatever that means) is a spiritual reality, and thus leaves the door open to the biblical description of human persons as being both finite, bounded, physical creatures, and at the same time possessing immortal, imperishable identity. Under closer scrutiny, the boundary lines NRP places around materialism/naturalism are difficult to discern and, depending upon how the idea of emergence is interpreted, it may be debated whether NRP actually succeeds in "squaring the circle" or falls into the same trap as eliminative materialism with respect to sustaining a coherent statement of material existence as something that can stand aloof from active relationality with the living God.

The whole premise of NRP swings on the hinge of *emergence*, as Brown explains,

> It must be emphasized that the term "emergent" does not here refer to emergent *entities* or to new physical forces, but rather to emergent *levels of causal efficacy*. If "emergence" is so restricted in meaning, the term "emergent monism" is generally equivalent to nonreductive physicalism.[21]

Note that Brown invokes here the term "monism" in order to defend his stance on NRP. This is an attempt to avoid the heretical teachings of dualism that divide human persons into two or more separate parts or substances—say, a physical body and a disembodied spirit/soul. Monism refers to the biblical view of the human person as being a unified whole—a person made in the image of God—and not two or more different things. Monism affirms the unity of the human person.

---

20. Brown, "Neurobiological Embodiment"; Murphy, *Bodies and Souls*.
21. Brown, "Neurobiological Embodiment," 65.

The metaphysical nuances required to sustain NRP as a theory of personhood might seem to raise more questions than they answer. Other theologians seem not to find warrant for a Christian apologetics that avoids spiritual reality as an aspect of human life. Barth, for one, embraces "concrete monism" as a reality that the living God sustains.

> It is to this concrete monism that we found ourselves guided by the biblical view and the biblical concept of the "soul." The abstract dualism of the Greek and traditional Christian doctrine, and the equally abstract materialist and spiritualist monism, are from this standpoint a thoroughgoing and interconnected deviation . . . It is the Spirit, i.e., the immediate action of God himself, which grounds, constitutes and maintains man as soul of his body. It is thus the Spirit that unifies him and holds him together as soul and body.[22]

Monism affirms the unity of soul and body as an inseparable, coherent whole, held together by "the immediate action of God." Ray Anderson prefers the term "contingent monism"[23] to emphasize the active, willful action of the living God in sustaining and bringing this unity about. For this reason, it is better to say that a person *is* a living soul, rather than a person *has* a soul.

Malcom Jeeves, neuroscientist and Christian philosopher of science, suggests the term, "irreducible, intrinsic interdependence":

> This way we avoid using words like monism, dualism, and physicalism . . . Thus, we see mental activity "embodied" in brain activity. The link is not a causal one in the most common way of using causal in science . . . The relationship is between two independent levels.[24]

Although NRP would seem to be the most promising attempt to posit a purely material basis for (whatever we mean by) "soul" or "soulishness," it stumbles against the witness of Scripture, tradition, and doctrine regarding the relational identity of human persons. It seems that a metaphysical understanding of the soul (or the experience of "soulishness") needs to move along other lines of theological anthropology that are not rooted in physicalism.

---

22. Barth, *Church Dogmatics*, III.2, 393.
23. Anderson, "On Being Human," 186.
24. Myers and Jeeves, *Psychology through the Eyes of Faith*, 23.

1 Cor 15:50: "I tell you this, brothers: flesh and blood cannot inherit the kingdom of God, nor does the perishable inherit the imperishable."

Question 8: Can an AI be spiritual or display "soulishness"?

Based on the foregoing theological interpretation, we can say that a purely physical machine or virtual machine (any form of AI) is not capable of becoming or being a soul, as the word is used in Scripture (see Q3).

This is not to deny that robots, virtual machines, and AIs may exhibit thought processes, communication skills, and behaviors that mimic human spirituality and the intractable qualities referred to as "soulishness" (see Q7). Indeed, it seems to be the norm that AI will continually do things that seem surprisingly human. This leads to an ironic but practical definition of AI: "Artificial Intelligence is the science and engineering of making computers behave in ways that, until recently, we thought required human intelligence."[25]

To ask whether a virtual machine could display "soulishness" is, in essence, merely a restatement of the Turing test. Alan Turing proposed in 1950 that the best way to settle the question of whether or not a machine could think would be to hide it behind a curtain and carry on a conversation with it. If the virtual machine could fool enough of the people enough of the time (Turing proposed 30 percent was good enough) into thinking that they were communicating with a real person, then it would be fair enough to say, yes, the machine is indeed thinking. This was a tongue-in-cheek proposal by Turing, who no doubt understood the difference between being a thinking person and mimicking the conversation of one.[26]

Another computer scientist famously quipped that asking whether a computer can think is like asking whether a submarine can "swim." The point is that observable behaviors do not prove ontological identities. This is certainly true when it comes to human dignity and the *imago Dei*.

The caveat in all this metaphysical musing is that sound theology stops short of telling God what God can or cannot do. On matters of mystery (and the soul is certainly a mystery), we may be obliged to remain apophatic.

Perhaps there is some mysterious possibility in the unforeseeable future that a merger of living persons and virtual machines might result in an

---

25. High, "Carnegie Mellon Dean." Douglas Hofstader puts it even more succinctly, paraphrasing Tesler's theorem: "AI is whatever hasn't been done yet" (Hofstadter, *Gödel, Escher, Bach*, 601).

26. Boden, *Artificial Intelligence*, 120.

identity that retains the in-breathed Spirit of God and becomes an instance of *nephesh-haya* ("living creature/soul"). With this sort of thought experiment, however, we have entered the realm of either fantasy or speculative theology. Such speculation takes us beyond the reach of biblical witness.

Suffice to say, a purely materialistic artifact is categorically different from a living soul, as described in Scripture.

> Isa 40:13: "Who has measured the Spirit of the Lord, or what man shows him his counsel?"
>
> Job 5:9: "God does great things and unsearchable, marvelous things without number."
>
> Rom 11:33: "Oh, the depth of the riches and wisdom and knowledge of God! How unsearchable are his judgments and how inscrutable his ways!"
>
> 1 Cor 15:51: "Behold! I tell you a mystery. We shall not all sleep, but we shall all be changed."
>
> John 1:18: "No one has ever seen God; the only God, who is at the Father's side, he has made him known."

Question 9: Can an artificial intelligence be evil?

The capacity to do good and evil flows from the freedom and willful power of a soul to make choices, act, and bear responsibility for those actions. AI, like countless other technologies that have come before, can be used as a tool and as a weapon, for good or evil purposes. The destructive power of the technology stems not from the device per se, but rather from the powers and principalities that unleash it and set it free to serve a false god, and from a goal that does not seek to bestow grace and *shalom* and to edify others, but rather to profit at the expense of others and corrupt God's creation.

The danger with the powerful new technology of AI stems from the opportunity for it to be used for evil through sins of selfishness, idolatry, or violence. The cyborg, robot, or AI lie outside of the relationship of communion with the Trinitarian God. Evil flows from spiritual power which they do not have.

The good news is that God makes all things new in the eschaton. God redeems the creation and heals the hurts and brokenness wrought by evil. The resurrection is the final word, not the word of evil.

Luke 6:45: "The good person out of the good treasure of his heart produces good, and the evil person out of his evil treasure produces evil, for out of the abundance of the heart his mouth speaks."

John 3:19: "And this is the judgment: the light has come into the world, and people loved the darkness rather than the light because their works were evil."

Eph 6:12: "For we do not wrestle against flesh and blood, but against the rulers, against the authorities, against the cosmic powers over this present darkness, against the spiritual forces of evil in the heavenly places."

Rom 2:9–10: "There will be tribulation and distress for every human being who does evil, the Jew first and also the Greek, but glory and honor and peace for everyone who does good, the Jew first and also the Greek."

Rev 21:1: "Then I saw a new heaven and a new earth; for the first heaven and the first earth had passed away, and the sea was no more."

2 Cor 5:17: "Therefore, if anyone is in Christ, he is a new creation. The old has passed away; behold, the new has come."

Question 10: What does being made in the image of God affirm about human identity?[27]

The Athanasian Creed affirms, "We worship one God in trinity and the trinity in unity, neither blending their persons nor dividing their essence." God is relational in God's very being. To be made in the image of God is therefore to be a person-in-relationship, or persons-in-communion,[28] to put it more accurately. Core to human identity is participation in the innertrinitarian life of God.

Humans are not defined in essential but relational terms. That is, unlike the philosophical stream running from Plato to Descartes and into the present, Scripture is not concerned with defining human life with reference to the necessary "parts." Nor does it concern itself with explaining, in what we may regard as a philosophically satisfying way, the nature of our physicality in life, death, and afterlife. Instead, Scripture presents the human person above all in relational terms. And it marks the human being as

---

27. *Study Catechism* of the PC(USA) (1998) asks a very similar question: "Question 17: What does our creation in God's image reflect about God's reality?"

28. For a fuller treatment of this concept, see Torrance, *Persons in Communion*.

genuinely human and fully alive only within the family of humans brought into being by Yahweh, in relation to the God who gives life-giving breath, and in harmony with the cosmos God has made.[29]

Human identity is inextricably bound up in this relationality. Ultimately, this is the *sine qua non* of human personhood that separates the human person from other creatures and from the artificial creations of human ingenuity. No matter how sophisticated its programming, how complex its mechanisms, how elaborate its circuitry, or how convincing its behavioral replication of human behavior and thought patterns, machines and virtual machines remain ontologically distinct from humans in this regard.

AIs will continually gain ground in their ability to match and exceed human thought and behavior in diverse ways. This does not, however, pose any threat to the affirmation of God's Trinitarian personhood and the image of this personhood borne by the human race.

> 1 Cor 13:12: "For now we see in a mirror dimly, but then face to face. Now I know in part; then I shall know fully, even as I have been fully known."
>
> John 1:1–4: "In the beginning was the Word, and the Word was with God, and the Word was God. He was in the beginning with God. All things were made through him, and without him was not anything made that was made. In him was life, and the life was the light of men."
>
> John 5:19: "So Jesus said to them, 'Truly, truly, I say to you, the Son can do nothing of his own accord, but only what he sees the Father doing. For whatever the Father does, that the Son does likewise.'"
>
> John 17:21–22: "That they may all be one, just as you, Father, are in me, and I in you, that they also may be in us, so that the world may believe that you have sent me. The glory that you have given me I have given to them, so that they may be one, as we are one."

Bibliography

Anderson, Ray. "On Being Human: The Spiritual Side of a Creaturely Soul." In *Whatever Happened to the Soul?: Scientific and Theological Portraits of Human Nature*, edited by Warren S. Brown, Nancey Murphy, and H. Newton Malony, 175–94. Theology and the Sciences. Minneapolis: Fortress, 1998.

Barth, Karl. *Church Dogmatics*. Translated by G.W. Bromiley, and T.F. Torrance. New York: T&T Clark, 2004.

---

29. Green, "Identity."

Boden, Margaret. *Artificial Intelligence: A Very Short Introduction*. Oxford: Oxford University Press, 2018.

Brown, Warren. "Neurobiological Embodiment of Spirituality and Soul." In *From Cells to Souls—and Beyond: Changing Portraits of Human Nature*, edited by Malcolm Jeeves, 58–76. Grand Rapids: Eerdmans, 2004.

Churchland, P.M. "Eliminative Materialism and the Propositional Attitudes." *Journal of Philosophy* 78 (1981) 67–90.

Cole, David. "The Chinese Room Argument." *Stanford Encyclopedia of Philosophy*. Edited by Edward N. Zalta. Stanford: Center for the Study of Language and Information, 2020.

Crick, Francis. *The Astonishing Hypothesis: The Scientific Search for the Soul*. New York: Scribner, 1994.

Du Sautoy, Marcus. *The Creativity Code: Art and Innovation in the Age of AI*. Cambridge: Belknap, 2019.

Green, Joel. "Identity." *Fuller Magazine* 15 (2019).

High, Peter. "Carnegie Mellon Dean of Computer Science on the Future of AI." *Forbes*, October 30, 2017. https://www.forbes.com/sites/peterhigh/2017/10/30/carnegie-mellon-dean-of-computer-science-on-the-future-of-ai/.

Hofstadter, Douglas R. *Gödel, Escher, Bach: An Eternal Golden Braid*. New York: Vintage, 1980.

Murphy, Nancey. *Bodies and Souls, or Spirited Bodies?* Cambridge: Cambridge University Press, 2006.

Myers, David G., and Malcolm A. Jeeves. *Psychology through the Eyes of Faith*. Rev. and updated ed. Through the Eyes of Faith Series. San Francisco: HarperSanFrancisco, 2002.

Plantinga, Alvin. *Where the Conflict Really Lies: Science, Religion, and Naturalism*. New York: Oxford University Press, 2011.

Reese, Byron. *The Fourth Age: Smart Robots, Conscious Computers, and the Future of Humanity*. New York: Atria, 2018.

The Study Catechism of the PC(USA). Louisville: Presbyterian Mission, 1998.

Tegmark, Max. *Life 3.0: Being Human in the Age of Artificial Intelligence*. New York: Alfred A. Knopf, 2017.

Torrance, Alan J. *Persons in Communion: An Essay on Trinitarian Description and Human Participation, with Special Reference to Volume One of Karl Barth's Church Dogmatics*. Edinburgh: T&T Clark, 1996.

Torrance, T.F. *God and Rationality*. Oxford: Oxford University Press, 1971.

Wilczek, Frank. "The Unity of Intelligence." In *Possible Minds: 25 Ways of Looking at AI*, edited by John Brockman, 66–75. New York: Penguin, 2019.

8

Artificial Intelligence, the Ascension of Jesus Christ, and Human Flourishing

NEAL D. PRESA

And the Word became flesh and lived among us, and we have seen his glory, the glory as of a father's only son, full of grace and truth.
—John 1:14 (NRSV)

Since, then, we have a great high priest who has passed through the heavens, Jesus, the Son of God, let us hold fast to our confession.
—Hebrews 4:14 (NRSV)

SPACEX FOUNDER ELON MUSK called it "the biggest existential threat" facing humanity—both today and on into the future.[1] The "it" is artificial intelligence (AI), a "mechanical creature which can function autonomously."[2] AI is ubiquitous in almost every part of our lives, whether seen or unseen. AI is used in assembly production lines that package foods that wind up on grocery store shelves. AI processes your credit card information on your Amazon Prime order. AI processes trillions of terabytes of data, providing information to policymakers, military officials, business leaders, investors, and consumers who make decisions that impact households, companies, and entire nations. AI is here to stay. And notwithstanding doomsday prognosticators who fear a cataclysmic takeover of the human race akin to the movie *Terminator*, AI's advent since the late 1940s and its ubiquity in our lives takes its place in a long

1. Gibbs, "Elon Musk."
2. Murphy, *Introduction to AI Robotics*, 3.

history of technological development: from the advent of paper to the wheel, to the light bulb, to the computer. This paper seeks to frame the question of AI's present-future through the lens of the Christian faith, specifically how human flourishing is understood in light of the Lord's ascension and within the comprehensive framework of life as living liturgy. Because so many aspects of life are directly or indirectly affected by AI (regardless of where one resides, works, or travels—whether in developed, developing, or non-industrialized countries), it is important that we read "the signs of the times." We must not do so with fear, but with the acuity of a scriptural exegete who looks at the challenges of the present context, while simultaneously naming the good news of God in Jesus Christ.

The thesis of this paper is that in order for AI to have a positive future and contribute to universal human flourishing, its makers and users must see it as an instrument and expression of human progress and must be committed to the mission, vision, and values of Jesus Christ, which is love.

In pursuit of this thesis, this paper will begin by briefly laying out the definition of AI and its basic operating principles. Subsequently, the paper will explore the ways that AI falls short in addressing the deep human needs foundational to human flourishing across all contexts, all cultures, and all circumstances. Finally, we will set this in contrast to how the Judeo-Christian faith understands the flourishing of humanity in light of the concepts of love, liturgy, and the ascension of Jesus Christ. As we will see, all of life is liturgy to the glory of God. On this point, we will be aided by Methodist theologian Geoffrey Wainwright's ecumenical trio of virtues from First Corinthians 13—faith, hope, and love—and French liturgical theologian Louis-Marie Chauvet's notion of gift and symbol.

The Definition and Nature of AI

AI is a kind of robot that functions autonomously. One of the first times the word "robot" was used was on January 25, 1921, in Prague when a character, Rossum, in Karel Capek's play *R.U.R.* (Rossum's Universal Robots), invented mechanical workers. Capek created that term, derived from the Czech word *robota*, which means repetitive labor.[3] Roboticists have joked that robots are good for jobs with the three Ds: dirty, dull, or dangerous.[4] And now-defunct company, Thinking Machines, Inc., quipped that they were "making machines that will be proud of us."[5] Initially, one primary

---

3. Murphy, *Introduction to AI Robotics*, 2–3.
4. Murphy, *Introduction to AI Robotics*, 16.
5. Murphy, *Introduction to AI Robotics*, 15.

function of robots was to protect humans. A major impetus for their development was the handling of nuclear materials following World War II. The telemanipulator was a robotic arm that enabled nuclear scientists and engineers to move past simple rubber gloves and a leaded glass shield. The telemanipulator evolved to industrial robotic manipulators which functioned either as open loop (consisting of a pre-programmed goal towards which a robot proceeded to carry out function without any course corrections) or close loop controls (where sensors guided the robot by noting any gaps or errors between the pre-programmed goal and current position). These telemanipulators, which were the genesis of AI today, were further developed for the space industry as engineers sought to control instrumentation from a great distance. Sometimes lacking complete control because of remote linkage, engineers relied upon sensors to acquire the needed data to make decisions on how to manipulate the robots.[6]

When AI's architecture is constructed, the data controls are applied depending on the type of application and the desired goal. Three predominant paradigms shape robotic architecture and its component connections. In the oldest paradigm, the Hierarchical Paradigm, robots work on a *sense-plan-act* sequence: sensing the world, planning the action, and then acting. The Reactive Paradigm works on a *sense-act* sequence where an input to an action is the output of the sensing. The robot's architecture may have couplings of these *sense-act* sequences, such as to turn a certain degree or to move backwards two feet. The Hybrid Deliberative/Reactive Paradigm follows the organization *plan, sense-act*, where planning happens as one step, then sensing and acting are done together.[7]

In all these paradigms, robotic architecture relies on a certain level and degree of human input. AI takes the human input on the front end and extrapolates from there certain options for action as the AI is learning and acquiring patterns. In the 1950s, mathematician Alan Turing proposed a test for a robot to receive five minutes of a text exchange to see if it could deceive real human partners. Known as the Turing test and used in the field of philosophy of artificial intelligence, it is a way to gauge the ability of a robot to learn human language if the human subject is unable to distinguish the robot's communication with that of the other human in the test. In a more recent example of AI's capacity for learning, Google's CEO, Sundar Pichai, oversaw the Google Brain initiative, one aspect of which was the Google Translate project, to have Google AI acquire and learn the vast array of human languages and to be able to communicate in such a way that was indistinguishable from

---

6. Murphy, *Introduction to AI Robotics*, 19–34, for a brief history.
7. Murphy, *Introduction to AI Robotics*, 6–10.

humans.[8] The ubiquity of AI in our lives was further catalyzed with the advent of the smartphones in the early twenty-first century, according to Gone! founder, Nicolas Bayerque.[9] With the use of iOT (Internet of Things) and chatbots, the connectivity of devices beyond and including our smartphones, such as Alexa and Google Assistant, has pervaded our human interactions, communications, and transactions exponentially. Large amounts of personal data are acquired, analyzed, organized, curated, and utilized by algorithms for increased communications—whether positively or negatively—resulting in increased connectivity of businesses with one another, people with their friends/family networks, as well as online purchases, marketing, and even conducting war games for statecraft.

The Limits and Risks of AI

While AI has increased connectivity, communication, and the market economy, there are increasing concerns of the role of AI in human affairs. While personal data is useful for a globalized market economy to market and sell their goods and services, breaches of that data on a massive scale, such as what occurred with Facebook and Cambridge Analytica, have called forth more regulations of AI. Futurist Amy Webb proposed fifteen principles to guide the use of AI, particularly among the nine technology leaders of the world (Google, Amazon, Apple, Microsoft, IBM, Facebook, Baidu, Alibaba, Tencent). The principles are:[10]

- "Humanity should always be at the center of AI's development."
- "AI systems should be safe and secure."
- These nine technology companies (their employees, investors) and the governments they work with must ensure safety.
- "If an AI system causes harm, it should be able to report out what went wrong, and there should be a governance process in place to discuss and mitigate damage."
- "[AI] systems should carry something akin to a nutritional label, detailing the training data used, the processes used for learning, the real-world data being used in applications and the expected outcomes."
- "Everyone in the AI ecosystem . . . must recognize that they are making ethical decisions all the time."

8. Lewis-Kraus, "Great A.I. Awakening," 14–34.
9. Bayerque, "Short History of Chatbots," 38–39.
10. Webb, *Big Nine*, 240–42.

- There must be development of and adherence to a "Human Values Atlas, which would define our unique values across cultures and countries."[11]
- Code of conduct for all those who work on designing, building, and deploying AI.
- "All people should have the right to interrogate AI systems."
- "The terms of service for an AI application—or any service that uses AI—should be written in language plain enough that a third-grader can comprehend it."
- "PDRs (personal data records) should be opt-in and developed using a standardized format, they should be interoperable, and individual people should retain full ownership and permission rights. Should PDRs become heritable, individual people should be able to decide the permissions and uses of their data."
- "PDRs should be decentralized as much as possible, ensuring that no one party has complete control."
- "To the extent possible, PDRs should be protected against enabling authoritarian regimes."
- A system of public accountability should be developed including "an easy method for people to receive answers to questions about their data and how it is mined, refined, and used throughout AI systems."
- "All data should be treated fairly and equally" without discrimination or bias.

Webb's recent publication is premised on the real danger that AI poses: the adverse consequences of mining, archiving, and using personal data for the purposes of increasing the profit margins of companies that use AI and the increased potential risks for AI and the data associated with AI to fall prey to evil intentions.

Underlying Webb's fifteen prescriptions are the centrality of humanity. After all, robots were first created in order to protect and to aid humans. Her proposal echoes Isaac Asimov's so-called Three Laws of Robotics from his 1942 short story, "Runaround": (1) robots must not harm humans nor allow humans to be harmed, (2) robots must obey laws/directives unless those laws/directives conflict with the first, (3) and robots must protect themselves unless protection conflicts with (1) and (2).[12] Our primary concern for the

11. Webb, *Big Nine*, 239.
12. Webb, *Big Nine*, 238.

future use of AI is the self-preservation and the advancement of humanity with as little adverse effects from AI as possible to enable humanity to advance and flourish. These are noble goals considering that the right use of each successive technological innovation can impact the way human life is supported and enhanced. There are, of course, inventions and technologies that have brought great harm, such as the atom bomb, even though one may argue from just war theory that the use of atomic technology—while killing Japanese citizens in Hiroshima and Nagasaki—spared millions around the world from the continuation of World War II.

Admittedly, everyone benefits from AI in some way. But where AI falls short—or more accurately—where AI's human designers, producers, and deployers fall short and where we consumers of AI are complicit, is in not attending to the basic human need to be loved. We can say further that with all attempts to have AI autonomously act as a learned, integrated response to prior data sets, algorithmic outcomes, learned behaviors, and other such components that constitute an AI's architecture, AI cannot fulfill the essence of human flourishing, which is to love and be loved.

Human Flourishing through Love and Liturgy

As children of God and followers of Jesus Christ, we can both embrace the positive aspects and benefits of AI and also critique the shortcomings of AI and its use. At the core of the critique is the question of what the key is to human flourishing. If the prescriptive correctives for AI's present-future use is to ensure that humanity is kept safe in its survival, we should then seek that which will enable humanity to thrive and flourish whether with AI or without AI. What AI can never deliver is love: the capacity to give love nor to mediate love. Saint Augustine spoke of the double love commandments as key to understanding Scripture and understanding life. To love God with all of our heart, with all of our soul, with all of our mind, and with all of our strength, and to love your neighbor as yourself both served as the criteria to determine the rightness of a scriptural interpretation. Love as exegetical hermeneutic brings to human relationships an upward call towards the Lord and a horizontal call towards other people. Love involves a comprehensive, holistic orientation that applies transcendently and immanently. What is affirmed in the double love hermeneutic encompasses Scripture, life, faith, the world, and our very humanity through God's love for us and our love to God and towards one another. Love is the key to our humanity. And it is love that is mediated to us by God in Jesus Christ through the Holy Spirit.

But love does not occur in a vacuum. Love is expressed in encounter, forged and shaped in contexts, in liturgical relationality. The Israelites encountered the living God through feasts, festivals, rituals, through the singing and storytelling of the Scriptures. The Lord called the first disciples and expressed his covenantal love through deeds of mercy and compassion, through meal fellowship, and ultimately through his death and resurrection. The "where" and the "how" of God's love in Christ being appropriated and mediated to us comes through liturgies, holy encounters which the Holy Spirit employs: encounters with the word—the word that is read, that is proclaimed, that is prayed, that is ritualized in bread, in cup, at the font. Even when crowds come forward at an evangelistic crusade and are invited to pray, say a confession of sin, and receive the grace of God, they are engaged in ritual action. When we offer signs of peace to each other, to express love to each other, we are engaged in a ritual encounter.

Methodist theologian Geoffrey Wainwright reminds us that the gifts in First Corinthians 13 of faith, hope, and love animate our life and the church's life towards unity.[13] These three gifts of the Spirit correspond to the ritual encounters of baptism, the Lord's Prayer, and the Eucharist. In baptism, faith is appropriated and attested, thus, incorporating the baptized into the body of Christ. In the Lord's Prayer, as we join the community of believers and as the Lord prays with and for us, the Holy Spirit enables us to hope in life, "thy will be done on earth as it is in heaven." The Lord's Prayer orients us to the heart of God. Finally, at the Eucharist, through the sharing of the one bread and drinking of the one cup, we are strengthened and assured by God's love in Jesus Christ, the Word made flesh, the one with whom our hearts are joined by the Holy Spirit. Thus, Calvin saw in the *sursum corda* the pivotal moment:[14]

> Pastor: The Lord be with you.
>
> People: And also with you.
>
> Pastor: Lift up your hearts (*sursum corda*)
>
> People: We lift them up to the Lord.

It was in that moment that the Spirit of the ascended Christ raises up the hearts of the gathered community to the One "who is seated at the right hand of God the Father Almighty, from thence He shall come to judge the quick and the dead," as the Apostles' Creed attests.

---

13. Wainwright, *Faith, Hope, and Love*.
14. Calvin, *Institutes*, IV.17.18.

It was in that sacramental, liturgical event whereby the assembly is united to the Lord Christ, and therefore the life of the community is strengthened and flourishes.

Christ's Ascension and Human Flourishing

We participate in Christ and in God's desire for communion with humanity and with the creation in Christ.[15] For Barth, Christ's ascension was about our participation in Christ, who communes with us and expresses that communion through three dimensions: justification, sanctification, and vocation. Justification is "the divine verdict that repudiates, displaces, removes, and pardons the being of sinful humanity that in its place establishes a new and truly human subject who receives the new humanity in faith as an act of pure and obedient gratitude."[16] Where in justification God decides the essential identity of humanity, in sanctification Jesus Christ is "God's direction, God's command to live as his children. He is not the command to enter into the kingdom of God, but rather the command to live as those who are in it already."[17] Vocation is the promised reality in Jesus Christ, the *telos* of justification and sanctification. Neder observes that Barth summarizes vocation by speaking about eternal life: "Eternal life is life in action . . . Barth chooses the word service (*Dienst*) as the leading concept in his description of eternal life precisely because it denotes a life of action: eternal life is 'a being in the service of God.'"[18] Christ's union with humanity in his ascension is a "union in distinction" which is a union in action, a "fluid and differentiated but genuine and solid unity." Christ makes us alive by making us his witnesses.[19] Neder says, "Union with Christ is not merely the privatistic reception of gifts. It is rather the perfect mutual coordination of Jesus Christ's active calling and the correspondingly active human response of witness to the grace and greatness of God."[20] In short, as aspects of God's work of reconciliation and communion, justification as divine verdict results in the Holy Spirit's gift of faith; sanctification as divine direction results in the Holy Spirit's gift of love; and vocation as divine promise results in the Holy Spirit's gift of hope. For Calvin and Barth, the mediation of the Holy Spirit in forging and forming life is done in community: the gathered community of the

15. Canlis, *Calvin's Ladder*, 48, 49.
16. Neder, *Participation in Christ*, 52.
17. Neder, *Participation in Christ*, 54.
18. Neder, *Participation in Christ*, 55.
19. Neder, *Participation in Christ*, 79.
20. Neder, *Participation in Christ*, 79.

church in her worship and service and in that community being sent by the Spirit to bear witness, to be salt and light of the earth in the world.

Conclusion

Putting in conversation artificial intelligence, liturgical theology, and ascension theology, what we see at stake is the present-future of humanity and what shapes and frames human flourishing with or without AI, with or without technology. Technology in any form either helps or hinders human flourishing. In either case, technology will always fall short in addressing the universal human need to love and be loved. Robots, while autonomous and possessing a form of mechanized intelligence, cannot have love, nor any of the two other parts of the trifecta charisms: faith and hope. These are gifts from God for the people of God—created beings in his image, with flesh, blood, and soul, and for whom the eternal Word was enfleshed to die, in the words of the late Orthodox liturgical theologian Alexander Schmemann, "for the life of the world."[21] Of course, Schmemann's use of that phrase, which also served as the title of his book, was in reference to the Eucharist, that in the eating of the bread and drinking of the cup, we are partaking of a foretaste of the heavenly banquet table, that in enacting the liturgy of the church, we are doing liturgy, we are doing theology, we are doing life, we are having life. AI has sometimes been referred to as *transhuman*, but there is nothing human about AI. For AI could never love nor partake of the liturgy, and, therefore, could never have true life, real life. Such a destiny is only for true humans, real humans, to which the Word became flesh, for the life of the world.

Bibliography

Bayerque, Nicolas. "A Short History of Chatbots and Artificial Intelligence." In *The Reference Shelf: Exploring Contemporary Issues with Selected Primary and Secondary Sources: Artificial Intelligence*, edited by H.W. Wilson, 37–40. Amenia, NY: Grey House, 2018.

Canlis, Julie. *Calvin's Ladder: A Spiritual Theology of Ascent and Ascension*. Grand Rapids: Eerdmans, 2010.

Gibbs, Samuel. "Elon Musk: artificial intelligence is our biggest existential threat." *Guardian*, October 27, 2014. https://www.theguardian.com/technology/2014/oct/27/elon-musk-artificial-intelligence-ai-biggest-existential-threat.

Lewis-Kraus, Gideon. "The Great A.I. Awakening." In *The Reference Shelf: Exploring Contemporary Issues with Selected Primary and Secondary Sources: Artificial Intelligence*, edited by H.W. Wilson, 9–36. Amenia, NY: Grey House, 2018.

---

21. Schmemann, *For the Life of the World*, 12.

Murphy, Robin. *Introduction to AI Robotics*. Cambridge: MIT Press, 2000.
Neder, Adam. *Participation in Christ: An Entry into Karl Barth's Church Dogmatics*. Columbia Series in Reformed Theology. Louisville: Westminster John Knox, 2009.
Schmemann, Alexander. *For the Life of the World*. Crestwood: St. Vladimir's Press, 2004.
Wainwright, Geoffrey. *Faith, Hope, and Love: The Ecumenical Trio of Virtues*. Waco: Baylor University Press, 2014.
Webb, Amy. *The Big Nine: How the Tech Titans and Their Thinking Machines Could Warp Humanity*. New York: Public Affairs, 2019.

9

On Human Transcendence, Artificial Intelligence, and the Gathering Gnostic Storm

MISSY BYRD DeREGIBUS

"I, for one, welcome our new computer overlords."

—KEN JENNINGS, long-time Jeopardy winner,
after losing to IBS's Watson in 1996

OVER TWO MILLENNIA AGO, Socrates famously fretted about the overly sanguine claims of the benefits of writing which promised to make the Egyptians wiser and would improve memory.[1] Socrates's response is worth repeating here.

> In fact, he said, it will introduce forgetfulness into the soul of those who learn it; they will not practice using their memory because they will put their trust in writing, which is external and depends on signs that belong to others, instead of trying to remember from the inside, completely on their own. You have not discovered a potion for remembering but reminding; you provide your students with the appearance of wisdom, not with its reality. Your invention will enable them to hear many things without being properly taught, and they will imagine that they have come to know much while for the most part they will know

---

1. Socrates's concerns are framed in the repetition of an ancient dialogue within a (then) contemporary dialogue.

nothing. And they will be difficult to get along with since they will merely appear to be wise instead of really being so.[2]

It is not without irony to note that we only know about Socrates's concerns because his pupil, Plato, saw fit to commit them to paper some decades later.

While it would be interesting to weigh Socrates's claims regarding the invention and rise of writing and the subsequent loss or gain to humanity, the purpose of this paper is to consider a larger question raised by Socrates: At what point does a tool, even one with undisputed benefits, cross the line and become a master? At what point does what is lost supersede what is gained?

Specifically, I will be examining Artificial Intelligence, its potential advantages as well as its possible moral hazards. Does AI cross a new threshold that previous tools of mankind have not? Consider the domestication of crops, the invention of the wheel, or the advent of antibiotics and its dramatic effect of lengthening lifespans.[3] Could it not be said that countless thresholds have already been crossed in human history and that these innovations resulted in a net gain?

The questions surrounding AI seem different in kind than previous creations of man. Is AI merely quantitatively bigger and faster, or is there something radically dissimilar to previous inventions, however momentous? Does AI have the potential not just to change human culture and captivate us, as have many inventions of the past, but also to take on a life of its own and actually take over, making human beings redundant? Might it be able to develop human abilities such as consciousness, qualia, or even moral agency? Just the massive scale and speed of development confronts us with unprecedented concerns. We will examine some of those stated concerns from within the industry as well as from theological grounds which may serve to guide us as we stand on the brink of what feels like a new era in human history.

It should be said from the outset that the term AI has been flung about rather promiscuously. Used commonly, it often seems to mean "really cool stuff we can't do now but hope to do in the near future," referring to high levels of computing that tend to downplay the intelligence part of the equation. This is known as the AI effect.[4] For the purpose of solidifying definitions, we will first look at the criteria used to delineate the different kinds

---

2. Plato, *Phaedrus*, 274e–275b.
3. Sigbeku, "Treasure Called Antibiotics," 56–57.
4. AIS researcher Rodney Brooks complains, "Every time we figure out a piece of it, it stops being magical; we say, 'Oh, that's just a computation'" (Kahn, "It's Alive!," para. 3).

of AI and use human intelligence as a point of comparison to allow for the greatest possible overlap of abilities.

It is no secret that technology has exploded exponentially, including the technology that allows for artificial intelligence of any kind, strong or weak. Gene sequencing, facial recognition, or even GPS from a smartphone are all uses of AI that would have seemed incredible to scientists in any field a scant half-century ago. The speed and pervasiveness at which advances are made are not just difficult but literally impossible to keep up with.

This is nowhere illustrated more concretely than with Moore's law, named after Intel CEO Gordon Moore from a paper he wrote in 1963, in which he made the observation that "the number of transistors in a dense integrated circuit doubles about every two years," a fact that has proven more or less accurate.[5] Moore's law has since been applied more broadly to describing the catalyst resulting in greater internet capacity, epidemiology, and even economic growth.[6] *The doubling every two years* (or other exponential models) of components, information, or productivity is what should get our attention, especially as we consider the possibilities for AI. For example, since the first paper on artificial neural networks was written in 1943, more than one hundred fifty thousand additional academic papers have been published on the topic.[7]

The predictive use of Moore's law has led some philosophers and scientists such as Nick Bostrom, Swedish philosopher at the University of Oxford and author of *Super Intelligence*, to speculate on the possibility of an information singularity, where information gathering and calculation accelerate at a clip that becomes at some point irretrievable, resulting in a super-intelligence.[8] It is this exponential explosion of information and ability that makes the future seem both limitless and literally unimaginable.

But that hasn't stopped people from trying to imagine it.

To picture the possible futures of AI, we need to distinguish between the three levels of AI: weak, strong, and super. The first level of AI is an intelligence that meets or surpasses human ability in a narrow sphere, such as IBM's Deep Blue did in chess, NASA's spacecraft did in landing a drone on Mars, or your countertop Siri does on an everyday basis. Although impressive, this weak form of AI has occurred in many ways and continues to have new applications daily. The second level of AI that can meet human competencies in a general or broad-based way is considered

5. Moore, "Cramming More Components," 114.
6. Tardi, "Moore's Law."
7. Bostrom, *SuperIntelligence*, 10.
8. Bostrom, *SuperIntelligence*, 4.

to be strong AI. Note that the word "general" used here does not mean vague, but rather multi-domained, as opposed to one specific sphere. Last, an intelligence that greatly exceeds human abilities in many domains of interest would qualify as a super intelligence.

Since weak AI has already been indisputably met and is familiar to us all, we want to address the second level of AI. For this, we look to Alan Turing, the English mathematician, computer scientist, and cryptologist. In a 1950s paper, Turing asked the not-so-original question, "Can machines think?" He proposed a test that changed the question to a more measurable one, "Can machines do what we do?" Specifically, can machines perform basic language functions in such a way as to be indistinguishable to a human third party? The Turing test in its original form was simple, conceived in a text-only version by keyboard and screen. Although it has not been without its critics, it nonetheless has served as a jumping-off place for much of the AI discussion since, including almost daily claims of success countered by speculation as to whether it has been passed or not.

Turing used humans as the comparison for intelligences. One might ask what qualifies as intelligence in humans, and while philosophers disagree on the exact list of what intelligence constitutes, for the most part they agree that intelligence is needed to represent knowledge, including commonsense knowledge; to be able to plan and learn; to communicate in natural language; to think abstractly and comprehend complex ideas; and to integrate all these skills towards common goals.[9] A strong AI would be able to do, or appear to do, these things that humans of normal intelligence do on a daily basis.

Moral capacity, however, involves something beyond mere computing abilities or even the more challenging general intelligence; it seems to require the presence of qualia and consciousness as the gateway for moral thinking, however flawed that thinking might be.[10] Consciousness allows for an awareness of oneself, others, and the ability to evaluate one's own ideas and perceptions, what philosophers call philosophy of mind.

---

9. This list of intelligent traits is based on the topics covered by major AI textbooks, including Russell and Norvig, *Artificial Intelligence*.

10. While qualia and consciousness are frequently conflated and disputed, we find the distinction made by Ned Block, philosopher of mind at NYU, to be compelling and helpful. He proposed as distinction between the two types of consciousness what he calls phenomenal (P-consciousness) which is "simply raw experience" and access (A-Consciousness) which is how we perceive, remember, and introspect on qualia. Generally speaking, it is P-consciousness that is considered the more difficult to understand and is referred to as *the hard problem of consciousness* (Block, *Nature of Consciousness*, 375–415).

Bostrom, not a believer, describes wisdom as the ability to get the big picture about right.[11]

It is the presence of qualia and consciousness in addition to rationality that form the possibility of moral agency. Such are the dreams and nightmares of science fiction, as are found in *Ex Machina*, *Battle Star Galactica*, *West World*, and a host of others. These futuristic dystopias are less concerned with a computer's ability to reason, which is presumed, but rather with the possibility of sentience. *Can it feel?* It is feeling, then judging, weighing, and interpreting beyond mere experience or calculation that makes humans moral beings.

To examine a theological framework for human moral abilities, we look to American theologian Reinhold Niebuhr, who wrote extensively on the nature of the human condition. Niebuhr's understanding was twofold. A person is a body, with all that implies: a history of genes, environmental influence, and spatial-temporal limits. But she is also transcendent, able to rise above her environment by means of rationality and imagination to experience a world far beyond her own. This combination of materiality and transcendence explains not only the everyday experience of humans, but also their access to a moral life. The cognitive ability to recognize the otherness of other humans and other animals, to imagine and to weigh counterfactuals, and to predict and fear one's own death are all unique to humans. Humans are free, even within their materiality, to observe, analyze, reject, and attempt reform of their environment. It is in this God-given sphere of human transcendence that both creativity and sin occur.[12]

Lest we imagine that this level of thinking is both sophisticated and rare, let me assert that it is instead sophisticated and commonplace. Consider the following hypothetical situation:

Imagine that I need to pay my property taxes at the local courthouse down on Main Street. I figure it won't take long and that I can do so and still make it to my 10:00 a.m. meeting, the first in a busy day. I find to my pleasure that there is one parking spot left and that I am able to deftly parallel park my car. I find to my annoyance that I do not have quarters for the meter. I make a quick calculation. If I run home to get quarters, I will not be able to get to my meeting on time. If I don't pay my taxes today,

---

11. Bostrom, *SuperIntelligence*, 67. As a biblical example, we might think of the woe of the Pharisees (Luke 11:42), which involved tithing of mint but neglecting the larger element of the law. Although the Pharisees' technical application was correct (see Lev 27:30, Deut 14:22, and others), according to Jesus, the Pharisees got the small rote thing right, but missed the broader value behind the specific. In other words, they missed the ethical forest for the moral trees.

12. DeRegibus, *Man as Moral Animal*, 4–6.

I will get fined. I figure it might take me about twelve minutes to get in and out of the courthouse if there are no long lines. What are the odds of getting a ticket in twelve minutes? I decide to take a chance. When I return to my car, having righteously paid my taxes like the good citizen I am, I find that I have indeed gotten a parking ticket for fifty dollars. I am outraged. I consider the unfairness of the system that punishes good citizens trying to do the right thing and imagine what unscrupulous ends my precious money will go to—probably paying for parties for meter nazis who have nothing better to do. I notice that the meter of the car in back of me has also expired, but that that car has not received a ticket. I have an idea. Perhaps I could move my ticket to their windshield! Perhaps the poor unsuspecting sot will not notice and pay the fine. After all, they deserve it just as much as I do. But wait! What if someone sees me? What if someone sees me that I know? I am a spiritual leader, for heaven's sake! "What a terrible thing to think," I tell myself. "What kind of person are you? *That's cheating.* You should be ashamed of yourself." Chastened, I consider that even though the system may be unfair, two wrongs do not make a right, and just maybe some of that money goes to fix potholes. I decide to pay the fine and resolve to carry quarters in my car hereafter.

All this thinking is done in about a minute, far faster than it takes to read it.

Could a computer ever do this kind of moral thinking? Two things are necessary and possibly sufficient to create a moral super-intelligence: a path to create a computer beyond our own capacities and the ability to imbue consciousness within that frame.[13]

Many scientists believe the possibility of creating a super AI is likely beyond the skill of mere humans. Nick Bostrom, among others, proposes that a human-created AI, working together with humans, could create a super AI that meets or surpasses the human-created AI. This human-created AI working with the super AI could then work together without human aid to make an even more powerful AI, creating a singularity far outstripping human abilities.[14] Most experts, however, tend towards skepticism regarding computers building more sophisticated versions of themselves. In the history of computer science "no programmer has created a code that can substantially improve itself."[15]

---

13. A mere strong AI, as opposed to a super AI, would likely not be sophisticated enough to house "consciousness."

14. As summarized by Bringsjord and Govendarajulu, "Artificial Intelligence."

15. Khatchadourian, "Doomsday Invention," para. 50.

Adding consciousness to even an advanced machine presents an additional set of challenges. Max Tegmark, MIT physicist and author of *Life 3.0*, speaks about the great difficulties inherent in understanding human consciousness and the mind-brain problem that it presents.[16] There are immense hurdles involved in a computer application[17] with no clear path to being able to encode or develop the kind of consciousness we see in humans. Without consciousness, there is no housing for moral agency. Without moral agency and acts of the will, there is no ability to have a malicious takeover; you can't have a malicious takeover in the absence of malice.

The future of an *intentional* super-intelligent computer takeover appears unlikely. However, in light of the rather frail history of humans' ability to accurately predict the future and a bit of the Christian virtue of humility, it might be best to not proclaim it impossible. A more tempered response might say that based on the data that we now possess, it looks unlikely that computers will end up possessing the consciousness and qualia necessary to become moral agents or that they will mount a conscious takeover.

This does not mean that there aren't serous worries about more modest versions of AI in scenarios that are very likely to happen or are already happening. Even without the presumption of sentience and perhaps without the possibility of a super-intelligent AI, many in the field have expressed grave concerns for the unintended consequences of the impending horizon.

The Future of Life Institute, founded by Max Tegmark, released a four-paragraph open letter in July of 2015 expressing the desire that AI research would "maximize its societal benefits while 'avoiding positional pitfalls.'"[18] Since its release, the letter has been signed by over eight thousand people, including such luminaries as Bill Gates, Elon Musk, and Stephen Hawking.[19] Linked to the open letter is a research priorities document which lists various examples where AI could be prone to nefarious ends. These include such things as the probable vastly disproportionate benefits between tech-haves and have-nots, security issues, liability issues such as those related to riderless cars, and the uncharted ethical quagmires regarding war and weaponry,

16. Tegmark, *Life 3.0*, 281–315.

17. Unfortunately, Tegmark conflates the concepts of goal and purpose with function, even applying them to non-conscious items such as a missile in a manner that would likely be cringe-worthy to most biologists and physicists. The works function and cause are usually considered more accurately descriptive of what a missile does, eliminating implied agency on the part of the missile.

18. Russell et al., "Research Priorities," 112.

19. Bill Gates, Tesla founder Elon Musk, and theoretical physicist Stephen Hawking all expressed concerns regarding unbounded artificial intelligence which could "spell the end of the human race," saying, "I don't know why people aren't worried." Musk called it "summoning the demon" (Holley, "Bill Gates," para. 10).

just to name a few. While the letter seems tempered in its approach, the motto at the top of the Future of Life Institute website is a bit more plainly blunt, reading, "Technology is giving life the potential to flourish like never before . . . or to self-destruct. Let's make a difference!"[20]

While the concerns listed in the research priorities document are undoubtably valid and require both theological attention and calls to action, I am struck by what is missing. The concerns have to do with loss of agency and various ethical conundrums. It is the agency lost by the disenfranchised. It is the abused agency of using AI for warfare in addition to curing cancer. It is the tyranny of a tech-manipulated market. It is the ethics of security, control, and liability in untested waters. These concerns are valid. The question of misused agency is a topic that dominates practical theology and reoccurs constantly in Scripture, and it deserves further study from the vantage point of new and existing AI strategies.

But I'd like to focus on what is not mentioned—so glaringly absent that I wonder if it is not considered to be a problem—and that is a missing sense of the inherent value of the body. The unspoken overarching *ethos* found in so much of this literature is that the body is a net loss to humanity; it is a weak link in a two-link chain. If you can shore it up indefinitely, fine, but if not, why not kick it to the corner? If you could intimately upload your consciousness to the cloud, would not the most important part of you remain and the expendable part be discarded like taking down scaffolding on a building that has been completed?

As a representative gnostic view, Nick Bostrom is quite explicit about this. In a *New Yorker* article, Khatchadourian notes,

> Bostrom has written more than a hundred articles, and his longing for immortality can be seen throughout. In 2008, he framed an essay as a call to action from a future utopia. "Death is not one but a multitude of assassins," he warned. "Take aim at the causes of early death . . . turn your biggest gun on aging, and fire. You must seize the biochemical processes in your body in order to vanquish by and by illness and senescence. In time, you will discover ways to move your mind to more durable media." [Bostrom] tends to see the mind as immaculate code, the body as inefficient hardware—able to accommodate limited hacks but probably destined for replacement . . . he suspects that the farther into the future one looks the less likely it seems that life will continue as it is . . . *humanity becomes transcendent, or it perishes.*[21]

---

20. Future of Life website at https://futureoflife.org.

21. Khatchadourian, "Doomsday Invention," para. 21, 31; emphasis mine.

It is clear that Bostrom does not use nor view the word transcendence in the same way that Niebuhr does. Niebuhr's concept of human transcendence is grounded and intimately intertwined in the good body, the experiences of the body, the senses of the body. Niebuhr rejects the Platonic image of the superiority of the mind's essential goodness warring against the frailties of the flesh as the source of evil. He's not having it: "The Bible," he says, "knows nothing of a good mind and an evil body."[22]

Bostrom's transcendence is of a cloud-floating consciousness unshackled by the constraints of the body. The body is the appendix that is no longer needed; its usefulness has been outgrown.

Our own culture is reflective of a schizophrenic view of the body, either idolizing its sensual nature in an Epicurean frenzy or despising its frailty and incessant demands. The latter saturates current culture both explicitly and implicitly. Nowhere is this attitude displayed more emblematically than the unfortunately named drink concoction Soylent,[23] developed by software engineer Rob Rhinehart who viewed food as "a time-consuming hassle" and resolved to treat it as an engineering problem.[24] While I suspect that most of us have some version of Soylent (what's wrong with Ramen?), Rhinehart's goal was to completely eliminate the need for eating and preparing food, and he would spend months subsiding exclusively on Soylent, presumably to allow him to sit for longer hours in front of the computer screen.

In strong contrast, the biblical witness is unambiguous: the material world, including the material body, is a good gift. The body is an inherently created good. It teaches us things beyond or at least differently than just abstract teaching, especially in relation to memory, knowing, and community. Even the weaknesses of the body, such as sickness or disability, remind us of our limitations and teach us things such as empathy and compassion that we cannot fully appreciate otherwise. We believe that the weak, including the physically weak in our human communities, are to be treated with special reverence, not discarded. We believe that physical presence of bodies creates an intimacy in time of grief, celebration, and hospitality. We know that the body acts as a check to hubris: death comes to all and curtails not only our ambitions, but also our evil.

We are awed by the joy and mystery of the Incarnation of Christ; our Lord came in a body, which was both a humbling and a gift, at once from and to and of God.

22. Niebuhr, *Nature and Destiny of Man*, 6.

23. Which you can buy online at soylent.com, marketed with the by-line of "Let us take a few things off your plate."

24. For enjoyment on a rainy day, I highly commend reading the entire Wikipedia article, especially the taste reviews of Soylent.

A worldly depreciation of the innate value of the body may naturally hasten to seek disembodied solutions to true and challenging material problems. Some solutions may be welcomed; others are inherently problematic. The imminent danger is not so much a Bostromian takeover of computers, but rather an intentional and relieved abdication of responsibility driven by a scarcity of resources.

Let us consider just one example of a current scarcity and how AI might be enlisted to address a very real problem.

The current and looming aging care crisis found in this country and throughout much of the world will serve to illustrate this problem. The world's aging population is expected to double in the next thirty years. This has profound implications for the burden of the treatment of disease and on the social and healthcare systems which are already unable to address the soaring demand even in resource-rich countries. A report titled *Crisis in Care* was published in the 2014 *Lancet*, a magazine not normally given to hyperbole. It highlights the depth of the caregiving disaster: "The figures we have uncovered are . . . catastrophic," says Caroline Abrahams, director of Age UK. John Schall of the United States-based Caregiver Action Network reports that the USA is heading towards a "caregiving cliff." Both report current unsustainable strain on families' emotional and financial resources even while unable to provide sufficient levels of care with dire predictions for the future.[25]

Technological advancements can no doubt be a part of a robust and ethically sound solution to the caregiving crisis. They can also provide some ethically dubious solutions. While housekeeping, monitoring vital signs, and preparing meals might well be done by not-too-future robotic assistance, surely end-of-life care, companionship, compassion, and assurance in old age should demand actual human beings who are physically present. But what if there are simply not enough human beings to go around? Shall we put robots in their place?

Lest this emotional robotic caregiving scenario seem unlikely, we look to a currently existing phenomena of the ELIZA effect. As long ago as 1966, MIT computer scientist Joseph Weizenbaum developed a computer program that crudely mimicked psychotherapist responses by rephrasing statements from his students posing as patients. Designed in the form of a question, the reply gave the appearance of a supportive reflection of their thoughts. For example, the statement, "I feel frustrated," would be met in the response of "Why do you feel frustrated?" He named the program ELIZA.

Weisenbaum was surprised and disturbed by the response of his students. Some exhibited "strong emotional connections" to his program; others even wanted to spend time alone with it. This occurred even though

---

25. See "Global Elderly Care in Crisis."

the students fully understood that they were conversing with a computer program; they still treated it as if it were a "real, thinking being that cared about their problems."[26] This study and many other similar ones that followed demonstrated what is now known as the ELIZA effect, where users seem to want to anthropomorphize computer communications to be expressing actual human emotion and intelligence.

Keep in mind that neither strong nor super AI is needed for the ELIZA effect to occur. It is not necessary for consciousness or even rationality to make this work, just clever coding. The ethical concerns surrounding the creation of seemingly empathetic computers worries even some roboticists. Sherry Turkle, founding director of the MIT's Initiative of Technology and Self, asks, "Should we be creating robots just to make people feel good? Should we be making artificial companions? Isn't this a statement that we've given up on offering actual human companions?"[27]

Although this is just one example, there are likely dozens with similar dilemmas. It is the nature of scarcity and poverty of options that anticipate just one of the moral hazards that lie very immanently ahead of us.

What then must we do? With our present understanding, the church has several imperatives before it.

We must develop a rich and deep understanding of technology in light of a robust theology of the body. While celebrating the benefits of technology, we recognize that, not unlike all tools, it has inherent limits and will have some applications that are possible but not beneficial, even abhorrent, and with dramatically destructive potentialities. This theological underpinning must incorporate and integrate the various theologies of the body already mentioned.

Because this theology has pragmatic implications for all humans, we should strive in every way possible to translate this message to the outside world in language that can be understood, language that is both compelling and winsome.

Finally, the church must teach, practice, and model heuristic applications of this theology within the church. As in the past, the practice of the church will likely be more compelling than the verbal teaching of the church. Simple practices that reflect our beliefs can prove a unique opportunity for faithful presence and an opportunity to be salt and light in a banal and darkened world.

---

26. Billings, "Rise of Roboethics," para. 6.
27. Thompson, "It's Alive!," para. 22.

Bibliography

Billings, Lee. "The Rise of Roboethics." *Seed Magazine*, July 16, 2007. https://web.archive.org/web/20090228092414/http://www.seedmagazine.com/news/2007/07/rise_of_roboethics.php.

Block, Ned. *The Nature of Consciousness: Philosophical Debates*. Massachusetts: MIT Press, 1998.

Bostrom, Nick. *SuperIntellegence: Paths, Dangers, Strategies*. Oxford: Oxford University Press, 2014.

Bringsjord, Selmer, and Naveen Sundar Govendarajulu. "Artificial Intelligence." *Stanford Encyclopedia of Philosophy*. Edited by Edward N. Zalta. Stanford: Center for the Study of Language and Information, 2020.

DeRegibus, Missy. "Man as Moral Animal: Reinhold Niebuhr's Theology of Human Transcendence in Light of the Recent Comparative Animal Studies." Unpublished paper, Regent College, Vancouver, 2017.

"Global Elderly Care in Crisis." *Lancet* 383.9921 (March 15, 2014) 927.

Holley, Peter. "Bill Gates on Dangers of Artificial Intelligence: 'I Don't Understand Why Some People Are Not Concerned.'" *Washington Post*, January 29, 2015.

Kahn, Jennifer. "It's Alive!" *Wired*, March 1, 2002. https://www.wired.com/2002/03/everywhere/.

Khatchadourian, Rafi. "The Doomsday Invention: Will Artificial Intelligence Bring Us Utopia or Destruction?" *New Yorker*, November 23, 2015. https://www.newyorker.com/magazine/2015/11/23/doomsday-invention-artificial-intelligence-nick-bostrom.

Moore, Gordon. "Cramming More Components into Integrated Circuits." *Electronics* 38.8 (April 19, 1965) 114.

Niebuhr, Reinhold. *The Nature and Destiny of Man*. New York: Charles Scribner's Sons, 1948.

Plato. *Phaedrus*. Translated by Alexander Nehamas and Paul Woodruff. Indianapolis: Hackett, 1997.

Russell, Stuart, Daniel Dewey, and Max Tegmark. "Research Priorities for Robust and Beneficial Artificial Intelligence." *AI Magazine* (Winter 2015) 106–14.

Russell, Stuart, and Peter Norvig. *Artificial Intelligence: A Modern Approach*. 2nd ed. Upper Saddle River, NJ: Prentice Hall, 2010.

Sigbeku, Operyemi. "The Treasure Called Antibiotics." *Annals of Ibadan Postgraduate Medicine* 14.2 (December 2016). https://www.ajol.info/index.php/aipm/issue/view/15440.

Tardi, Carla. "Moore's Law Definition." *Investopedia*, February 24, 2021. https://www.investopedia.com/terms/m/mooreslaw.asp.

Tegmark, Max. *Life 3.0: Being Human in the Age of Artificial Intelligence*. New York: Knoff, 2017.

Thompson, Clive. "It's Alive!" *Wired*, January 1, 2007. https://www.wired.com/2007/01/alive/.

10

In the Image of Our Choosing?

Personhood, the Image of God, and the Ethics of Gene Editing[1]

NATHAN A. BARCZI

IMAGINE A LARGE TUB sitting on the floor in front of you. In the tub is some water and a heap of material containing mostly carbon, nitrogen, calcium, phosphorous, and smaller amounts of about twenty other elements—basically, mud. Legally and ethically, you could do whatever you wanted with this stuff: buy it, sell it, run experiments on it, or just toss it in the trash.

But take that same material and arrange its molecules just so, and they become something very different—a person, with autonomy and inalienable rights. We universally recognize that these otherwise common materials have dignity and autonomy. They become a human person, someone who cannot be bought or sold or experimented upon without his or her express permission, even if the person has died.

Why is this? This might seem like a silly question. On some level, most of us instinctively recognize the difference between a human being and a pile of dirt, such that it would seem strange even to ask the question of *why* the person ought to be treated with dignity and respect. But on the other hand, our history suggests that the dignity of the human person is not something which can merely be taken for granted; there are too many examples of its denial, not all of them in the past. Humans have frequently

---

1. Early versions of this chapter were co-authored by Chad Baldanza for presentation at the Personal Genetics Education Project Industry Forum in May 2016 and the Cambridge Roundtable discussion seminars in fall 2016.

violated the dignity of other humans—through murder, genocide, rape, bullying, and oppression of every kind. And often, such oppression is preceded precisely by *dehumanization*; if the other is less than human, then we have the right to mistreat them.[2]

Moreover, we need to remind ourselves that the progress of liberal humanism has proved no impediment to dehumanizing tendencies. In support of his own anti-Semitic policies, Adolf Hitler pointed to the American eugenics movement of the early twentieth century. At that time, Charles William Eliot, a Harvard president, was an outspoken opponent of immigration and intermarriage between races (including not only blacks marrying whites, but Irish Catholics marrying Anglo-Saxon Protestants), and a supporter of the forced sterilization of those considered "feebleminded" or "criminalistic."[3] No less a scion of liberal progressivism than Chief Justice Oliver Wendell Holmes Jr. wrote the majority opinion in *Buck v. Bell*, which upheld the forced sterilization of Carrie Buck, a woman designated "feebleminded" by the state of Virginia. "Three generations of imbeciles are enough," wrote Holmes, referring to Buck's mother and infant daughter. The stakes, it is clear, are too high to take the dignity of the human for granted.

Recently, those stakes have been raised by the advent of CRISPR gene editing technology, which has radically increased the ease and accuracy of our capacity to edit the human genome[4]—including, most controversially, in "germline" cells that will pass any changes on to all subsequent generations. With startling speed—CRISPR was only developed in 2013 by teams of researchers in Cambridge, Massachusetts, and Berkeley, California—it has become clear the question is when, not whether, precise and relatively cheap genetic modification of human embryos will be available to prospective parents.

It has not escaped notice that this technology raises a number of novel ethical concerns. While CRISPR holds out tremendous potential to alleviate the suffering that follows from genetic diseases such as sickle cell anemia and Huntington's disease, it could eventually also make possible, to those with access to the technology, the selection of traits such as height, eye color, and greater strength and intelligence.[5]

2. For a catalog of such examples, see Smith, *Less Than Human*.
3. Cohen, "Harvard's Eugenics Era."
4. Think of editing the genome like a "find-and-replace" function: a tool finds, removes, and replaces a specific sequence of genetic material. In older methods of gene editing, the search is done using protein structures, which are laborious to construct and not terribly precise. Instead, CRISPR uses RNA, which can be cheaply and quickly constructed by most good graduate students working in a lab.
5. Regalado, "Eugenics 2.0."

Some Christians who have wrestled with such issues have allowed cautious support for the technology. The Vatican, for instance, which takes a relatively conservative line on questions of bioethics, has expressed qualified support for "strictly therapeutic intervention."[6] It has even written that "[g]erm line genetic engineering with a therapeutic goal in man would in itself be acceptable were it not for the fact that is it is hard to imagine how this could be achieved without disproportionate risks,"[7] such as embryo loss and unintended genetic changes. But questions remain, including the question of what it means for humanity to be the sort of being that desires and can exercise such control over itself.

The strongest concern is that we will begin to conceive of humanity as something that we can reshape to suit our own wishes. This is, in general, characteristic of technology—as Paul Graham, founder of the technology accelerator Y Combinator, puts it: "Technological progress means making things do more of what we want."[8] But implicit in this project is an ontological gulf between ourselves and our technology. We can fashion it according to our desires without ethical concern because we are its maker. But as moral theologian Oliver O'Donovan has written, this is not how we relate to other humans, not even our own children.[9] We are not their maker. To use a biblical term, we *beget* our children, the difference being that what is begotten and not made is ontologically equal, rather than being other or inferior. (Christian theology refers to the Son as eternally *begotten* of the Father precisely in order to emphasize the equality of the persons of the Trinity. To refer to the Son as the creature of the Father, as Arius would have had it, would have been to reject Jesus' divinity.)

There are those who argue not only that we may, but that we are obligated to take all available steps to enhance ourselves and our offspring genetically.[10] And post-humanists such as Gregory Stock see a future of ubiquitous genetic enhancement as inevitable: "In the first half of the twenty-first century, biological understanding will likely become less an end in itself than a means to manipulate biology. In one century, we have moved from observing

---

6. Ratzinger, *Instruction on Respect for Human Life*.
7. International Theological Commission, "Communion and Stewardship," no. 90.
8. Graham, "Acceleration of Addictiveness," para. 2.
9. O'Donovan, *Begotten or Made?*
10. Julian Savulescu, Uehrio Professor of Practical Ethics at Oxford University, for instance, is a strong proponent of procreative beneficence, the putative moral obligation of parents to employ preimplantation genetic diagnosis to select those children with the greatest genetic prospects.

to understanding to engineering."[11] The question posed by this essay is: What can Christian faith and doctrine contribute to this debate?

One immediate answer can be provided here at the outset. Christians confess God the Creator. This is above all a doctrine about *God*, but is indirectly a teaching about all things in relation to God—specifically that all things are his *creation*. To say this is to imbue the world with meaning and to confess that its meaning is determined by God, not by mankind. In other words, what things are, and what things are for, is given by God, and those givens determine how they may be used. The task of exercising *faithful* dominion over God's creation, then, is a matter of rightly discerning how we may put the creation to use in service not to our every whim, but to rightly ordered desires, subject to his Lordship over all.

This creational frame is literally turned on its head by what Neil Postman called "technopoly," by which he meant a society in which our understanding of the good life is laid out in technological terms. A creational view says that things have natures given by God and that this determines how they may be used in service to rightly ordered desires. In a technological society, we begin with our desires, then put things to use in order to satisfy those desires, and finally delude ourselves into imagining that the way we can use things defines what they are.

A particularly stark example of this way of thinking arose from the world of gene editing in 2017. In that year, the journal *Nature* reported[12] on an experiment carried out at the Oregon Health and Science University in Portland. In this experiment, for the first time, CRISPR was used to edit the genome of viable human embryos—in other words, embryos which would, if implanted, develop normally to birth. In response to the outcry that followed, prominent Stanford Law School ethicist Hank Greely downplayed its significance, noting on Twitter that the experiment had only involved "research embryos not to be transferred for possible implantation. Not a big deal."[13] What is it that defines these embryos—*viable* human embryos,

---

11. Stock, *Redesigning Humans*, 7. This is a situation C.S. Lewis warned of in *The Abolition of Man*: "It is in Man's power to treat himself as a mere 'natural object' and his own judgments of value as raw material for scientific manipulation to alter at will. The objection to his doing so does not lie in the fact that this point of view (like one's first day in a dissecting room) is painful and shocking till we grow used to it. The pain and the shock are at most a warning and a symptom. The real objection is that if man chooses to treat himself as raw material, raw material he will be; not raw material to be manipulated, as he fondly imagined, by himself, but by mere appetite . . ." (84).

12. Ma et al., "Correction of a pathogenic gene mutation."

13. Hank Greeley (@HankGreeleyLSJU), "In US? Not signif to me. & not particularly in any event—research embryos not to be transferred for possible implantation. Not a big deal," Twitter, July 26, 2017, 7:42 p.m. https://twitter.com/HankGreeleyLSJU/status/890371791947833344.

physically indistinguishable from what you or I or any of our children were like at an earlier stage in our own lives—as research embryos? It would seem to be nothing other than the intention of the researcher. From a technological frame, the fact that we desire to cure diseases based in genetic mutations—a noble aim—and can use a human embryo to make progress toward that desire appears to allow us to define the embryo as "only a research embryo." A belief in creation does not allow us that power; from the frame of creation, what humanity is, is defined for us and sets us apart.

But why is this? Assuming, as Christianity does, that God defines what humanity is and what humanity is for, what exactly is it that sets humanity apart?[14] Christianity's answer is that every human being, regardless of characteristics or capacities, is made to bear the image of God in the world.[15] The purpose of this essay is to explain what that means and to draw some ethical implications from this idea.

To summarize our argument in advance, Christianity argues (along with Judaism and some forms of Islam) that the fact that humanity is made in the image of God is what confers incalculable dignity on every human being. Human dignity is not, in other words, simply assumed. There is a clear reason that humanity is set apart. But what sets humanity apart is not in the first instance a set of capacities, but a calling. The image of God is a vocation, and the capacities that indicate humanity and make it unique—such as our rationality, linguistic capabilities, creativity, and so on—are given in service to that vocation. It is the vocation that is primary. The capacities are not themselves the vocation, which is the image of God, and so the loss of capacities does not entail the loss of that image or of human dignity.

What is that vocation? Simply put, it is to manifest God's presence within the world. This way of phrasing it, used by Marc Cortez,[16] captures

14. There are, of course, those who would argue that humans are *not* set apart—that some other subset of the animal kingdom, or all animals, or all life, or even the whole of the cosmos, ought to be treated equally. This essay will not address their arguments directly, but it will present the Christian case that humans are indeed unique and why.

15. The concept of the image of God has long been at the center of Christian anthropology. Marc Cortez notes several examples of theologians attesting to this centrality. John Paul II, for example, referred to the *imago Dei* as "the immutable basis of all Christian anthropology" (*Apostolic Letter Mulieris Dignitatem*).

16. Cortez, *ReSourcing Theological Anthropology*. Owen Strachan has recently argued for a similar understanding of the image of God as "an ontological reality that leads into function . . . The human race is a living testimony to its Creator" (Strachan, *Reenchanting Humanity*, 29–30). John F. Kilner offers a similar account (in which the image indicates that humanity bears a special connection to God and is intended to reflect God and glorify him) in his expansive treatment of the *imago Dei*, albeit with a dynamic at its center in which even pre-fall humanity was always destined to be made fully the image of God in union with Christ, who alone *is* the image (Kilner, *Dignity and Destiny*, esp. ch. 7).

two separate facets of what it means to bear the image of God. First, humanity manifests God's presence in a *representational* sense: in some way, by our very existence, we show what God is like. And second, humanity manifests the presence of God in a *representative* sense: we are called to care for God's creation in service to our Creator, bringing order where there is chaos. In the rest of this essay, we will first develop this argument and then offer some ethical implications for questions surrounding gene editing. We have two main conclusions. First, the notion that the image of God is a vocation that involves the nurture and development of the world generates tremendous enthusiasm for the work of scientists, including geneticists, whose work is one of the most fruitful ways for humanity to serve that calling. Second, however, the image of God also raises robust barriers to all forms of dehumanization and preserves space to question critically the development of technologies which may violate the dignity of human persons, regardless of their benefits.

The Image of God in the Bible and Theology

The Image of God in Genesis 1

"Man is neither angel nor beast," wrote Pascal,[17] but neither is humanity a hybrid of the two, according to the book of Genesis. The Bible presents humanity as spiritual and yet irreducibly material, a psychosomatic unity of body and soul. Humanity is an animal and yet set apart from the rest of the animals and given charge to rule over and care for them.

The creation account found in the first chapter of Genesis begins with the world "formless and void"—a chaos, uninhabited and uninhabitable.[18] The first chapter of Genesis presents God's work of creation as an ordering of the chaos. He forms what is formless, separating and ordering the chaotically mixed elements of the cosmos: light from darkness, waters above from waters below, dry land from sea. Then he fills what is empty, populating his creation with sun and moon, with birds and sea creatures, with vegetation and animals. And at the apex of his creation on the sixth day, before the great rest that completes his work on the seventh, is humanity.

The text of Genesis 1 is highly structured, full of rhythmic patterns. God speaks his creation into existence with ten words, introduced with

17. Pascal, *Pensées*, no. 257.
18. The Christian doctrine of *creatio ex nihilo*, that God creates from nothing, rather than from anything pre-existing his act of creation, is derived from other biblical texts and metaphysical and theological reflection. See McFarland, *From Nothing*, for a recent survey of the doctrine, or the more classical treatment in May, *Creation Ex Nihilo*.

the phrase "And God said . . ."[19] Eight times God speaks the words "Let there be . . ." or "Let the earth bring forth . . ."; six times we hear the repeated phrase, "And there was evening and there was morning . . ." But the creation of humanity breaks many of these patterns, indicating its uniqueness. The text reads:

> Then God said, "Let us make man in our image, after our likeness; and let them have dominion over the fish of the sea, and over the birds of the air, and over the cattle, and over all the earth, and over every creeping thing that creeps upon the earth." So God created man in his own image, in the image of God he created him; male and female he created them. And God blessed them, and God said to them, "Be fruitful and multiply, and fill the earth and subdue it; and have dominion over the fish of the sea and over the birds of the air and over every living thing that moves upon the earth." (Gen 1:26–28)

The pattern-breaks are numerous. Earlier in the creation narrative, the text speaks of God appointing the sun and moon to rule over their respective realms of day and night (Gen. 1:16), but here God grants humanity "dominion" over *all* of creation. As Bruce Waltke writes, "The impersonal 'let there be' (or its equivalents) of the seven preceding creative acts is replaced by the personal 'let us.' Only in the creation of humanity is the divine intent announced beforehand. The formula 'and so it was' is replaced by a threefold blessing. In these ways, the narrator places humankind closer to God than the rest of creation."[20] As Blocher puts it, "man was created . . . for a purpose and for a person: on the one hand, in order to subdue the earth; on the other hand, the man was made to be with the woman, and the woman with the man."[21]

Most striking is the statement by God that "man (is) in our image, after our likeness." "Whereas the other creatures are created 'according to their kinds' (Gen. 1:21, 24, 25)," Waltke writes, "humanity is made 'in the image of God.'"[22] What does this mean? At its simplest, the text simply indicates

---

19. Commentators since ancient Judaism have noted that the ten words of creation correspond to the ten "words"—commandments—given by God to his people through the prophet Moses.

20. Waltke, *Genesis*; Sarna, *Genesis*, 11. Calvin wrote that "God certainly might here command by his bare word what he wished to be done. But he chose to give this tribute to the excellency of man—that he would, in a manner, enter into consultation concerning his creation. This is the highest honor with which he has dignified us" (Calvin, *Genesis*, 25).

21. Blocher, *In the Beginning*, 90.

22. Waltke, *Genesis*, 65; Lints, *Identity and Idolatry*, 58; Clines, "Humanity as the Image of God," 448.

that humanity reflects God in some unspecified way.[23] And yet, the concept is central to the biblical understanding of human dignity. Later in Genesis, God will prohibit the taking of human life, "for God made man in his own image" (Gen 9:6). The New Testament letter of James condemns cursing humanity, "who are made in the likeness of God" (Jas 3:9).[24] And so it is worth asking, despite the immediate text's relative silence, what it means to say that humanity is made in the image of God.

The Image as Capacities

The image of God has always been recognized by the Christian tradition as central to its understanding of humanity, though its interpretation has undergone shifts. Up through the middle of the twentieth century, with some exceptions, Christian theological reflection on the meaning of the image of God tended to focus on capacities and characteristics such as rationality, morality, emotion, and spirituality.[25]

Saint Augustine, for instance, wrote that "man's excellence consists in the fact that God made him to His own image by giving him an intellectual soul, which raises him above the beasts of the field."[26] Elsewhere Saint Augustine writes that God made humanity "after His own image, not as regards the possession of a body and of mortal life, but as regards the rational mind with the power of knowing God, and with the superiority as compared with all irrational creatures which the possession of reason implies."[27] Thomas Aquinas followed a similar logic, tying the image of

---

23. Lints, *Identity and Idolatry*, 57. Westermann argues that "Gen. 1:26f. is not making a general and universally valid statement about the nature of mankind; if it were, then the Old Testament would have much more to say about this image and likeness. The fact is that it does not, and this has been noted on a number of occasions" (Westermann, *Genesis*, 155).

24. Contrary to some theologians who have argued that sin deprives mankind of the image of God, it is worth noting that both of these references occur after the fall in Genesis 3.

25. For the sake of space we mention only a few major examples here; for a more complete survey, see Blocher, *In the Beginning*, 80; Berkhof, *Systematic Theology*; Hodge, *Systematic Theology*; Strong, *Systematic Theology*; and for surveys of patristic thought see McGuckin, *Westminster Handbook*, and Wilken, *Spirit of Early Christian Thought*. This interpretation originated at least as early as Philo and the apocryphal Wisdom of Solomon (Blocher, *In the Beginning*, 80).

26. Augustine, *Literal Meaning of Genesis*, VI.12.193.

27. Augustine, *Reply to Faustus the Manichæan*, 318.

God in man to his rationality and intellect, which "is that whereby the rational creature excels other creatures . . ."[28]

Following the Reformation, John Calvin extended the image of God beyond the mind, but continued to define it in terms of capacities, arguing "that the image of God extends to everything in which the nature of man surpasses that of all other species of animals . . . And though the primary seat of the divine image was in the mind and the heart, or in the soul and its powers, there was no part even of the body in which some rays of glory did not shine."[29] He points in particular to the perfections of Adam as he was created prior to humanity's fall into sin, so "that at the beginning the image of God was manifested by light of intellect, rectitude of heart, and the soundness of every part."[30] Reformed Scholastic John Owen argued along similar lines: "We were created in the image of God. Whatever was good or comely in us was a part of that image, especially the ornaments of our minds, the perfections of our souls. These things had in them a resemblance of, and a correspondency unto, some excellencies in God."[31]

Certainly, all of these may be valid *indicators* of humanity and what makes it unique. But to treat any such qualitative characteristic or capacity as being *constitutive* of humanity is problematic because this would imply that if a particular human being loses the capacity, his or her humanity is lost as well.[32] If humanity is grounded in capacities, then human dignity

28. Aquinas, *Summa Theologiae*, I.93.

29. Calvin, *Institutes*, I.xv.3.

30. Calvin, *Institutes*, I.xv.4.

31. Owen, *Works of John Owen*, 497. Earlier, Owen writes that Adam was "created in the image of God, full of that integrity, righteousness, and holiness, which might be and was an eminent resemblance of the holiness of God" (Owen, *Works of John Owen*, 103).

32. One response to this concern would be to say that qualitative definitions don't operate at the level of the individual, but at the level of what is *ordinarily* true of the *species*. In other words, if we take language as the defining characteristic of humanity, then a person who suffered a traumatic brain injury and could no longer speak would still be human, because they remain a member of a species which *ordinarily*—absent traumatic brain injury—enjoys language. This response has the advantage of affirming—in line with the creational view outlined above—that there is such a thing as created human nature, and that the loss of speech due to injury represents disorder relative to the goodness of that nature, as created. Nevertheless, two concerns remain with this approach. One is that since we are considering questions including germline editing, this response does not seem to resolve the status of a person in whom the capacity for language has been removed, both in him and in all of his descendants. Does this represent a permanent change to the nature of that person and his descendants? Does the person belong to a new, non-human species? The other problem is that, philosophical questions aside, human dignity is acknowledged one individual at a time, and historical examples of dehumanization have often revolved precisely around an argument that a given individual or group is *deficient* in some qualitative sense, such that they can be treated as less than human, precisely by being *excluded* from the community of humanity.

is something that can be acquired and something that can be lost. As John Swinton warns, "If personhood is defined by whether someone does or does not have certain characteristics, qualities, and abilities then the tone and focus of the discussion does inevitably change. But that change is not necessarily for the better."[33] If we define the image according to capacities, then it is the capacities that we value—not the person.

The Image as Vocation

The characterization of the image of God in terms of capacities held sway among Christian scholars until the middle of the twentieth century. But more recently, driven in part by archaeological research that has provided insights into the original Ancient Near Eastern (ANE) context of the book of Genesis, a shift has taken place. Today, the dominant view among biblical scholars is that the image of God refers rather to humanity's vocation or calling, the purpose for which humanity was created—that is, that it provides an account of human identity and the meaning of human existence, rather than a metaphysical account of human nature.[34]

Recent biblical scholarship stresses the covenantal nature of the relationship into which God calls humanity in the early chapters of Genesis and even the covenantal structure of the texts themselves.[35] Mendenhall, in particular, noted the similarities between Israelite covenant texts and a contemporaneous group of documents known as Hittite suzerainty treaties—both, in turn, structured similarly to the Pentateuch as a whole and individual texts within it (such as the book of Deuteronomy).[36] In these texts, a covenantal relationship between two parties (often a lord and his vassal, e.g., an emperor and a subordinate regional king) would be established by a historical prologue, followed by sections detailing how the parties would relate from that point. In this view, the book of Genesis serves as just such a historical prologue.

In light of this context, it is unlikely that the image of God refers primarily to attributes, capacities, or the metaphysical nature of humanity, and more likely that the author is concerned with the nature of the role humanity is called to play within its covenantal relationship to its Creator.[37] Various capacities may set humanity apart from the rest of

33. Swinton, "Introduction," 8.//
34. Lints, *Identity and Idolatry*, 23; Kelsey, "Personal Bodies," 139–58.//
35. Kline, *Images of the Spirit*.//
36. Lints, *Identity and Idolatry*, 45.//
37. Lints, *Identity and Idolatry*, 35, 60; Blocher, *In the Beginning*, 87; Brueggemann, *Theology of the Old Testament*, 451.

the creation; rationality and language may be valid *indicators* of what is unique to humanity. But the capacities are not *constitutive* of the image of God, because the image is a vocation, and capacities are given in service to the vocation. As Marc Cortez has put it:

> Traditionally, people have associated the image with one or more human capacities (e.g., rationality). On the divine presence view, however, such capacities cannot *define* the image since a divine being does not depend on the capacities of the idol to manifest its presence. . . . We would thus need to say that the basic meaning of the *imago Dei* has nothing to do with any particular capacities of the human person, even though capacities remain necessary for the ways in which we live in response (function) to the reality of being made in the image of God (essence). We are called to use whatever capacities we do have to carry out the divinely intended functions as a consequence of the truth that we are images of the living God.[38]

Or, as theologian Richard Lints writes, "the question of the qualities inherent in humankind (the image-bearer) is derivative from and secondary to the teleological claim of Genesis 1 that the *imago Dei* reflects God."[39]

Can we be more precise about what this reflection entails? In the original Hebrew text, man is said to be made in the image (*tselem*) and likeness (*demut*) of God. Current scholarship has made the following points about these words:

First, the word *tselem* typically refers to a concrete image or statue of a god, as in Num 33:52.[40] Indeed, as Lints has pointed out, beyond the first chapters of Genesis, the word almost always refers to an idol, a physical manifestation of one of the gods of Israel's neighbors.[41] As numerous theologians and scholars across the Christian tradition have pointed out, God's command to make no image of him for use in worship (the second commandment, Exod 20:4–6) must be understood in correlation to his creation of man in his image: man is to create no image of God because God has already created his own image, which is humanity itself.

Second, it is notable that the text says that *humanity* is made in the image of God—not the body alone, nor the soul, nor the mind, but the "psychosomatic unity" that is the human being, explicitly including the diversity of male and female.[42] Thus the image of God is borne in full by

---

38. Cortez, *ReSourcing Theological Anthropology*, 113.
39. Lints, *Identity and Idolatry*, 60.
40. Blocher, *In the Beginning*, 84.
41. Lints, *Identity and Idolatry*, 79.
42. Waltke, *Genesis*, 65; Clines, "Image of God in Man," 53–103.

the totality of every individual human being. Lints writes that "according to Genesis 1 the whole human person represents God's royal rule, without any intended emphasis on the spiritual or physical aspects of human identity carrying on this role."[43]

Third, an image is *representational* of its original. In reflecting God, humanity in some fashion shows the rest of creation what God is like and represents God's presence within creation,[44] albeit in a way utterly derivative of and dependent on the original.[45]

Fourth, the image is also *representative* of the original. An image "functions as a ruler in the place of the deity." Here Waltke cites Hart:

> In the Ancient Near East it was widely believed that a god's spirit lived in any statue or image of that god, with the result that the image could function as a kind of representative or substitute for the god wherever it was placed. It was also customary in the ANE to think of a king as a representative of a god; obviously the king rules, and the god was the ultimate ruler, so the king must be ruling on the god's behalf. It is therefore not surprising that these two separate ideas became connected, and a king came to be described as an image of a god.[46]

Although this interpretation has only recently gained sway among biblical scholars, it has ancient provenance, dating back to ancient Judaism.[47] But today, the understanding of "image" as indicating representation and representative rule "has become the dominant interpretation, supplanting the interpretation of image as 'spiritual qualities.'"[48]

Cortez summarizes, "We need to view the *imago Dei* as a declaration that God intended to create human persons to be the physical means through which he would manifest his own divine presence in the world."[49] It is worth noting the radically democratizing effect of this definition. As

---

43. Lints, *Identity and Idolatry*, 71n38.

44. Waltke, *Genesis*, 65–66; Clines, "Image of God in Man," 53–103.

45. Lints, *Identity and Idolatry*, 29, 59; Blocher, *In the Beginning*, 82; see also Beale, *We Become What We Worship*, 16.

46. Waltke, *Genesis*, 66; Clines, "Image of God in Man," 53–103; Hart, "Genesis," 315–36; Lints, *Identity and Idolatry*, 69.

47. Blocher, *In the Beginning*, 80.

48. Waltke, *Genesis*, 66n46; Blocher writes, "No exegete defends this distinction [referring the image of God solely to humanity's spiritual dimension] any longer" (Blocher, *In the Beginning*, 80). Lints cites Westermann, *Genesis*, as arguing that "royal representation is the majority view for interpreting the meaning of the image of God" (Lints, *Identity and Idolatry*, 69).

49. Cortez, *ReSourcing Theological Anthropology*, 115.

Waltke points out, the Hebrew text stands apart from its ANE counterparts in applying the concept of the image of God not only to the king, but to all of humanity. He cites a letter written to a seventh-century Assyrian king, Esarhaddon, which says in part that "a (free) man is as the shadow of god, the slave is as the shadow of a (free) man; but the king, he is like unto the (very) image of God."[50] Blocher cites a study by Erik Hornung adducing many more examples of this phenomenon.[51] In contrast, Hart writes that the Hebrew "text is saying that exercising royal dominion over the earth as God's representative is the basic purpose for which God created man," adding that "man is appointed king over creation, responsible to God as the ultimate king, and as such expected to manage and develop and care for creation, this task to include actual physical work."[52]

Does the additional statement that man is made in the "likeness" (*demut*) of God add anything to the concept? Here opinions have varied. Patristic and medieval theology considered that the "image" of God referred to rationality, while "likeness" referred to an original righteousness lost at the fall.[53] Scholarship since the Reformation (including Calvin), on the other hand, has tended to assume that the words are synonyms.[54] Waltke argues that it is unlikely that the words are mere synonyms, but also disputes the medieval distinction. In his view, "the word *likeness* serves to clearly distinguish God from humans in the biblical worldview."[55] In other words, *likeness* emphasizes that humanity, while made in the image of God, is not divine—a creature, not the Creator.[56]

---

50. Pfeiffer, *State Letters of Assyria*, quoted in Clines, "Image of God in Man," 84.

51. Blocher, *In the Beginning*, 86.

52. Waltke, *Genesis*, 66; Hart, "Genesis," 322, 324. See also Lints, *Identity and Idolatry*, 69; Mathews, *Genesis*, 169; Levenson, *Creation and the Persistence of Evil*, 114, 116. We should acknowledge that there remain some modern scholars who continue to focus more on attributes than vocation in defining the image of God, such that even those who acknowledge humanity's royal commission see this as being something for which he is fit *by virtue of* the image, e.g., capacities. Von Rad, for instance, writes that "This commission to rule is not considered as belonging to the definition of God's image; but it is its consequence, i.e. that for which man is capable because of it" (Von Rad, *Genesis*, 57, cited by Lints, *Identity and Idolatry*, 69n29; see also Bray, "Significance of God's Image in Man," 195–225; and Blocher, *In the Beginning*, 90).

53. Luther followed this interpretation as well (Blocher, *In the Beginning*, 81).

54. Waltke, *Genesis*, 66; Calvin, *Genesis*, 26.

55. Waltke, *Genesis*, 65–66, 66n51; Clines, "Image of God in Man," 53–103; Lints, *Identity and Idolatry*, 32.

56. Blocher, *In the Beginning*, 82.

Summary of Christian Reflection on the Image of God

To summarize, we have argued that the teaching that man is made in the image of God refers primarily to a vocation by which humanity reflects its Creator. This vocation, described in Gen 1:26–28, is expressed in two particular tasks: humanity is to "be fruitful and multiply, and fill the earth and subdue it."[57] The vocation exists within a covenantal relationship in which humanity exercises representative rule over creation on behalf of the Creator—which implies that the subduing of the earth is not a matter of capricious domination, but of nurture and care, continuing God's creative work of bringing order where there is chaos.[58] Waltke and G.K. Beale have noted a connection between the twofold vocation. In Genesis, humanity is placed within a garden, a bounded place of great order and beauty, outside of which lies tillable ground and then wilderness. But as Adam and Eve fulfill their calling to "be fruitful and multiply," they will necessarily have to push back the borders of the garden to accommodate a growing population—they will be required, that is, to "subdue the earth" as they fill it.[59] In other words, the creation narrative indicates that the image of God consists of the vocation—common to every person regardless of individual capacities or characteristics—to make of all the earth an ordered place, a place literally more *humane*, fit for God to dwell with his people.[60]

---

57. Note that while the sun and moon are appointed to *rule* over the day and night on the fourth day of creation (Gen 1:18), the sea creatures and birds are commanded to "[b]e fruitful and multiply and fill the waters in the seas, and let birds multiply on the earth" (Gen 1:22). The fact that the vocation given to humanity combines these two is another indication of the uniqueness and supremacy of humanity within God's creation.

58. For the sake of space, we have focused on the major theme of representative rule in describing this covenantal relationship, drawing on imagery depicting God as Lord over creation and humanity as his vassal king. But it is worth noting that the biblical texts are richer in metaphor than this. Scholars including those cited here—Waltke, Beale, Lints, among others—have noted the *liturgical shape* of the creation narrative in Genesis, suggesting that in creating the cosmos, and Eden in particular, God has constructed a temple and appointed humanity as his priest. Likewise, ANE covenant documents often presented the parties in filial terms, with the superior party acting as an adoptive father. In their context, these images do not compete with one another, but add dimensionality to the understanding of the vocation that is constitutive of being made in the image of God.

59. Waltke, *Genesis*, 186; Beale, "Eden," 11–12.

60. Support for this contention comes from the last chapters of the Bible, in which the Apostle John's vision of the ultimate state of all things includes what appears to be a garden city, and the declaration that, "Behold, the dwelling of God is with men. He will dwell with them, and they shall be his people, and God himself will be with them;

The value placed upon the whole of the human being is most clearly demonstrated in the one to whom the Bible refers as the perfect Image of God, Jesus Christ (Col 1:15; Heb 1:3).[61] In him, God himself took on humanity, including a human body. He suffered and died and was raised from death, in that same body, never to abandon it (Phil 2:5–11; John 20:24–29; Luke 24:36–43; Acts 1:1–9; Phil 3:20–21). The Bible talks of him as only the "firstfruits": in the resurrected body of Christ, we have a picture of the ultimate status of all human bodies, which are not to be discarded but restored to perfection (1 Cor 15). The image of God introduced in Genesis is the beginning of Christian reflection on the nature of what it means to be human, but Christians ultimately see what it means to be human, and the value that God places on our full humanity, in the person of Jesus.

Ethical Implications of the Image of God

We now draw some preliminary ethical conclusions from these reflections.

The image of God confers incalculable worth and dignity on every human being, because it means that every human being—regardless of capacity or characteristics, strength, intelligence, creativity, health, age, etc.—is called to reflect and represent its Creator. Because, as we have argued, capacities are not themselves the image, but are given in service to the vocation that is the image, a human's status as an image-bearer cannot be acquired, merited, or lost. Neither can the image exist in degrees, according to levels of intelligence or any other capacity.[62]

Humanity, not the human mind or soul, is created in the image of God. The book of Genesis does not present humans as souls inserted into bodies, but as psychosomatic unities. It is the human person—body, mind, and soul, taken as a whole—that bears the image of God and is thus considered sacred.

---

he will wipe away every tear from their eyes, and death shall be no more, neither shall there be mourning nor crying nor pain any more, for the former things have passed away" (Rev 21:3b–4). This argument, of course, assumes that the biblical canon can be read as a whole.

61. Recent theological anthropology, as with theology more generally, has exhibited a "Christological turn," emphasizing the need not only to end but to begin reflection on what it means to be human with the person of Jesus; Cortez, *ReSourcing Theological Anthropology*, is an excellent and accessible recent example. There is much to commend in this approach, notwithstanding the greater focus we have applied to the text of Genesis 1 here.

62. Some dolphins are more intelligent than some humans; nevertheless we recognize the dignity of the incapacitated human over against that of the animal.

As gene-editing technology advances, it is critical that the church engage its theological tradition to deliberate over and give voice to its understanding of what it means to be human. We have much to be grateful for in our liberal democratic society, but it is unlikely that that society has within itself the resources to provide any robust set of ethical norms to guide the debates we should be having, outside of calls to make science safe, efficacious, and broadly accessible to individuals, to whom ultimate choices are always left.[63] The concern, as Amy Laura Hall has put it, is that "political liberalism is not ultimately capable of engendering and fostering hospitality toward people with overt, recalcitrant needs. The norms encircling the liberal axis of individual autonomy cannot easily accommodate lives dedicated to the care of perpetually dependent individuals, or admit the intrinsic value of these individuals."[64] Or again, Hans Reinders warns that

> given the fact that our society accepts that we are entitled to our own conceptions of the good, there is no limit . . . to the range of biological conditions that may be targeted as the appropriate object of genetic manipulation as long as our aspirations to do

---

63. In 2017, the National Academy of Sciences issued a report assessing the use of gene editing technology (Brier and Helaine, *Human Genome Editing*, available at http://www.nap.edu/24623). It proposed that the following considerations should govern its application: promoting well-being, transparency, due care, responsible science, respect for persons, fairness, and transnational cooperation. It further recommended that germline editing be used in clinical research trials "only for compelling purposes of treating or preventing serious disease or disabilities, and only if there is a stringent oversight system able to limit uses to specified criteria," and that gene editing not be permitted for purposes of enhancement until substantial public debate has addressed non-therapeutic uses (*Human Genome Editing*, 10). In elaborating on the principle of "respect for persons," the report noted: "The principle of respect for persons requires recognition of the personal dignity of all individuals, acknowledgment of the centrality of personal choice, and respect for individual decisions. All people have equal moral value, regardless of their genetic qualities. Responsibilities that flow from adherence to this principle include (1) a commitment to the equal value of all individuals, (2) respect for and promotion of individual decision making, (3) a commitment to preventing recurrence of the abusive forms of eugenics practiced in the past, and (4) a commitment to destigmatizing disability" (*Human Genome Editing*, 9). On the whole, Christians in the sciences or engaging with science in public debate should be encouraged by the substantial common ground indicated by these recommendations; it is noteworthy that these considerations formed the basis of the universal condemnation, within the scientific community, of Dr. He Jiankui's editing of the genomes of two embryos born as twins in 2018. Nonetheless, there is nothing in the report or the extant scientific literature to indicate *why* persons are worthy of dignity, and we should be wary of assuming that this principle will continue to hold sway without some robust account of human nature, which is what Christian theology should promote within this ongoing public debate.

64. Hall, "To Form a More Perfect Union," 92.

so do not violate other people's legitimate interests. By the same token, there is no limit to the range of biological conditions that can be targeted as a "disability." Any attempt to impose limits to medical interventions of a certain kind—for example, interventions qualified as "genetic enhancement"—will sooner or later be exposed as morally arbitrary.[65]

What sort of guidelines or guardrails would Christian ethical deliberation centered on the concept of the image of God deliver? I conclude, briefly, by offering two implications that Christian reflection on the image of God can provide for the work of scientists and of geneticists in particular.

First, it generates tremendous enthusiasm for the work that scientists do, because science is one of the most powerful ways that humans fulfill their calling to subdue the earth, bringing order where there is chaos. As scientists work to cure disease, expand supplies of food and water, and alleviate suffering of every kind, the knowledge and practical wisdom that they gain and apply is nothing less than an expression of the care for creation into which God calls humanity as his representative on earth.

Second, however, reflection on the image of God will raise high barriers against dehumanization of every kind. Any desecration of humans is forbidden, from murder to rape to bullying. It is noteworthy how often such acts of violence are preceded by subtle—or sometimes quite explicit—dehumanization, in which the perpetrator reduces the victim below the status of being human. Hans Reinders warns of our capacity to employ genetic technologies in ways that can dehumanize, writing, "Not only does our society allow us to decide how many children we will have, and when and by whom, but it also allows us to decide what kind of children we want, and—by implication—what kind of children we do not want."[66] Similarly, Francis Collins has worried that "the application of germline manipulation would change our view of the value of human life. If genomes are being altered to suit parents' preferences, do children become more like commodities than precious gifts?"[67] The technological mindset treats all things in the world as bare, neutral material, a "standing reserve" waiting for us to define it according to how it can be used. But if our children, and all humans for that matter, are not commodities, but gifts, then we need to remind ourselves what is involved in receiving a gift—namely, that we develop in ourselves habits of submitting to the reality of what is given, letting our hearts be formed by a response not of mastery, but of gratitude.

65. Reinders, "Life's Goodness," 166.
66. Reinders, "Life's Goodness," 165.
67. Skerrett, "Debate."

As Blocher points out, Jesus's joining of the two great commandments—to love God and to love one's neighbor—follows the logic of man being made in God's image.[68] "And who is my neighbor?" Jesus was asked. In response, he told a story of a man who discerned the humanity of another not by observation, but quite simply by love (Luke 10:25–37).[69] "We may decide," writes Oliver O'Donovan, "whether or not any being manifests 'personality' by testing for it . . . But we cannot decide in this way whether or not any being is a *person*. We discern persons only by love, by discovering through interaction and commitment that this human being is irreplaceable."[70] John Swinton writes:

> Love means recognizing and welcoming . . . Love speaks the words: "It's good that you exist; it's good that you are in this world," and embodies them in acts of hospitality that reveal the authenticity of that love . . . To say to someone that they are not welcome here because they are different or because they will cause us problems is deeply hurtful. To pretend that they are welcome and then to engage in social practices which are designed to ensure that their existence "won't happen again" is loveless and inhospitable.[71]

And if we discern persons not according to their capacities, but by love and commitment, then that to which we commit ourselves is, quite simply, the person, rather than this or that characteristic that we may find or fail to find in them. We simply love this *someone*, called into being with a purpose that is not ours to give, made in the image of God.

Bibliography

Aquinas, Thomas. *Summa Theologiae*. Translated by Fathers of the English Dominican Province. Canton: Pinnacle, 2017.

Augustine of Hippo. *The Literal Meaning of Genesis*. Translated by John Hammond Taylor. New Jersey: Paulist, 1983.

———. *Reply to Faustus the Manichæan*. In *St. Augustine: The Writings Against the Manichaeans and Against the Donatists*, edited by Philip Schaff, translated by

---

68. Blocher, *In the Beginning*, 86.

69. The context of Jesus's parable of the Good Samaritan makes this distinction explicit; as his hearers would have known very well, the cultural norms of the day would have given the Samaritan every reason to *fail* to find human dignity in the Jew who fell among thieves.

70. O'Donovan, *Begotten or Made?*, 59.

71. Swinton, "Introduction," 19.

Richard Stothert, 171–426. Nicene and Post-Nicene Fathers 4. Buffalo, New York: Christian Literature, 1887.
Beale, G.K. "Eden, the Temple, and the Church's Mission in the New Creation." *Journal of the Evangelical Theological Society* 48 (2005) 5–31.
———. *The Temple and the Church's Mission: A Biblical Theology of the Dwelling Place of God*. Downers Grove: InterVarsity, 2004.
———. *We Become What We Worship: A Biblical Theology of Idolatry*. Downers Grove: InterVarsity, 2008.
Berkhof, Louis, *Systematic Theology*. Grand Rapids: Eerdmans, 1939.
Blocher, Henri. *In the Beginning*. Downers Grove: InterVarsity, 1984.
Bray, Gerald. "The Significance of God's Image in Man." *Tyndale Bulletin* 42 (1991) 195–225.
Brier, Rona, and Helaine Resnick, eds. *Human Genome Editing: Science, Ethics, and Governance*. Committee on Human Gene Editing. Washington, DC: National Academies Press, 2017.
Brueggemann, Walter. *Theology of the Old Testament*. Minneapolis: Fortress, 1997.
Calvin, John. *Genesis*. Edited by Alister McGrath and J.I. Packer. Crossway Classsic Commentaries. Wheaton: Crossway, 2001.
———. *Institutes of the Christian Religion*. Edited by John T. McNeill. Translated by Ford Lewis Battles. Library of Christian Classics XX–XXI. Philadelphia: Westminster, 1960.
Clines, D.J.A. "Humanity as the Image of God." In vol. 2, *On the Way to the Postmodern: Old Testament Essays, 1967–1998*, 447–97. Sheffield: Sheffield Academic, 1998.
———. "The Image of God in Man." *Tyndale Bulletin* 19 (1968) 53–103.
Cohen, Adam S. "Harvard's Eugenics Era." *Harvard* Magazine (March–April 2016). https://harvardmagazine.com/2016/03/harvards-eugenics-era.
Cortez, Marc. *ReSourcing Theological Anthropology: A Constructive Account of Humanity in Light of Christ*. Grand Rapids: Zondervan Academic, 2018.
Graham, Paul. "The Acceleration of Addictiveness." *Paul Graham*, July 2010. http://www.paulgraham.com/addiction.html.
Hall, Amy Laura. "To Form a More Perfect Union: Mainline Protestantism and the Popularization of Eugenics." In *Theology, Disability, and the New Genetics: Why Science Needs the Church*, edited by John Swinton and Brian Brock, 75–95. London: T&T Clark, 2007.
Hart, I. "Genesis 1:1—2:3 As a Prologue to the Books of Genesis." *Tyndale Bulletin* 46 (1995) 315–36.
Hodge, C. *Systematic Theology*. Grand Rapids: Eerdmans, 1986.
International Theological Commission. "Communion and Stewardship: Human Persons Created in the Image of God." *Vatican*, 2002. http://www.vatican.va/roman_curia/congregations/cfaith/cti_documents/rc_con_cfaith_doc_20040723_communion-stewardship_en.html.
John Paul II. *Apostolic Letter Mulieris Dignitatem*. Vatican City: Libreria Editrice Vaticana, 1988.
Kelsey, D. "Personal Bodies: A Theological Anthropological Proposal." In *Personal Identity in Theological Perspective*, edited by Richard Lints, Michael Horton, and Mark R. Talbot, 139–58. Grand Rapids: Eerdmans, 2006.
Kilner, John F. *Dignity and Destiny: Humanity in the Image of God*. Grand Rapids: Eerdmans, 2015.

Kline, Meredith. *Images of the Spirit*. Grand Rapids: Eerdmans, 1980.

———. *Kingdom Prologue*. Eugene, OR: Wipf & Stock, 2006.

———. *Treaty of the Great King*. Grand Rapids: Eerdmans, 1963.

Levenson, J. *Creation and the Persistence of Evil: The Jewish Drama of Divine Omnipotence*. San Francisco: Harper & Row, 1988.

Lewis, C.S. *The Abolition of Man*. New York: Macmillan, 1955.

Lints, Richard. *Identity and Idolatry*. Downers Grove: InterVarsity, 2015.

Ma, H., et al. "Correction of a pathogenic gene mutation in human embryos." *Nature* 548 (2017) 413–19.

Mathews, K.A. *Genesis 1—11:26*. New American Commentary. Nashville: Broadman & Holman, 1996.

May, Gerhard. *Creatio Ex Nihilo: The Doctrine of "Creation out of Nothing" in Early Christian Thought*. Translated by A.S. Worrall. London: T&T Clark International, 1994.

McFarland, Ian. *From Nothing: A Theology of Creation*. Louisville: Westminster John Knox, 2014.

McGuckin, John Anthony. *The Westminster Handbook to Patristic Theology*. Louisville: Westminster John Knox, 2004.

Meilaender, Gilbert. *Bioethics: A Primer for Christians*. Grand Rapids: Eerdmans, 2013.

Mendenhall, George E. *Law and Covenant in Ancient Israel and the Ancient Near East*. Pittsburgh: Biblical Colloquium, 1955.

O'Donovan, Oliver. *Begotten or Made?* Oxford: Oxford University Press, 1984.

Owen, John. *The Works of John Owen, Volume 6*. Edited by William H. Goold. Edinburgh: T&T Clark, 1966.

Pascal, Blaise. *Pensées*. Edited by Anthony Levi. Translated by Honor Levi. Oxford: Oxford University Press, 2008.s

Pfeiffer, R.H. *State Letters of Assyria*. Connecticut: American Oriental Society, 1935.

Regalado, Antonio. "Eugenics 2.0: We're at the Dawn of Choosing Embryos by Health, Height, and More." *MIT Technology Review*, November 1, 2017. https://www.technologyreview.com/s/609204/eugenics-20-were-at-the-dawn-of-choosing-embryos-by-health-height-and-more/.

Reinders, Hans S. "Life's Goodness: On Disability, Genetics, and 'Choice.'" In *Theology, Disability, and the New Genetics: Why Science Needs the Church*, edited by John Swinton and Brian Brock, 163–81. London: T&T Clark, 2007.

Ratzinger, Joseph. *Instruction on Respect for Human Life in Its Origin and on the Dignity of Procreation: Replies to Certain Questions of the Day*. Rome: Sacred Congregation for the Doctrine of the Faith, 1987. http://www.vatican.va/roman_curia/congregations/cfaith/documents/rc_con_cfaith_doc_19870222_respect-for-human-life_en.html.

Sarna, N. *Genesis*. JPS Torah Commentary 1. Philadelphia: Jewish Publication Society, 1989.

Skerrett, Patrick. "A Debate: Should We Edit the Human Germline?" *STAT News*, November 30, 2015. https://www.statnews.com/2015/11/30/gene-editing-crispr-germline/.

Smith, David Livingstone. *Less Than Human: Why We Demean, Enslave, and Exterminate Others*. New York: St. Martin's, 2011.

Stock, Gregory. *Redesigning Humans: Our Inevitable Genetic Future*. Boston: Hougton Mifflin, 2002.

Strachan, Owen. *Reenchanting Humanity: A Theology of Mankind*. Fearn: Christian Focus, 2019.
Strong, Augustus H. *Systematic Theology*. Rochester: E.R. Andrews, 1886.
Swinton, John. "Introduction: Re-imagining Genetics and Disability." In *Theology, Disability, and the New Genetics: Why Science Needs the Church*, edited by John Swinton and Brian Brock, 1–26. London: T&T Clark, 2007.
VanDrunen, David. *Bioethics and the Christian Life: A Guide to Making Difficult Decisions*. Wheaton: Crossway, 2009.
Von Rad, Gerhard. *Genesis*. Old Testament Library. London: Westminster John Knox Press, 1972.
Waltke, Bruce. *Genesis: A Commentary*. Grand Rapids: Zondervan, 2001.
———. *An Old Testament Theology: An Exegetical, Canonical, and Thematic Approach*. Grand Rapids: Zondervan, 2007.
Westermann, C. *Genesis 1–11: A Commentary*. Minneapolis: Augsburg Fortress, 1984.
———. *Genesis: An Introduction*. Minneapolis: Augsburg Fortress, 1992.
Wilken, R. *The Spirit of Early Christian Thought: Seeking the Face of God*. New Haven: Yale University Press, 2005.

11

Fearfully and Wonderfully Made?

Christians and Embryos in an Era of Biotechnology

JEFF HARDIN

MOST SATURDAY AFTERNOONS I take my adult autistic son, Christopher, to a local indoor pool and then for a long drive in the country near our home. The drive has given me many opportunities to listen to audiobooks, including that staple of high school English literature, Aldous Huxley's *Brave New World*. As a professor who studies the cellular intricacies of early embryonic development, I find Huxley's postapocalyptic vision of a dystopian society dominated by the cult of technology—including chemical treatments that produced numerous identical embryos that could be reared and prenatally conditioned in artificial wombs in central "hatcheries"—not only chilling, but, for a scientist, uncanny in its prescience.[1]

In 1932, Huxley knew very little of the things we now take for granted, including the fundamental discovery that DNA carries our genetic information, and our ever-increasing ability to engineer that DNA for our own purposes. But we in the twenty-first century live in an era that many have called the century of biology. Nowhere is the dizzying pace of biotechnology more evident than in our ability to manipulate human embryos. The announcement of Louise Brown, the first "test-tube baby" in 1978, to recent startling claims of the first live births of humans whose genomes had

---

1. Although space precludes further discussion, scientists have achieved unprecedented success with *ex vivo* culturing of mammalian embryos in ways that Huxley predicted. See Aguilera-Castrejon, "Ex Utero Mouse Embryogenesis," 119–24.

been intentionally edited[2] have all occurred since I graduated from high school in 1977. For us, what was once fodder for science fiction is quickly becoming scientific fact.

Helping the church to think biblically about bioethics in a way that encourages care for humans from their tiniest, earliest moments to the end of life is a pressing need. The year 2019 marked the fiftieth anniversary of a very important small book, *Fabricated Man*, by Christian ethicist Paul Ramsey. Writing at the time of the founding of what we now call bioethics, Ramsey cogently argued from a profoundly Christian perspective. Since then, however, as sociologist John Evans has chronicled, bioethics gradually excluded explicitly religious viewpoints from the discussion.[3] As a result, ordinary Christians often feel left out of ethical discussions. Now more than ever, Christian voices are sorely needed in the public marketplace of ideas.

The Wonder of Embryonic Development

How should Christians respond to recent developments regarding the earliest moments of human life? An appropriate place to start is with a profound sense of *wonder*. Any of us who have had the privilege of holding a newborn baby cannot help but be absolutely astonished at how incredibly delicate, yet intricately structured newborns are. Every spring, on the first day of class in my undergraduate course on embryonic development, I point out that people have been pondering embryonic development for millennia. I then read from an ancient piece of Hebrew poetry, Psalm 139:13–14.

> For You formed my inward parts; You wove me in my mother's womb. I will give thanks to You, for I am fearfully and wonderfully made; wonderful are Your works, and my soul knows it very well. My frame was not hidden from You, when I was made in secret, and skillfully wrought in the depths of the earth; Your eyes have seen my unformed substance; and in Your book were all written the days that were ordained for me, when as yet there was not one of them. (NASB)

I explain to my students that whether they share the psalmist's worldview—as I do as a Christian—or not, the psalmist's sense of wonder is a valuable model for the developmental biologist. Embryonic development is certainly wonderful! Each of us started as a single cell smaller than the period at the

---

2. Nature News has followed this story closely since the fall of 2018; e.g., Cyranoski, "CRISPR-baby Scandal," 440–42.

3. Evans, *History and Future of Bioethics*.

end of this sentence.[4] Eventually, that single cell gives rise to five trillion cells at birth, specialized and arranged to form the human body. Building the embryo is a truly staggering challenge, and what developmental biologists like myself find so fascinating and beautiful.[5]

What processes give rise to the incredible complexity of an organism? Reliable development depends on two fundamental processes. One is *differentiation*—how parts of the embryo become different. The ear is different from the finger, which is different from the eye, which is different from any other specialized tissue in the body. Differentiation crucially depends on regulatory proteins that act like genetic switches, known as *transcription factors*. When a cell makes a particular set of these proteins, a whole host of genes and their expression are regulated, which leads to the cell's differentiation. One exciting achievement of modern developmental biology is the realization that some of these regulatory switches show remarkable conservation among all animals.[6]

Differentiation is not enough, however. The different cells of the body must be constructed into an organized whole, a process known as *morphogenesis* (literally the "genesis of form"; *morphe* is the Greek word for "form"). Some assembly is definitely required! Morphogenesis requires cells to move to new locations and to push and pull on one another in a self-construction project of staggering complexity. It is this delicate cellular choreography that my own research group studies intensively.

Scientists have identified several crucial landmarks during this self-organizing process and are unlocking the secrets of these events at the cellular and molecular level. The first and most obvious event is *fertilization*. When a human sperm unites with an *oocyte*, it awakens the resulting fertilized egg—the *zygote*—physiologically, eliciting dramatic changes that will allow it to undergo its first cell division. Fertilization ultimately unites the genetic material of sperm and egg. Fertilization is a highly contingent event: in the case of a typical fertilization not carried out using *in vitro* technology, a single sperm has a 1 in 250 million chance of uniting with an oocyte, defining the moment at which each of us began our biological existence.

Following fertilization, and while the embryo is in the fallopian tube moving towards the uterus, the zygote undergoes several cell divisions,

---

4. For brief overviews of embryonic development, see Nilsson and Hamberger, *Child Is Born*; Gilbert et al., *Bioethics and the New Embryology*; Wolpert, *Developmental Biology*; Bancewicz, *Wonders of the Living World*, ch. 5.

5. For some of my own thinking, see Bancewicz, *God in the Lab*, especially chs. 6 and 7. See also Bancewicz, *Wonders of the Living World*, ch. 5.

6. For a popular treatment, see my colleague Sean Carroll, *Endless Forms Most Beautiful*.

collectively known as *cleavage*. As one cell divides into two, two into four, and four into eight, eventually the embryo resembles a loose cluster of grapes under the microscope. Midway through the eight-cell stage, however, the cells of the embryo produce an adhesion protein—a molecular glue known as a *cadherin* that my own laboratory investigates—that causes the cells of the embryo to become tightly compacted. As cleavage continues, interior cells become different from exterior ones, eventually becoming the *inner cell mass*, a group of cells at one end of the embryo. Cells on the exterior (called the *trophoblast*) eventually line a fluid-filled cavity (called the blastocoel, pronounced "blasto-seel"). The embryo at this stage is called a *blastocyst*. The inner cell mass is what eventually gives rise to a baby. As we will see, the inner cell mass cells are developmentally flexible in the extreme. Trophoblast cells above the inner cell mass will eventually specialize and allow the embryo to implant in the uterine lining, establishing a pregnancy.

After the blastocyst stage cells derived from the inner cell mass separate into layers. Then groups of cells begin to migrate within the embryo during a signature morphogenetic event known as *gastrulation,* dramatically transforming it as the basic body plan emerges. As gastrulation proceeds in humans, a group of cells collects along the central region of the embryo from head to tail known as the *primitive streak*. Cells move *en masse* at this time into the interior of the embryo to create a new, middle layer of cells (known as the *mesoderm*; meso- is from a Greek word for "middle"). The movements of gastrulation are one of the most complicated bits of cellular choreography we know of. Powerful modern microscopes are allowing us to watch these cellular movements with ever-increasing detail in non-human embryos; the processes that operated in each of us are very similar. The cells of the gastrula are covered by other cells, collectively known as *extraembryonic* cells because they are not the part of what forms the fetus (*extra-* means "outside of"). Ultimately, these will be left behind when a baby is born.

Following gastrulation, the embryo bends towards its ventral, or belly, side. At this stage, each of us, if our extraembryonic tissues had been removed, would have borne an uncanny resemblance to a tiny burrito. During this stage, a flat sheet of cells on the dorsal (back) side of the embryo rolls into a tube in a process known as *neurulation*. The resulting tube, known as the *neural tube*, forms the embryonic spinal cord. Eventually that simple tube undergoes infolding and enlargement over a period of months to form the brain; at the same time, other organ systems form during the complicated processes of *organogenesis*, which is accompanied by the growth of the fetus.

Ultimately, the processes of embryonic development lead to exceedingly complicated organisms like you and me. Differentiation and morphogenesis work together throughout development in a spiraling cycle of increasing spatial organization and complexity over time. Crucially, these processes result from the self-organization of the embryo, given a suitable environment, from the one-cell stage onward, as potentialities present in the one-celled zygote unfold. Stanford bioethicist William Hurlbut has said that "fertilization initiates the most complex chemical reaction in the known universe: a self-directing, purposeful integration of organismal development."[7] Fearfully and wonderfully made, indeed!

The biological facts of early development are clear. As the Ramsey Colloquium has said, "The [embryo] is human . . . Any being that is human is a human being. If it is objected that, at five days or fifteen days, the embryo does not look like a human being, it must be pointed out that *this is precisely what a human being looks like—and what each of us looked like—at five or fifteen days of development*."[8] Indeed, based on this clear biological watershed, many argue that the biology of development is sufficient to establish a clear, bright line that establishes our moral responsibility towards the embryo.[9] And yet those in the public square who agree on the biology can have diametrically opposed views of the moral implications.[10] Clearly, moral reasoning about embryos requires additional inputs based on our worldview. For Christians, then, it is appropriate to pause and ask several important, inherently *theological* questions.

The Bible, Theology, and Embryos

The first question is one asked by the most probing practical theologian in my household, my wife Susie. An objection she might raise would be the following: "I thought life is a miracle. Haven't you taken all of the mystery out of it by studying it in such detail?" This might be a danger if the goal of scientific study of the embryo were mere dissection. But I would argue that by understanding the detailed mechanisms of embryonic development, scientists ought to have a heightened—not diminished—appreciation for each of our lives from their tiniest beginnings. For a Christian, deeper understanding of biological processes is also an exciting new opportunity to see God at work. Charles Kingsley, the nineteenth-century British theologian, said it this way: "Are we to reverence Him less or more, if we hear that His

---

7. Hurlbut, "Personal Statement," 268.
8. Ramsey Colloquium, "Inhuman Use of Human Beings"; emphasis mine.
9. A classic statement of this view is in George and Tollefson, *Embryo*.
10. See the fascinating point/counterpoint I use in my teaching by Roman Catholic legal scholar Robert George and Nobel laureate David Baltimore, "Stem Cell Research."

might is greater, His wisdom deeper, than we ever dreamed? We knew of old that God was so wise that He could make all things: but, behold, He is so much wiser than even that, that He can make all things make themselves."[11] Kingsley was talking about biological evolution as a new way of thinking about God's unfolding providence through process. I would argue the same is true for each of us as God's providence unfolds in the ordered, yet highly contingent, processes of embryonic development.

A second key question is, how should we integrate information from biology with the witness of the Scriptures and the history of orthodox Christian doctrine?[12] Decades ago, Christian geneticist V. Elving Anderson wisely said, "What inner resources will individuals have for coping with future discoveries? It is sometimes claimed that questions of the future will be so unique that 'old values' will be inadequate but I have not found any basic questions that will not profit from consideration of a biblical perspective."[13] One of the challenges of bringing the Bible to bear on modern biology, however, is that the human authors of Scripture knew nothing about the earliest steps of embryonic development. Nevertheless, several key biblical ideas can provide important guidance in this area.

Biblically, human beings are distinctive in *bearing God's image* (Gen 1:26–27). God's design is procreation in "one-flesh" relationships (Gen 2:23–24) that yields children who are "begotten gifts" (Ps 127:3–5). Whatever we may say theologically about the nature of the *imago Dei*, the Bible testifies that because we are all image-bearers, each human individual is deserving of protection, especially the weakest among us (Exod 22:22; Deut 10:18; Isa 1:17). In this sense, image-bearers are ends in themselves. As image-bearers, we are also vice-regents who carry out God's kingdom purposes in the world, and who act as *stewards* of creation (Gen 1:28, 2:15). In the twenty-first century, the stewardship mandate includes thinking about engineering ourselves.

And yet this immediately raises a key question: Are embryos image-bearers? Although the biblical writers knew nothing about blastocysts, they certainly had a sense that God was there with each of us throughout the intricate choreography of embryonic development, something that Psalm 139:13–16 affirms. Crucially in context, there is nowhere the psalmist could ever go, including before his birth, where God has not been. God

11. Kingsley, *Westminster Sermons*, xxvii.

12. Helpful resources here include the following: Buratovich, *Stem Cell Epistles*; Hui, *At the Beginning of Life*; Meilaender, *Bioethics*, 3e; Ramsey, *Fabricated Man;* Walters and Cole-Turner, *God and the Embryo*. Also see the Center for Bioethics and Human Dignity website: http://cbhd.org.

13. Anderson, "Biological Engineering," 169–170.

is seen as shaping the psalmist's "unformed substance" (Hebrew *golem*; v. 16) through a carefully crafted process, as the Hebrew verb "skillfully wrought" (*rāqam*; v. 15) indicates.[14] Indeed, God was superintending the formation of the psalmist's organ systems as an embryo (*kilyōṯ*, "inward parts," is literally "kidneys"). Psalm 139:13–16 also affirms the *continuity of embryo and adult*. The psalmist as worshipper and as embryo are one and the same person. Such continuity resonates with other passages (e.g., Ps 51:5; Job 10:8–12), with passages in which embryos are included as part of God's plan (Isa 49:1; Jer 1:5), and places in which embryos seem to have personal identity *in utero* (Luke 1:39ff).

The Bible provides further guidance in thinking about biotechnology. Humans have *inherent limitations*. God gave Adam and Eve certain boundaries in the garden *before* they fell into disobedience (Gen 2:16–17). Now, of course, technology is wielded by creatures who have a universal bent toward sin (Rom 3:23). Humanity's tendency toward sinful behavior means that human beings are perpetually at risk of misusing technology. Christians then have a unique perspective, because they ultimately believe that the fundamental problems that we face as humans are not genetic nor biological, but spiritual.

A final theological resource for thinking about embryos is the Incarnation. Although there is, and always will be, great mystery here, the historical affirmations of the church through two millennia provide a rich backdrop for thinking about embryos.[15] The Apostles' Creed says succinctly that "Jesus was conceived by the Holy Spirit" and "born of the Virgin Mary." Between these two poles is the process of embryonic development. Analytic theologian Oliver Crisp has recently suggested that, in order to avoid classical theological errors regarding the hypostatic union of Christ's divine and human natures, Christ's human nature is best understood to be present immediately, at fertilization.[16] At a far less abstract level, classical doctrine suggests a profoundly personal notion: the Second Person of the Trinity has dignified embryonic development by taking it up into the divine life, and has thereby dignified the lives of all humans from our earliest moments.

How should these considerations temper how we think about manipulating embryos? Space precludes extensive discussion, but several principles emerge. First, *we should aim to treat the embryo as a patient, a begotten gift, rather than a means to some other end*, at *all* stages of

---

14. The *qal* participle of *rāqam* is used elsewhere of weaving the tapestry for the Tabernacle (e.g., Exod 26:36).

15. Helpful studies include Jones, *Soul of the Embryo*; Mackellar, *Image of God*.

16. See Crisp, *Christ and the Embryo*.

development. Secondly, *we must balance two realities of our relationship to technology*. On the one hand, Christians are called to love, which means we ought to use technology to prevent disease. On the other hand, we should be wary of excessive technological optimism. Finally, simple prudence means we should be *cautious*, as Christian ethicist Gilbert Meilaender urges, "If we are genuinely baffled about how best to describe the moral status of that human subject who is the unimplanted embryo, we should not go forward in a way that peculiarly combines metaphysical bewilderment with practical certitude by approving even limited [use] for experimental purposes."[17] With these principles in mind, it is time to consider examples of technical manipulation of human embryos.

Preimplantation Genetic Diagnosis

A commonly used technology today is *preimplantation genetic diagnosis* (PGD). As is true for many key procedures, PGD relies on *in vitro* fertilization. Space precludes discussing this important topic here, except to acknowledge that Christians do not agree on whether it is ever appropriate to use *in vitro* fertilization. However, our focus here will be on whether there are appropriate uses of PGD and whether there are alternatives.

PGD is possible because human embryos, like others from a group of animals called deuterostomes, are incredibly resilient.[18] We know from common experience that humans display the same malleability: monozygotic twins (often misleadingly called "identical" twins) can form from a splitting of the early embryo. It is this resilience of the early embryo that allowed the original version of the PGD assay, which involved removing one cell from an uncompacted eight-cell human embryo using a pipette. Remarkably, the remaining seven-eighths of the embryo can survive to form a baby. The removed cell or its progeny, cultured in a dish, can be genetically assessed to determine the genotype (genetic makeup) of the embryo from which they came. More recently, PGD is commonly performed using cells

---

17. Meilaender, "Begetting and Cloning," 43–44.

18. A standard text that describes these experiments is Barresi and Gilbert, *Developmental Biology*, 12e. The original experiments that showed the resiliency of deuterostome embryos were done in sea urchins by German embryologist Hans Driesch at the end of the nineteenth century. Driesch showed, in a classic experiment, that separating the four cells of a four-cell embryo results in four well-proportioned embryos. Driesch was so flummoxed by this experiment that he eventually abandoned science to become an early twentieth-century vitalist philosopher!

removed from the exterior of the embryo (*trophoblast* cells), which is gentler and less dangerous to the remainder of the embryo.[19]

How should we assess PGD? There are some uses of this technology that are widely criticized. For example, PGD is being used heavily in certain countries, such as India and China, for sex selection.[20] In other cases, the goal of PGD is to assess an embryo for devastating, invariably lethal genetic disorders, such as Tay Sachs disease.[21] This is certainly a compassionate motivation. Typically, however, if the genotype of the embryo is found to be incorrect, then the embryo is intentionally destroyed. From a biblical perspective, alternative diagnostic technologies should be sought that circumvent destroying embryos. One alternative, though technically challenging and less powerful, is to genetically test an oocyte prior to fertilization.[22] This is possible because the sister cell of the oocyte, called the first *polar body*, contains DNA that can be sampled, in some cases allowing unambiguous assessment of the genotype of the oocyte prior to fertilization.

Pluripotent Stem Cells

In our whirlwind tour of early human development, we discussed a special group of cells at one end of the blastocyst called inner cell mass (ICM) cells. ICM cells are very flexible in terms of their developmental capabilities. They are *pluripotent*: this means that they can produce any specialized cell type in the embryo proper, the part of the embryo that produces a baby. ICM cells can be isolated from embryos and grown in a dish. The most common approach relies on treating blastocyst stage embryos with antibodies that cause the outer cells to slough off, allowing the ICM cells to be harvested. The isolated cells, grown in a dish, act as *embryonic stem* (ES) cells: they can divide to produce more daughter cells like themselves, or they can produce daughter cells that can become more specialized.[23]

Tremendous optimism surrounded the development of human ES cells. ES cells are very flexible, making them potentially useful for developing therapies; by coaxing them along certain lines of differentiation, they could—in theory—be used to replace tissues that are missing in a

---

19. See, for example, this older but serviceable reference: Harper, *Preimplantation Genetic Diagnosis*.

20. See "Gender-biased Sex Selection."

21. E.g., see the National Tay Sachs and Allied Diseases website: https://www.ntsad.org/family-planning.

22. See Harper, *Preimplantation Genetic Diagnosis*, ch. 9.

23. See, for example, National Institutes of Health, "Introduction to Stem Cells."

patient. Aside from substantial practical obstacles to their successful use in patients thus far, including formation of tumors, immune rejection, and other issues,[24] a major problem from a biblical perspective is that generating ES cells requires the destruction of an embryo. It is for this reason that my colleague at the University of Wisconsin-Madison, James Thomson, who pioneered ES cell technology, has said, "If human embryonic stem cell research does not make you at least a little bit uncomfortable, you have not thought about it enough."[25]

Since ES cell production typically involves intentional destruction of embryos, alternatives are preferable. Such an alternative has become available due to the work of Shinya Yamanaka and colleagues. Yamanaka received a Nobel prize in 2006 for his work, which identified the proteins that pluripotent cells make that maintain them in a pluripotent state, which are now colloquially called "Yamanaka factors." In a bit of cellular alchemy, Yamanaka and colleagues found that if they forced cells to make these proteins, they would become pluripotent, or *induced pluripotent stem cells* (iPS cells).[26] A major advantage of iPS cells beyond avoiding embryo destruction is that specialized cells from a patient can be converted into iPS cells and then redifferentiated to replace missing or damaged cells from the patient with cells that are an exact genetic match to the patient.

Scientists are working very hard to develop iPS cells for use in therapeutic applications. In the next several decades it seems likely that iPS cell and related technologies will find a place in the toolkit of regenerative medicine in treating disease. As is true for many technologies, however, there have been several indirect consequences of this technology. One arises from the very flexibility of iPS cells. Scientists have found ways, currently somewhat imperfectly, but with rapidly improving technology to turn iPS cells into cells that can produce gametes, i.e., sperm and oocytes.[27] This includes the possibility that cells from a genetically XY individual could be converted into cells that can generate oocytes. The same is true of genetically XX individuals, whose cells could be converted into sperm-producing cells. While technically unfeasible currently, it may be possible one day for same-sex couples to use such engineered gametes, combined with *in vitro* fertilization or artificial

---

24. For example, see this candid assessment of clinical successes with ES cells originating from my own institution marking the twenty-year anniversary of ES cells: "Today, proven therapies based on trading out diseased cells for healthy lab grown cells remains a clinical aspiration" (Devitt, "Twenty Years On," para. 5).

25. Kolata, "Stem Cell War."

26. For a retrospective, see Scudellari, "How iPS Cells Changed," 310–12.

27. See, for example, Yamashiro, "Generation of Human Oogonia," 392–94.

insemination in procreation. Christians will need to anticipate and respond to such possibilities, which go far beyond biblical norms.

A second approach made possible by iPS cells and ES cells is that they, much like cells in a normal embryo, are capable of remarkable feats of self-organization.[28] When treated in various ways, iPS cells can form what appear to be strikingly like organ rudiments, or *organoids*. Such structures are useful for basic biology, and some hope that one day organoids will be used to produce replacement cells for use in patients. The self-organizing capabilities of pluripotent cells are truly remarkable. In some cases, what looks remarkably like an eye rudiment can be coaxed to arise in a dish. In other cases (called cerebral organoids), neural structures that are associated with folding the cerebral cortex can form that are capable of producing brain waves.[29]

While current cerebral organoids do not mimic key aspects of brain function associated with cognition, extrapolating organoid technology into the future raises many questions. What are the capacities of self-organized neural tissues? How would we know? These questions are magnified by what have been called *gastruloids*. Pluripotent cells can be coaxed to self-organize into something that looks remarkably like a gastrulating embryo. Some have called these SHEEFs, for "Synthetic Human Entities with Embryo-Like Features."[30] One investigator at the University of Michigan working on gastruloids realized that the term "synthetic embryo" implies something significant: "We have to be careful using these terms, synthetic human embryo, because some people are not happy about it."[31] Scientists are rapidly developing ways to achieve correct differentiation of the neural tubes produced from gastruloids.[32] As these structures ever more closely resemble fully functioning embryonic central nervous systems, careful thought will be required regarding these self-organized embryonic tissues.

Finally, recently scientists have placed pluripotent cells into specialized tiny containers that coax them to produce structures that closely resemble blastocysts. These *iBlastoids* produced what appear to be inner cell mass-like cells and exterior, trophoblast cells that, to the untrained eye

---

28. For a catalogue of these technologies, see El Azhar and Sonnen, "Development in a Dish."

29. For a highly publicized example of brain organoids, see, e.g., Hernandez, "Engineered Mini Brain Models."

30. The term was used in Aach et al., "Addressing the Ethical Issues," 6. For Christian analysis of SHEEFs, see Zeiger, "Embryoids," 14–15; Daly, "Synthetic Human Entities," 93–105.

31. Regalado, "Artificial Human Embryos."

32. See, for example, Rifes, "Modeling Neural Tube Development," 1265–73.

look very much like embryos.³³ While current blastoids do not have the full capabilities of embryos and therefore do not appear to require moral consideration, it is clear that these technologies are becoming ever more refined. Christian voices have much to contribute to the discussions surrounding embryo-like entities.

Chimeras

We saw with PGD that removing cells from human embryos causes widespread changes in differentiation that allow the partial embryo to develop into a baby. It turns out that the same is true when embryos contain *additional* cells. This can be shown directly with mouse embryos. Remarkably, if three mouse embryos prior to compaction are placed together, at compaction they will form a single unified embryo. If the three embryos have different genetic constitutions (e.g., fur color), the resulting mouse will contain islands of cells with these different genetic makeups. These and many other experiments indicate that the early development of mice is remarkably malleable.

As we saw with cloning, typically, if an experiment can succeed in other mammals, it will succeed in primates, including humans. In 2012, scientists at Oregon Health Sciences University announced that they had produced a monkey made from a combination of six embryos.³⁴ Such embryos are called *chimeras* ("chimera" comes from the hybrid monster from Greek mythology). Chimeras can also be made by injecting extra inner-cell mass cells into a blastocyst. In mice, monkeys, and other mammals, the injected cells will typically take part in development, contributing to the embryo proper (the part that makes the baby mammal).

Recently, chimeric embryos that are a combination of human and other mammalian cells have been produced,³⁵ including monkey/human chimeras.³⁶ Why would one want to make chimeric embryos using human cells? Some scientists involved in this work are simply curious about mixing cells from two species. Others, such as the atheist biologist and provocateur David Barash, advocate producing "humanzees" to prove a point about the

---

33. See, among others, Liu et al., "Modelling Human Blastocysts," 62732; and Yu et al., "Blastocyst-like Structures," 620–26.

34. Tachibana et al., "Generation of Chimeric Rhesus Monkeys," 285–95. For news coverage, see Akst, "World's First."

35. Wu et al., "Interspecies Chimerism," 473–86.

36. Tan et al., "Chimeric contribution," 2020–32. For a news report, see Subbaraman, "First Monkey–Human Embryos," 497.

lack of uniqueness of humans.[37] Beyond what appear to be such modern reiterations of H.G. Wells's *The Island of Doctor Moreau*, why might one wish to exploit chimeras? Another proposed use of chimeras is for organ transplantation. If human cells could be introduced into an animal embryonic host, for example, a genetically modified pig embryo, in such a way that the human cells are confined to a particular organ, then the human tissue from the chimera could be used to replace organs in human patients.

Many ethical questions arise from such work beyond the technical feasibility. If a sufficient number of human cells found their way into the brain of the host, what might this mean for the function and nature of the resulting chimeric brain? In a *Nature News* article, bioethicist Insoo Hyun from Case Western Reserve University remarked, "Some people may see that you're creating morally ambiguous entities."[38] Indeed. How should Christians think about such cross-species experiments in light of the unique status of humans as image-bearers?

Conclusions

The foregoing examples highlight just a few of the vexing ethical questions surrounding manipulation of human embryos. Biomedical technology is moving at breakneck speed. Pastor theologians must work closely with scientific experts to help the church think well about these issues so that thinking about thorny bioethical issues is not something left to the "experts." Biblically grounded, thoughtful Christians can and should learn about new biotechnologies in biblical perspective. Our ability to do so will be crucial in shaping the future.

Bibliography

Aach, John, Jeantine Lunshof, Eswar Iyer, and George M. Church "Addressing the Ethical Issues Raised by Synthetic Human Entities with Embryo-like Features." *eLife* 6.e20674 (March 21, 2017).

Aguilera-Castrejon, A., et al. "Ex Utero Mouse Embryogenesis from Pre-gastrulation to Late Organogenesis." *Nature* 593 (2021) 119–24.

Akst, Jef. "World's First Chimeric Monkeys." *Scientist*, January 5, 2012. https://www.the-scientist.com/the-nutshell/worlds-first-chimeric-monkeys-41511.

Anderson, V. Elving. "Biological Engineering and the Future of Man." In *Horizons of Science: Christian Scholars Speak Out*, edited by Carl F. H. Henry, 156–74. Contemporary Evangelical Thought. San Francisco: Harper & Row, 1978.

---

37. Barash, "Human Chimp Hybrids."
38. Subbaraman, "First Monkey-Human Embryos," 592, 497.

Bancewicz, Ruth M. *God in the Lab: How Science Enhances Faith*. Grand Rapids: Monarch, 2015.

———. *Wonders of the Living World: Curiosity, Awe, and the Meaning of Life*. London: Lion Hudson, 2021.

Barash, David P. "It's Time to Make Human-chimp Hybrids." *Nautilus*, March 8, 2018. http://nautil.us/issue/58/self/its-time-to-make-human_chimp-hybrids.

Barresi, Michael J.F., and Scott F. Gilbert. *Developmental Biology*. 12th ed. New York: Oxford University Press, 2019.

Buratovich, Michael A. *The Stem Cell Epistles: Letters to My Students about Bioethics, Embryos, Stem Cells, and Fertility Treatments*. Eugene, OR: Wipf and Stock, 2013.

Carroll, Sean B. *Endless Forms Most Beautiful: The New Science of Evo Devo*. New York: Norton, 2005.

Crisp, Oliver D. "Christ and the Embryo." In *God Incarnate: Explorations in Christology*, 103–21. New York: T&T Clark, 2009.

Cyranoski, David. "Stem Cells: Egg Engineers." *Nature* 500 (2013) 392–94. https://doi.org/10.1038/500392a.

———. "The CRISPR-baby Scandal: What's Next for Human Gene-editing?" *Nature* 566 (2019) 440–42. https://doi.org/10.1038/d41586-019-00673-1

Daly, Todd. "Synthetic Human Entities with Embryo-Like Features (SHEEFs) and the Incarnation." *Ethics and Medicine* 34 (2019) 93–105.

Devitt, Terry. "Twenty Years On, Measuring the Impact of Human Stem Cells." *UW-Madison News*, November 1, 2018. https://news.wisc.edu/twenty-years-on-measuring-the-impact-of-human-stem-cells/.

El Azhar, Yasmine, and Katharina F. Sonnen. "Development in a Dish—*In Vitro* Models of Mammalian Embryonic Development." *Frontiers in Cell and Developmental Biology* 9 (2021) 655–993. https://doi.org/10.3389/fcell.2021.655993.

Evans, John. *The History and Future of Bioethics*. New York: Oxford University Press, 2014.

George, Robert P., and David Baltimore. "Stem Cell Research: A Debate." *Wall Street Journal*, July 30, 2001.

George, Robert P., and Christopher Tollefson. *Embryo: A Defense of Human Life*. New York: Doubleday, 2008.

"Gender-biased Sex Selection." *United Nations Population Fund*, July 27, 2020. https://www.unfpa.org/gender-biased-sex-selection.

Gilbert, Scott, Anna L.Tyler, and Emily J. Zackin. *Bioethics and the New Embryology: Springboards for Debate*. New York: W.H. Freeman, 2005.

Harper, Joyce C., Joy D. A. Delhanty, and Alan H. Handyside, eds. *Preimplantation Genetic Diagnosis*. 2nd ed. Cambridge: Cambridge University Press, 2009.

Hernandez, Daniela. "Engineered Mini Brain Models Show Patterns of Activity That 'Resemble Babies.'" *Wall Street Journal*, Aug. 29, 2019.

Hui, Edwin C. *At the Beginning of Life: Dilemmas in Theological Bioethics*. Downers Grove: InterVarsity, 2002.

Hurlbut, William B. "Personal Statement." In *Human Cloning and Human Dignity: An Ethical Inquiry*, 267–76. Washington, DC: National Bioethics Advisory Commission, 2003.

Huxley, Aldous. *Brave New World*. New York: HarperCollins, 2006. First published 1932.

Jones, David Albert. *The Soul of the Embryo: An Enquiry into the Status of the Human Embryo in the Christian Tradition*. New York: Continuum, 2003.

Kingsley, Charles. *Westminster Sermons*. London: Macmillan, 1871.
Kolata, Gina. "Man Who Helped Start Stem Cell War May End It." *New York Times*, November 22, 2007.
Liu, Xiaodong, et al. "Modelling human blastocysts by reprogramming fibroblasts into iBlastoids." *Nature* 591 (2021) 627–32. https://www.nature.com/articles/s41586-021-03372-y.
Mackellar, Callum. *The Image of God, Personhood and the Embryo*. London: SCM, 2017.
Meilaender, Gilbert. "Begetting and Cloning." In *Flesh of My Flesh: The Ethics of Cloning Humans*, edited by Gregory Pence, 39–44. Lanham: Rowman & Littlefield, 1998.
———. *Bioethics: A Primer for Christians*. 3rd ed. Grand Rapids: Eerdmans, 2013.
National Institutes of Health. "Introduction to Stem Cells." *US Department of Health and Human Services*, 2016. https://stemcells.nih.gov/info/basics.
Nilsson, Lennart, and Lars Hamberger. *A Child Is Born*. 4th rev. ed. New York: Random House, 2003.
Ramsey, Paul. *Fabricated Man*. New Haven: Yale University Press, 1970.
Ramsey Colloquium. "The Inhuman Use of Human Beings." *First Things*, January 1995. https://www.firstthings.com/article/1995/01/the-inhuman-use-of-human-beings.
Regalado, Antonio. "Artificial Human Embryos Are Coming, and No One Knows How to Handle Them." *MIT Technology Review*, September 19, 2017. https://www.technologyreview.com/2017/09/19/149089/artificial-human-embryos-are-coming-and-no-one-knows-how-to-handle-them/.
Rifes, Pedro, et al. "Modeling Neural Tube Development by Differentiation of Human Embryonic Stem Cells in a Microfluidic WNT Gradient." *Nature Biotechnology* 38 (2020) 1265–73. https://doi.org/10.1038/s41587-020-0525-0.
Scudellari, Megan. "How iPS Cells Changed the World." *Nature* 534 (2016) 310–12. https://doi.org/10.1038/534310a.
Subbaraman, Nidhi. "First Monkey–Human Embryos Reignite Debate over Hybrid Animals." *Nature* 592 (2021) 497. https://www.nature.com/articles/d41586-021-01001-2.
Tachibana, Masahito, et al. "Generation of Chimeric Rhesus monkeys." *Cell* 148 (2012) 285–95. https://doi.org/10.1016/j.cell.2011.12.007.
Tan, Tao, et al. "Chimeric Contribution of Human Extended Pluripotent Stem Cells to Monkey Embryos Ex Vivo." *Cell* 184 (2021) 2020–32.
Walters, Brent, and Ronald Cole-Turner, eds. *God and the Embryo: Religious Voices on Stem Cells and Cloning*. Washington, DC: Georgetown University Press, 2003.
Wells, H.G. *The Island of Dr. Moreau*. Edited by Steven Palmé. Dover Thrift Editions. New York: Dover, 1996. First published 1896.
Wolpert, Lewis. *Developmental Biology: A Very Short Introduction*. New York: Oxford University Press, 2011.
Wu, J., et al. "Interspecies Chimerism with Mammalian Pluripotent Stem Cells." *Cell* 168 (2017) 473–86. https://doi.org/10.1016/j.cell.2016.12.036
Yamashiro, Chika, et al. "Generation of Human Oogonia from Induced Pluripotent Stem Cells In Vitro." *Science* 362 (2018) 356–60.
Yu, Leqian, et al. "Blastocyst-like Structures Generated from Human Pluripotent Stem Cells." *Nature* 591 (2021) 620–26.
Zeiger, Heather. "Embryoids: Unique Entities or Protected Like Human Embryos?" *Dignitas* 24.4 (2017) 14–15.

12

The Technology of Reading[1]

KAREN SWALLOW PRIOR

IN *THE PHAEDRUS*, PLATO writes of a dialogue between Socrates and the titular Phaedrus in which Socrates relays the story of Theuth, a mythical god who bestowed on the king of Egypt, among other inventions, the gift of writing.

> This, said Theuth, will make the Egyptians wiser and give them better memories; it is a specific both for the memory and for the wit. Thamus replied: O most ingenious Theuth, the parent or inventor of an art is not always the best judge of the utility or inutility of his own inventions to the users of them. And in this instance, you who are the father of letters, from a paternal love of your own children have been led to attribute to them a quality which they cannot have; for this discovery of yours will create forgetfulness in the learners' souls, because they will not use their memories; they will trust to the external written characters and not remember of themselves. The specific which you have discovered is an aid not to memory, but to reminiscence, and you give your disciples not truth, but only the semblance of truth; they will be hearers of many things and will have learned nothing; they will appear to be omniscient and will generally know nothing; they will be tiresome company, having the show of wisdom without the reality.[2]

---

1. Some material here is drawn from my book *On Reading Well*, as well as from previous talks and lectures.

2. Plato, *Phaedrus*, 274e–275b.

In this rendering, Plato deigns the written word to be merely an image of the spoken word, and thereby inferior.

I, in the interests of full disclosure, am not a Platonist. Yet Socrates's dialogue here is a good reminder that writing is indeed a technology. And all technologies, as Marshall McLuhan reminds us, bring both gains and losses. As "extensions of man," McLuhan famously puts it in his seminal work, *Understanding Media*, technologies (which, of course, includes media) have both a prosthetic and amputational effect. "Any extension," he says, "whether of skin, hand, or foot, affects the whole psychic and social complex."[3] The wheel, then the automobile, extend the foot, for example, but amputate our closeness to the land and each other. The telephone amplifies the voice, but amputates writing. (Texting perhaps brings back "writing," but amputates linguistic complexity.)

All language, whether spoken or written, is an extension of the human body, McLuhan says. It is an extension of our inner thoughts, feelings, and ideas. Language is, he explains, the extension "that enables the intellect to detach itself from the vastly wider reality. Without language . . . human intelligence would have remained totally involved in the objects of its attention."[4] Written language is a further extension of spoken language. And in a 1970 interview, McLuhan (an adult convert to Catholicism) made an interesting observation.

> I don't think it was accidental that Christianity began in the Greco-Roman culture. I don't think that Christ would have suffered under Ghengis Khan with the same meaning as under Pontius Pilate. The Greeks had invented a medium, the phonetic alphabet, which, as Eric Havelock explains in his book *Preface to Plato*, made it possible for men to have for the first time in history a sense of private identity. A sense of private substantial identity—a self—is to this day utterly unknown to tribal societies. Christianity was introduced into a matrix of culture in which the individual had enormous significance: this is not characteristic of other world cultures.[5]

Indeed, from the carving of the Ten Commandments to the writing of the Torah, to the copying and distribution of scrolls and letters in the early church, God's plan was for his people to read. The words God carved into stone at Mount Sinai include a caution against images, setting up a peculiar word-based relationship with his followers that contrasted starkly

---

3. McLuhan, *Understanding Media*, 4.
4. McLuhan, *Understanding Media*, 79.
5. McLuhan, "Electric Consciousness and the Church," 81.

with the image-worshiping pagan nations surrounding the Israelites—an observation famously made by Neil Postman, following McLuhan, in *Amusing Ourselves to Death*.[6]

And even before Sinai, in the garden of Eden, the skins with which God covered Adam and Eve after they sinned were a type, or foreshadowing, of the skin that would cover God himself in the Incarnation, who then, thus incarnated, would then "cover" the sin of all believers. As David Lyle Jeffrey explores in depth in *People of the Book: Christian Identity and Literary Culture,* even the animal skins (the vellum) on which early Scriptures were later written also remind us of this skin covering. (It's fascinating, too, to ponder how a leather-bound book is similar to a person—covered by skin, dead but made alive and eternal by the presence of the word within.) This motif of the book continued through church history, according to Jeffrey. Medieval paintings frequently depict Mary, other biblical figures, and church fathers anachronistically holding the Bible.

Such images, even—or especially—when anachronistic (bound books did not exist when Mary bore Christ, of course), symbolize the centrality of reading to Christian faithfulness and point out the concrete, tangible nature of the word. In many of these paintings, the subject is depicted with a finger inserted into the book's pages, suggesting active reading. Such paintings reflect how Thomas needed to put his fingers into Christ's body in order to know and believe. God's Word, both written and incarnate, beckons us to come close and engage with it—with him—in a tactile, concrete, bodily, incarnational aesthetic relationship.

As we read in John 1:14, "The Word became flesh and dwelt among us, and we have seen his glory, glory as of the only Son from the Father, full of grace and truth" (ESV). Some human beings even got to touch him. One even held him in her womb—as the old, orthodox hymn sings to Mary: "He whom the entire universe could not contain was contained within your womb."

Despite the centrality of the Word (and words) from the beginning of God's revelation, many generations of believers were unable to read the Bible for themselves. Before the Reformation, biblical words passed through priests and were supplemented by images depicted in stained glass windows and in itinerant drama troupes performing biblical stories. These symbols offered rich beauty, but images alone, so the Reformers asserted, cannot convey the abstractions of doctrine. Thus, in the pre-literate age preceding the Reformation, the Bible was delivered and understood only in pieces—not as a whole body.

---

6. Postman, *Amusing Ourselves to Death*, 9.

The Reformation's focus on reading and the resulting age of literacy it birthed were, in some ways, the culmination of the logocentrism that runs through the Bible and God's relationship with creation. "In the beginning was the Word, and the Word was with God, and the Word was God" (NIV) from John 1:1, is a direct echo of Genesis 1, when God created the world through his words. While the "word of the Lord" refers to all the ways God reveals himself, whether spoken (Genesis 1), in a vision (Gen 15:1), or written (Exod 24:12; 2 Tim 3:16), his word is logical, linear, and coherent.

Likewise, the key feature of a literate age is the cultivation, not only of the ability to read, but of the propensity to think in a logical, linear, coherent fashion. It is significant that the act of reading is not natural to the human brain. While scientists see reading in terms of evolution and adaptation, reading is, in some way, supernatural, or at least unnatural. As our reading becomes more immersed in a digital rather than a print culture, the more we return to some qualities of the pre-literate world. We are reading more, but the way we read on the internet replicates the effects of the discrete images of stained-glass windows more than the sustained, logical, and coherent linearity of a whole book. Digital technology and the internet extend our eyes and ears—but amputate, it seems, our focus and our feelings—or, in other words, attention and aesthetics.

In *Reader, Come Home: The Reading Brain in a Digital World*, neuroscientist Maryanne Wolf explains that reading is not hardwired in the human brain the way language is. Not only does the remarkable plasticity of the human brain make reading possible, but the activity of reading creates new circuits in the brain. These aid in learning abstract and creative concepts that go beyond the brain's genetically programmed functioning. Reading demands "extraordinary cerebral complexity," Wolf says, and the brain requires years for "deep-reading processes to be formed." Our reading habits, therefore, have the potential to shape our brains, for good or ill.[7]

Deep reading activates regions of the brain related to touch, motion, and feeling, and helps develop the background knowledge that we bring to further reading and living. "The consistent strengthening of the connections among our analogical, inferential, empathic, and background knowledge processes generalizes well beyond reading," Wolf explains. "When we learn to connect these processes over and over in our reading, it becomes easier to apply them to our own lives."[8] Her findings seem to confirm the truth of Psalm 119:11: "I have hidden your word in my heart that I might not sin against you" (NIV).

7. Wolf, *Reader, Come Home*, 6.
8. Wolf, *Reader, Come Home*, 6.

Cognitive science further shows that our brains work one way when accustomed to reading in logical, linear patterns, and another way when continually bouncing from tweet to tweet, picture to picture, and screen to screen. Wolf's research shows that reading on digital devices does not create the same kind of brain circuits as deep reading. In *The Shallows: What the Internet Is Doing to Our Brains,* Nicholas Carr cautions, "Calm, focused, undistracted, the linear mind is being pushed aside by a new kind of mind that wants and needs to take in and dole out information in short, disjointed, often overlapping bursts—the faster, the better."[9]

Likewise, in *The Gutenberg Elegies,* Sven Birkerts examines the many differences between a print culture and an electronic culture and, as the title suggests, laments the losses to human culture—indeed our very humanity—that he sees as we transition from the former to the latter. In extolling the gifts of reading, Birkerts writes,

> Through the process of reading, we slip out of our customary time orientation, marked by distractedness and surficiality, into the realm of duration. Only in the duration state is experience present as meaning. Only in this state are we prepared to consider our lives under what the philosophers used to call "the aspect of eternity," to question our origins and destinations, and to conceive of ourselves as souls.[10]

He continues,

> Reading, pledged to duration, refuses the idea of time as simple succession. Reading argues for a larger conception of the meaningful, and its implicit injunction . . . is that we change our lives, that we strive to live them in the light of meaning . . . What reading does, ultimately, is keep alive the dangerous and exhilarating idea that a life is not a sequence of lived moments, but a destiny. That, God or no God, life has a unitary pattern inscribed within it.[11]

As the way we process information shifts from print to digital, we enter what Birkerts calls a culture of "contemporaneity."[12] "In less than half a century we have moved from a condition of essential isolation into one of intense and almost unbroken mediation."[13] With it have come, Birkerts says,

9. Carr, *Shallows,* 10.
10. Birkerts, *Gutenberg Elegies,* 32.
11. Birkerts, *Gutenberg Elegies,* 85.
12. Birkerts, *Gutenberg Elegies,* 26.
13. Birkerts, *Gutenberg Elegies,* 50.

- a fragmented sense of time
- less space for experiencing a sense of reverie
- reduced attention spans and less patience for sustained inquiry
- distrust in institutions
- loss of a sense of history or narrative as offering form to individual and subjective experience
- loss of a sense of a vision for the future
- estrangement from community and place[14]

Technology, he says,

> in every way encourages in the user a heightened and ever-changing awareness of the present. It works against historical perception, which must depend on the inimical notions of logic and sequential succession. If the print medium exalts the word, fixing it into permanence, the electronic counterpart reduces it to a signal, a means to an end.[15]

But in addition to what is already lost, Birkerts predicts further developments that are likely with an all-electronic future. This is what he predicts:

1. Language erosion: "simple linguistic prefab" replaces "ambiguity, paradox, irony, subtlety, and wit"

2. Flattening of historical perspectives: "history (cognate with "story") is affiliated in complex ways with its texts . . . The printed page is itself a link, at least along the imaginative continuum, and when that link is broken, the past can only start to recede."

3. The waning of the private self as expressed in Joseph Brodsky's 1987 Nobel Prize acceptance speech,

> If art teaches . . . anything it is the privateness of the human condition . . . Aesthetic choice is a highly individual matter, and aesthetic experience is always a private one. Every new aesthetic reality makes one's experience even more private; and this kind of privacy, assuming at times the guise of literary (or some other) taste, can in itself turn out to be, if not a guarantee, then a form of defense, against enslavement.[16]

---

14. Birkerts, *Gutenberg Elegies*, 27.
15. Birkerts, *Gutenberg Elegies*, 123.
16. Quoted in Birkerts, *Gutenberg Elegies*, 128–32.

This is a rather shocking claim, isn't it? That art, through the privacy of aesthetic experience, is a defense against enslavement. Let's examine this relationship a bit, particularly in considering literary art. Because language is the mediating filter through which we process all of our experiences, reading literature—whether fiction, poetry, drama, or a well-crafted essay—allows us to practice and refine the tool by which we "read" our real lives. The fullness of literary language deepens that practice even more. Language used to inform is flat and technical. Literary language is formative, rich, and resonant. The ability to understand figurative language, language in which "a word is both itself and something else," is unique to human beings and is, one cognitive psychologist explains, "fundamental to how we think" because it is the means by which we can "escape the literal and immediate."[17]

Reading and interpreting literature notoriously lack hard and fast rules. Reading well depends upon a kind of freedom, one that flourishes when the responsibility for reading is taken seriously. It is this very quality that makes literature exciting for some, frustrating for others. There is no one right reading of a literary text—but there are certainly erroneous readings, good readings, and excellent readings. While the highest levels of biblical and literary hermeneutics can sometimes confound us, a basic and valid interpretive lens for reading the Bible can be as straightforward as approaching a great literary work. (Of course, as most college students will tell you—and this English professor will confirm—skillful reading doesn't come naturally. It must be learned.)

Like literary texts, the inspired word of God, the Bible, is also a literary work—it's more than that, but it's also that—written with artistry, a narrative arc, and themes both major and minor. Just as there are valid and invalid approaches to reading *Huckleberry Finn,* for example, there are right and wrong ways to read the Bible. As readers, whether the text we hold is God-breathed or merely mortal, we must take into account genre, purpose, audience, structure, and point of view. We find meaning by understanding each passage only within the context of the whole. As essayist, novelist, and short story writer George Saunders explains, "A story means by how it proceeds."[18]

This is the difference between learning propositional truth through reading history or an argumentative essay, and the knowledge gained aesthetically through the process of reading a fictional narrative.[19] As Birkerts

---

17. Oatley, *Such Stuff as Dreams,* 28–30.

18. George Saunders, lecture presented at Festival of Faith and Writing, Calvin College, April 15, 2016.

19. Taylor, "Sympathy and Insight in Aristotle's Poetics," 265–80.

points out, "Narration is sequence that claims significance. Animals, for example, do not narrate, even though they are well aware of sequence and of the consequences of actions."[20]

Consider the problem of the reliability of the narrator. A certain level of readerly maturity, skill, and critical distance is required to discern between a reliable narrator and an unreliable one. When Huck Finn tells us that his conscience is troubled for treating Miss Watson "so mean" by assisting her runaway slave, recognizing the *unreliability* of Huck as a narrator is imperative to grasping the meaning of the text as a whole. On the other hand, when the narrator of *A Tale of Two Cities* tells us, "It was the best of times, it was the worst of times," the astute reader intuits that the narrative voice reflects the view of the implied author. Similarly, the skilled reader of the Bible can distinguish between description and prescription, between ceremonial law and moral law, between abolishment and fulfillment of the law.

One obstacle I have noticed in nearly three decades of teaching literature is that many readers have been conditioned to jump so quickly to interpretation and evaluation of a text that they often skip the fundamental, but essential, task of comprehending what the words actually, literally mean. This habit of the mind can even be seen in the body. During classroom discussions, I often ask students to describe or restate what a line or passage says. Frequently, the students' first response to such questions is to turn their eyes upward in search of a thought or idea rather than to look down at the words on the page in front of them where the answer actually lies. Reading well begins with understanding well the words on the page. Attending to the words on the page is a skill that improves with practice.

My students' responses serve also as a reminder that reading is an aesthetic experience. It is embodied. Literature—like all art—cannot be understood or appreciated apart from its form. To attend to the form of a work is by its very nature an aesthetic experience. Reading is clearly an intellectual experience. This is the way in which we are accustomed to thinking about reading: as conveying ideas—good, bad, or in-between—to our minds. Yet, we tend not to think so much about reading as an aesthetic experience, as an embodied practice. We are conditioned today to focus on content at the expense of form. When we read (or watch a film, or view a work of art), we tend to look for themes, worldviews, gripping plots, relatable characters, and so forth, but often neglect the form. Part of this tendency is the fruit born of a culture influenced by a utilitarian emphasis on function and practical use at the expense of beauty and structure. Yet, we know from real-life relationships and communication that how something is communicated is

---

20. Birkerts, "Reading in the Digital Age," 31.

just as, if not more, important than what is communicated. As McLuhan is most famous for saying, "The medium is the message."[21] Birkerts observes, "I would not argue that the *Anna Karenina* read on an e-reader is different from the one read on the page. But the act of reading it *is* somewhat different, in both its mechanics and its outer signification, and that difference bears on our collective assessment."[22]

The aesthetic experience of literature—its formative quality—differs from its intellectual or informative qualities. To read a work of literature is to have a kind of experience, one mediated through language—which is the same medium we use to interpret and narrate back to ourselves our real-life experiences and their significance.

In *Caring for Words in a Culture of Lies,* Marilyn McEntyre cautions that "with the loss of the subtlety, clarity, and reliability of language, we become more vulnerable to crude exercises of power."[23] Thus literary reading is not only a political act, but a moral act, too. It is "morally consequential," McEntyre says, arguing,

> How we choose to read, how we submit to or question or resist the terms set by the writer, are choices that shape the habits of our minds and the habits of our hearts. Those habits determine the degree to which we are open to truth in its various guises, and capable of discerning the difference between the ring of truth and the metallic clang of lies.[24]

Reading is also a spiritual act. As Graham Ward explains in "How Literature Resists Secularity," human beings "inhabit language." He explains that "although the best writers of literature demonstrate a phenomenal control over their language, associations escape, rhythms beat out older and more sacred patterns, and words carry memories of previous use."[25] Words carry resonances that spill beyond the bounds of logic and even conscious thought. Ward says of literary texts, "their acts of naming and our acts of reading" cannot but conjure the possibilities of transcendence, "particularly when we attend to experience rather than dictionary definitions, as either a writer or a reader."[26] The fullness of literary language echoes meaning—and reminds us that there is, in fact, *meaning*.

---

21. McLuhan, *Understanding Media*, 7.
22. Birkerts, *Changing the Subject*, 134.
23. McEntyre, *Caring for Words*, 6.
24. McEntyre, *Caring for Words*, 69.
25. Ward, "How Literature Resists Secularity," 82.
26. Ward, "How Literature Resists Secularity," 85.

However, as we engage in deep reading less and superficial skimming more, these resonances gradually flatten out. The breadth and extent of the worldwide web engenders, Birkerts says, the "gradual displacement of the vertical by the horizontal—the sacrifice of depth to lateral range . . . from intensive to extensive reading" and the "more complex and sophisticated our systems of lateral access, the more we sacrifice in the way of depth."[27]

Beautiful words, however, return depth to our experience. Birkerts says that what "art adds to life" is "an adequacy of attention. The rendering is not more beautiful than the event, but the rendering directs our attention; it frames it."[28] Beauty by its very nature pulls us out of ourselves, through what Elaine Scarry calls a "radical de-centering" of ourselves.[29] By drawing attention away from ourselves, beauty reminds us of the layeredness of existence and, by implication, the fact that we are not alone. As an echo of its ultimate source, beauty is a kind of metaphor for God, reflecting the fact that all language is metaphorical.

Literature, in general, and metaphor, in particular, are merely ways of "understanding and experiencing one kind of thing in terms of another,"[30] and "metaphoric reasoning" is the means by which human beings make sense out of experience.[31] As metaphors writ large, stories, drama, and poetry put flesh on ideas so they can dwell among us.

In *Metaphors We Live By*, Mark Johnson and George Lakoff show how even our conceptual systems and therefore our very thought processes themselves are largely metaphorical.[32] Furthermore, the metaphors that form and flood human thinking and language derive from physical, embodied experience (note the metaphorical nature of the words just used here: *form* and *flood*). For example, Lakoff and Johnson show that the orientational metaphors that pervade our language express the way our spatial experience grounds so much of our experience: we wake *up*, we *rise* early, we *fall* ill, we *fall* asleep, we take control *over*, we *decline* an invitation, we feel *inclined*, we feel *down*, we are on *top* of the situation.[33] Other categories of common metaphors used to process human experience, Lakoff and Johnson show, include containment metaphors (by which concepts are understood to be *in* or *out*) visual metaphors (*see* what I mean?), entity and substance

---

27. Birkerts, *Gutenberg Elegies*, 26.
28. Birkerts, *Changing the Subject*, 158.
29. Scarry, *On Beauty and Being Just*, 111.
30. Lakoff and Johnson, *Metaphors We Live By*, 5.
31. Johnson, *Moral Imagination*, 3.
32. Lakoff and Johnson, *Metaphors We Live By*, 4, 6.
33. Lakoff and Johnson, *Metaphors We Live By*, 15.

metaphors (in which abstract concepts are expressed in terms of quantity, as in *I have been standing in this line for a lot of time*), as well as personification, metonymy, and countless other figures of speech.

The metaphors in our language express "the felt qualitative unity of situations" that underlies our propositions and articulated beliefs.[34] Literary language and other forms of symbolic information work with a human nature that makes meaning—even within our pre-lingual state of development—through metaphorical structures. Metaphors, a form of exchange and communication, by nature transcend the personal and private. They are, in this way, by their very nature political—and moral—as well as aesthetic. Metaphors reflect what Charles Taylor observes in *A Secular Age* of other kinds of symbolic gestures: meanings which inhabit a space of a "horizontal, simultaneous mutual presence, which is not that of a common action, but rather of mutual display. It matters to each one of us as we act that the others are there, as witnesses of what we are doing, and thus as co-determiners of the meaning of our action."[35] Thus, Sven Birkerts asks, "If a person turns from print—finding it too slow, too hard, irrelevant to the excitements of the present—then what happens to that person's sense of culture and continuity?"[36] Like all artistic forms, literature assumes this sort of witness and co-determination of the meaning of our actions, not only to ourselves, but to others and within the world.

It is in these relations of our bodies to the world and to others in the world that meaning is formed. Human meaning is made by metaphor, metaphors which develop out of embodied experience as connections and similitudes are perceived. This rootedness of human thinking in metaphors derived from physical, embodied experience leads to an understanding that—contra Rene Descartes's *cogito ergo sum*—all human experience and meaning begins with the body. Meaning is embodied; it is sensory, *aesthetic*. Mind and body are therefore not two separate aspects of being, Johnson argues, "but rather aspects of one organic process, so that all our meaning, thought, and language emerge from the aesthetic dimensions of this embodied activity."[37] Johnson explains,

> Every aspect of human being is grounded in specific forms of bodily engagement with an environment. Change your brain, your body, or your environment in nontrivial ways, and you will

---

34. Johnson, *Meaning of the Body*, xv.
35. Taylor, *Secular Age*, 481.
36. Birkerts, *Gutenberg Elegies*, 20.
37. Johnson, *Meaning of the Body*, 1.

> change how you experience your world, what things are meaningful to you, and even who you are.[38]

Anyone who has experienced physical trauma, geographical relocation, or dramatic bodily changes can attest to this relationship of the bodily orientation to the world (as I can as of late). Indeed, Johnson, argues,

> From the moment of our entrance into the world, and apparently even in the womb, we begin to learn the meaning of things at the most primordial bodily level. Things are meaningful by virtue of their relations to other actual or possible qualities, feelings, emotions, images, image schemas, and concepts.[39]

While we have come to use the terms "feeling" and "emotion" interchangeably, it is important to note that emotion occurs first (in the body, a motion drawn out from it), and feelings result from how we interpret that emotion or what we imagine surrounding it. Emotion is the bodily fact; feeling is what we imagine about that fact. We make sense out of our feelings (our "consciously experienced bodily processes"[40]—visceral responses such as a surge of adrenaline, increased heartbeat, a fluttering stomach) by making connections to past experiences and current knowledge, and from there employ reason (or don't). In *Real Presences,* George Steiner writes, "The meanings of poetry and the music of those meanings, which we call metrics, are also of the human body. The echoes of sensibility which they elicit are visceral and tactile."[41]

If meaning begins bodily, then so literary forms—indeed, all forms of art—literally express these impressions. While "information imposes shape," "imagination creates shape," Birkerts explains in his more recent book, *Changing the Subject* (a title that has profound implications). This shape-creating power of the imagination affects not only the artist, but the audience as well. Art "not only gives us the human experience," says Birkerts, but "it also asks from us some of the same attention that first triggered the artist's impulse . . . Art serves the soul not least by demanding and creating attention."[42]

To pay attention to words and to the forms they take and make is—as the etymology of the word "attention" suggests—to stretch toward something. Notably, the proto-Indo-European root "ten," from which the

38. Johnson, *Meaning of the Body,* 1–2.
39. Johnson, *Meaning of the Body,* 279.
40. Johnson, *Meaning of the Body,* 59.
41. Steiner, *Real Presences,* 9.
42. Birkerts, *Changing the Subject,* 22–23, 24.

word "attention" is derived, is the same root for the word "temple," a place marked out and reserved as sacred by ropes or cloth stretched out and over, like the skin over our own temples, the bodily space where all sense of the aesthetic is felt and understood.

McLuhan points out that the "effects of technology do not occur at the level of opinion or concepts but alter sense ratios or patterns of perception steadily and without any resistance." In other words, technology alters our attention. McLuhan calls "the serious artist" the only one "able to encounter technology with impunity, just because he is an expert aware of the changes in sense perception."[43] If we believe McLuhan, then we understand that the artist is not limited to the roles of professional painter, pianist, or poet. Rather, McLuhan says, "The artist is the man, in any field, scientific or humanistic, who grasps the implications of his actions and of new knowledge in his own time. He is the man of integral awareness."[44] The artist is, therefore, simply, one who possesses an artistic perspective (who pays attention), a perspective that belongs, most properly and profoundly, it would seem, to the preacher, the pastor, and the prophet.

The attention demanded by art, literature, the word of God, and flesh-and-blood people, is something qualitatively different from the pull of our screens, a drawing in whose very nature and purpose is to draw us immediately away to the very next tweet, like, post, or ad. I find—and perhaps you do as well—that there is nothing more "relaxing" than mindlessly scrolling through my Twitter feed. I understand what Simone Weil means when she says, "There is something in our soul which has a far more violent repugnance for true attention than the flesh has for bodily fatigue."[45] "Attention, taken to its highest degree, is the same thing as prayer. It presupposes faith and love. Absolutely unmixed attention is prayer."[46] In contrast to the siren's song of digital media, genuine attention is, says Weil, "the rarest and purest form of generosity."[47] Speaking of an even deeper kind of attention—contemplation—Birkerts says,

> Contemplation is not a subset category, not just one kind of thinking among many. It is the *point* of thinking, its alpha and omega. Contemplation directs itself at the existential, which is to say, at that which pertains to the possible *why* of our being. It abuts the religious, but also has a powerful secular formation.

---

43. McLuhan, *Understanding Media*, 18.
44. McLuhan, *Understanding Media*, 65.
45. Weil, *Waiting on God*, 56.
46. Weil, *Gravity and Grace*, 117.
47. Weil, *Gravity and Grace*, 117.

> Contemplation is what almost inevitably follows as soon as we allow the possibility that existence is neither trivial nor incidental; it is the mind, the spirit, looking to ask why not.[48]

Later, he explains,

> We need not just attention, but also *sustained* imagination. And these—I will risk vast generalization—are the two human attributes most at risk. Our fragmented, dispersed living is wreaking havoc on both, pushing at us the steady-breaking wave of competing stimuli on the one hand, and on the other offering the proxies that entertain us so effortlessly, sapping from us the special projective impetus that makes imagining possible.[49]

Perhaps the antidote to the technology of digital distraction, then, is the technology of reading. Not reading that is the mere skimming and decoding of words as a way to consume information. But rather the practice of deep, immersive reading that we wish to (if we do not already) practice in reading the Bible, or reading a work of good literature, or reading the look on a beloved's face, or reading a fine painting, or reading the signature of the Creator on a blazing sunset.

As a "People of the Book," Christians have a particular calling to preserve and promote the gift of deep reading—reading in both its literal and its metaphorical senses. The ability to read well is central to a Word-centered faith. Literary reading is central to cultivating the ability to use and understand language. Let us not neglect to be attentive to words, to contemplate the aesthetic aspect of our reading, to hold books in our hands, savoring the words, placing our finger inside to remind ourselves that the words—and the word of God—are not merely abstract symbols and signs—but ideas that take on flesh and dwell among us.

Bibliography

Birkerts, Sven. *Changing the Subject*. Minneapolis: Graywolf, 2015.
———. *The Gutenberg Elegies*. New York: Farrar, Straus, and Giroux, 2006.
———. "Reading in the Digital Age." In *The Edge of the Precipice: Why Read Literature in the Digital Age*, edited by Paul Socken, 27–41. Canada: McGill-Queen's University Press, 2013.
Carr, Nicholas. *The Shallows: What the Internet Is Doing to Our Brains*. New York: Norton, 2011.

---

48. Birkerts, *Changing the Subject*, 93.
49. Birkerts, *Changing the Subject*, 184.

Jeffrey, David Lyle. *People of the Book: Christian Identity and Literary Culture.* Grand Rapids: Eerdmans, 1996.
Johnson, Mark. *The Meaning of the Body.* Chicago: University of Chicago Press, 2007.
———. *Moral Imagination: Implications of Cognitive Science for Ethics.* Chicago: University of Chicago Press, 1993.
Lakoff, George, and Mark Johnson. *Metaphors We Live By.* Chicago: University of Chicago Press, 1980.
McEntyre, Marilyn. *Caring for Words in a Culture of Lies.* Grand Rapids: Eerdmans, 2009.
McLuhan, Marshall. "Electric Consciousness and the Church." In *The Medium and the Light: Reflections on Religion and Media*, edited by Eric McLuhan and Jack Szklarek, 79–88. Eugene, OR: Wipf and Stock, 2010.
———. *Understanding Media: The Extensions of Man.* Massachusetts: MIT Press, 1994.
Oatley, Keith. *Such Stuff as Dreams: The Psychology of Fiction.* Sussex: Wiley-Blackwell, 2011.
Plato. *Phaedrus.* In *The Collected Dialogues*, edited by Edith Hamilton and Huntington Cairns, 475–525. Translated by R. Hackforth. Princeton: Princeton University Press, 1989.
Postman, Neil. *Amusing Ourselves to Death: Public Discourse in the Age of Show Business.* New York: Penguin, 1985.
Prior, Karen Swallow. *On Reading Well: Finding the Good Life in Great Books.* Grand Rapids: Brazos, 2108.
Scarry, Elaine. *On Beauty and Being Just.* Princeton: Princeton University Press, 1999.
Steiner, George. *Real Presences.* Chicago: University of Chicago Press, 1989.
Taylor, Charles. *A Secular Age.* Cambridge: Belknap, 2007.
Taylor, Paul A. "Sympathy and Insight in Aristotle's Poetics." *Journal of Aesthetics and Art Criticism* 66.3 (2008) 265–80.
Ward, Graham. "How Literature Resists Secularity." *Literature and Theology* 24.1 (2010) 73-88.
Weil, Simone. *Gravity and Grace.* London and New York: Routledge, 2002.
———. *Waiting on God.* Oxon: Routledge, 2010.
Wolf, Maryanne. *Reader, Come Home: The Reading Brain in a Digital World.* New York: HarperCollins, 2018.

13

Digital Life and Social Media as Secular Liturgy

A Matter of Christian Formation

FELICIA WU SONG

TWO SUMMERS AGO, I left Facebook. I didn't deactivate my account. I didn't figure out how to archive or erase all my earlier posts. I didn't even say goodbye. I just sort of stopped checking one day and walked away. This is fairly unusual for me. I usually do a lot of research and thinking before I make any dramatic changes in my digital life. But leaving Facebook just kind of happened. I was fed up with Facebook's egregious disregard for its users' privacy, and I was disgusted by Zuckerberg's willful blindness about its growing role in damaging our democracy and exacerbating the fragility of so many others around the world.

Admittedly, there are times when I miss it. I feel a bit of an outcast because I am no longer on social media. There was the time my brother and his wife had vacationed in London and had assumed that I knew because they had posted travel photos on Facebook. Or those moments when something outrageous happens in the political world, I find myself wondering what my quick-witted grad school friends are saying about it. I do miss discovering the curated gems of news articles or essays that my friend Kate would post on her feed. I also miss the sunny feeling of affection that comes from seeing pictures of my friends' kids as they grow up, graduate high school, and move in on their first days of college.

With all that said, there are significant aspects of being on Facebook that I don't miss at all. I don't miss feeling that hankering to check my newsfeed every time I wake up, come out of a meeting, or sit in the car waiting to pick up my child from school. I don't miss feeling fidgety after I've posted something, constantly wondering if anyone has liked it. And I *really* don't miss experiencing that strange inversion in my psyche when my embodied life becomes background noise to my online life, which somehow comes to feel charged with an exclusive aura of excitement and significance.

The truth of the matter is, being without Facebook for over a year has helped me see more clearly how it had been shaping my sense of self and my relationships. When I was on Facebook and regularly experiencing the deliciously satisfying river of digital affirmation, I sometimes felt like I needed to engage, post, and publish in order to exist. At times, I had come to even feel that my relationships were primarily cultivated in terms of transactions and reciprocity as I liked or commented my way into trusting interdependence with others.

In my post-Facebook life, when I look around me in coffee shops or airport terminals, I am always taken by how many of us regularly wade through the thick rapids of social media, email, and messaging—and how it all has come to feel so remarkably normal. For isn't this how it feels and looks to be connected and to belong? Isn't it what it feels like and looks like to be productive? To be successful? And frankly, to be modern?

Every age is defined by a social imaginary. Charles Taylor explains that a social imaginary "incorporates a sense of the normal expectations we have of each other, the kind of common understanding that enables us to carry out the collective practices that make up our social life."[1] A social imaginary is a kind of story that a culture tells itself about what we believe to be our human condition and how we ought to live life together.

The main focus of this essay is to explore this distinctive story, the social imaginary that our digital practices are training us into, and how it is that it feels so remarkably normal, so desirable, so compelling—that is, until we encounter a startlingly different social imaginary. Consider the one that is embedded in Tish Harrison Warren's description of corporate confession found in Anglican Christian practice:

> In church each week, we repent together . . . Confession reminds us . . . our failures or successes in the Christian life are not what define us or determine our worth before God or God's people. Instead, we are defined by Christ's life and work on our behalf. We kneel . . . We confess and repent . . . And then—what a wonder!—the word of absolution: "Almighty God have mercy on you, forgive you all your sins through our Lord Jesus Christ,

---

1. Taylor, *Modern Social Imaginaries*, 24.

strengthen you in all goodness, and by the power of the Holy Spirit keep you in eternal life."

And then she goes on:

> When we confess and receive absolution together, we are reminded that none of our pathologies, neuroses, or sins, no matter how small or secret, affect only us. We are a church, a community, a family. We are not simply individuals with our pet sins and private brokenness . . . If we are saved, we are saved together—as the body of Christ, as a church. Because of this, I need to hear my forgiveness proclaimed not only by God but by a representative of the body of Christ in which I receive grace, to remind me that though my sin is worse that I care to admit, I'm still welcome here. I'm still called into this community and loved.[2]

After we have been drinking deeply of our digital world and its social imaginary, running across such an account of Christian confession and the church is to come up against something that feels positively alien. Warren's description brings into sharp relief the vast distance between the posture we practice when we are steeped in the social imaginary of our digital ecology and the posture that Christian spirituality encourages. Our normalized digital practices of keeping up, grasping for attention, and seeking the reward of affirmation begin to feel paltry and thin against the sheer magnificence of what is promised in the ritual of confession and absolution: to be invited to freely admit our failures and discover that we are still loved and welcomed.

What interests me most is the *pathos* of our contemporary circumstances: despite what we may profess in our faith, most of us float along, waking from time to time to discover how much we have strayed from this kingdom reality. Preoccupied by the circumstances and demands of daily life and ever trying to keep from getting left behind, we simply lose track of who or where we even are. We lose track of the fact that the Christian tradition produces a social imaginary that understands our embodiment, our worth, our relationship with time and the other in terms that are completely opposite from the story we are trained in when enmeshed within the contemporary digital ecology. In losing track, we live lives that often express a story that does not quite match up with the theological and faith commitments that so many of us profess to be true. This essay will first seek to examine this social imaginary that our digital practices are training us towards, consider the impact and implications of this story, and

---

2. Warren, *Liturgy of the Ordinary*, 58.

conclude with a reflection on how the church can and should respond and engage this cultural narrative that is powerfully shaping what we imagine it means to be human.

Our Digital Social Imaginary

One key feature of the social imaginary that comes with our digital ecology is the normalized expectation that we experience permanent connectivity. When you look at the history of mass communications and telecommunications, the promise of connection has been there from the start—from the telegraph, to radio, to television. At the core of the internet, in all of its amazing networking capacity, was a desire to connect, to share. But "being connected" in today's world means something dramatically different from what it meant back in the 1990s when the internet of yesteryear was accessed through a boxy desktop computer dialed into the walls of our homes or workplaces. In fact, "being connected" today is closer to a state of consciousness—a human condition—than a discrete behavior. Unlike the World Wide Web of old, the character of today's digital technologies and social media push us towards living in what media scholars call a state of permanent connectivity.

A major part of this shift occurred when the internet slipped beyond our desktop computers and into our phones and tablets. It became mobile and ubiquitous. With our digital devices ever in our pockets, in our bags, on our wrists, and even beneath our pillows when we sleep, we move through our days and nights draped with the immanent sense of the digital. Ever available and accessible, it is perpetually poised to tend to our desires, living and breathing at our sides. What also makes our current state of permanent connectivity so compelling and seemingly inevitable is the fact that the digital media and technology of today have become the primary portal to our social lives. Unlike the chat rooms from the 1990s which gave us contact to strangers, today's social media platforms like Facebook, Twitter, and Instagram capitalize on our existing networks of friends, family, colleagues, and professional contacts. Today, we are often drawn to the internet not because it connects us to the "information superhighway" or a limitless shopping extravaganza, but because it promises to connect us to those we love.

While going online today offers the possibility of communing with those we belong to in far-flung places, it is precisely because our digital experiences are thoroughly social that its ubiquity and mobility can become a problem. In her poignantly insightful books, *Alone Together* and *Reclaiming Conversation,* Sherry Turkle explores what it means that friends and family are now digitally tethered. Undoubtedly, on the plus side, to be constantly tethered to loved ones can be reassuring and pleasurable. But Turkle points out that it can also come to serve as a crutch when we become people incapable of solitude, fearful of being alone with ourselves, and prone to turning to our screens and away from our immediate surroundings whenever we feel awkward, bored, or anxious. Furthermore, being digitally tethered can foster a growing expectation of constant availability to one's friends and family regardless of time or day. Just as the digital is always accessible to us, we come to expect the same of people.

While our psychological longings to stay connected to the people we love may keep us in a constant state of vigilance and responsiveness to notifications at a moment's notice, our condition of permanent connectivity is further fed by the infinite novelty that is designed into our current digital media and services. From the moment a young person gets her own smartphone, she knows that she is gaining access to a mode of life that is perpetually filled with possibility. Her social media feeds are ceaselessly "refreshed," her games and apps are always "updating," and there are always new texts, new snaps, new "stories" to tend. When the mobile, social, and infinitely novel aspects of the contemporary digital experience are mixed together, the result is a psychological cocktail of pleasures, anxieties, and felt expectations. This is what it means to live in permanent connectivity: with our devices in our possession, the promise of fulfillment, completion, and emotional connection feels ever within a few inches of our reach. It is these key features that make the digital experiences of today very difficult to resist. Indeed, even if our devices are not powered on (or even in one's possession), our consciousness has become sufficiently trained and thoroughly immersed in the habits of mind formed by an unceasing awareness of the constantly shifting landscape of what is being said and posted in the digital realm. As Dalton Conley has described, life is constantly "being lived elsewhere" as our bodies are in one place, but our minds and consciousness dwell on the stuff of our screens.[3]

Mark Edmundson presciently captured this shift in consciousness all the way back in 2008, when he wrote about how the internet was changing the literature students he was teaching.

> Classes matter to them, but classes are just part of an ever-enlarging web of activities and diversions. Students now seek to master their work—not to be taken over by it and consumed. They want to dispatch it, do it well and quickly. Then get on to the many other things that interest them. For my students live

3. Conley, *Elsewhere, U.S.A.*

in the future and not the present... They dwell in possibility...
The idea is to keep moving, never to stop.[4]

After class, Edmundson observed what many professors still notice—the cell phones come out: "[Our students] need to disperse themselves again, get away from the immediate, dissolve the present away." With the infinitely novel content of digital media inevitably accruing over the course of a ninety-minute class, our students grasp for their phones at the end of class like oxygen tanks. As if we had submerged them underwater in our classes, they are finally coming up for air. Our classes have become the interruption in their lives, and they eagerly "dispatch" of their coursework as quickly as possible in order to get on with their "actual lives" which are mediated through their hand-held screens.

If we are honest, we know that college students are not the only ones who live like this. When we are at work, watching our kids, having lunch, or sitting through a meeting, our regular use of our digital devices has trained us to feel this sense that something else is always happening, something potentially more important, and we feel the itch to peek and know. The result is that, whatever is taking place around us, no matter what proximate reality we are submerged in, it begins to feel less interesting, more stifling, and more like something we want to be released from or bypass altogether.

It is no wonder that a professor of literature lamented this psychological outcome of digital technologies. For a teacher who has invested his life in guiding students to appreciate the richness embedded in the slow and steady work of story in our lives, it is a travesty to see students who seem constitutionally unable to disconnect from the digital flow. What becomes of us when we, too, become people so permanently connected to whatever streams of reality are being piped through our digital devices that we are incapable of allowing ourselves to be consumed, engulfed by the presence of another—whether it be a person, a piece of literature, or the triune God we profess to worship? In all this, I can't help but wonder if it might be rather apt to borrow the biblical notion of "abiding" to describe our relationship with our technologies today? In the same way that Jesus called his disciples to abide in him as he would abide in them, we, too, have become a people who abide in the digital, and the digital abides in us.

---

4. Edmundson, "Dwelling in Possibility," B7.

The Impact of the Digital Social Imaginary

A few years ago, a study reported that young people use their smartphones an average of five hours a day—roughly one-third of their total waking hours.[5] But what is actually more interesting about this study is the fact that, when participants were asked how much they thought they were on their phones, it turns out that they massively underestimated their use of their smartphones. What the researchers found was that participants used their devices roughly twice as much as they thought they did. Such a huge gap between perception and reality suggests that we are a people who have little or no awareness of what we are actually doing with our devices. The researchers write that these five hours often go by with little reflection because they are an accumulation of micro-moments—in between meetings, in between classes, waiting in line, waiting for the hot water to turn on. The digital practices that characterize our lives are largely habitual, automatic, and even compulsive.

In 2018, a Google study noted that our constant exposure to social media, email, and news apps on our smartphones is creating a "constant sense of obligation, generating unintended personal stress."[6] As our cortisol levels rise and we feel growing discomfort, we are driven to check our phones even more in order to relieve that anxiety. However, once we check again, we usually encounter something *else* that causes our cortisol levels to rise and the cycle of stress and connectivity begins again. Add on other trends in the collective disruptions in sleep we are experiencing: the vast majority of us sleep with our phones in our bedrooms within reach and are therefore prone to check our phones in the middle of the night to respond to a text, resume a game, or check our social media feeds. A 2012 seven-country poll found that over 70 percent of respondents eighteen to thirty-four years old reported sleeping with their phones in their bedrooms within reach. Additionally, 55–70 percent of adults thirty-five to sixty-four years old did the same.[7] All of these habits and outcomes are hardly surprising when we consider how the digital media industries are invested in securing and keeping our attention and unabashedly searching for new and more efficient ways to monetize our most basic needs for relationship and belonging.

Most users are unaware, or often forget, that social media like Instagram, Snapchat, Twitter, and YouTube are designed with the leading-edge insights of behavioral psychology and brain science to draw us in and keep us ensnared. The same experts that design casinos and other addictive

---

5. Andrews et al., "Beyond Self-Report."
6. Aranda and Baig, "Toward 'JOMO.'"
7. Khazan, "How Smartphones Hurt Sleep."

industries are brought in to consult about what types of notifications, what color buttons and badges, what types of emotional content are optimal for training our brains to become activated with dopamine that charge up the pleasure and novelty pathways of our brains. Brilliantly calculated algorithms have been painstakingly developed to chew through the trail of data that we have consented to have collected about ourselves—whose posts we respond to, what videos we watch and ignore, our click patterns, our viewing times, keywords in our emails in order to calculate the optimal way to keep us tethered to their site. All this data is used to deliver the content that these platforms think we want, but not necessarily the nuances and complexities of reality that we so desperately need individually and collectively.

While digital compulsions and collective sleep deprivation (and the role that the digital media industry may play in intentionally engineering such tendencies) may be seen as some of the troublesome effects of our permanent connectivity, I want to return to the question of our digital ecology's social imaginary—the particular story that it tells about the human condition—and nudge us in a more explicitly sociological direction. Max Weber classically laid down a foundation for thinking about the effects of industrialization on our modern human condition, and since then, contemporary theorists have drawn on Weber to argue that the logic and techniques of bureaucracies and corporate management have come to impact the most intimate of our relational experiences in family and friendship. In kind, I believe that social media and our digital ecology have the effect of industrializing our relationships by shaping the postures and expectations we bring to our mediated communications and interactions online. Here are just three brief examples of how this happens.

1. The Drive to Quantify

The social media industry has not only constructed an elaborate digital ecology that collects quantified data about us, but it perpetually frames and infuses our experience of relationships, communication, and information with numbers. If we stop and think about it, what does it mean to predominantly sustain relationships through platforms where we are encouraged to evaluate the quality of our social lives through lists and counts of followers, friends, likes, shares, posts, comments, or even a single number that so publicly quantifies our degree of influence and worth? Of course, it might sound silly and perhaps even pathetic to suggest that we *actually* base our sense of self or our social standing on these numbers, but how many of us can honestly say that we aren't mildly injured when few people (or, my heavens, when *no one!*) gives our post a thumbs up or like? How many of us can honestly say that we don't feel a jolt of satisfaction when someone finds so much value added by what we have offered on the altar of the social media feed that they actually "share" or "retweet" it?

When we daily interface within a digital environment that encourages us to measure the chances of success or failure in our social lives as a matter of quantity of connections, rather than their quality, can we be so confident as to assert that our imaginations and appetites are not shaped—in some small but substantive way—by what the industry has defined as important? As social media perpetually updates our numbers, so too do we perpetually check them. And when we check, what exactly are we looking for? What do the numbers mean and what do they mask? Is it an assurance of belonging? Legitimacy? Being desired?

2. *The Drive to Reify*

The fun of social media is that, like satellite TV or a Las Vegas buffet, there is always something new to consume. Unlike the scarcity of relationships that humans have historically had to make do with, the blessing of social media is the promise of abundance. Unfortunately, like many things in life, the blessing also becomes the curse. As we typically straddle multiple platforms each day, the sheer volume of interaction and content that we are privy to forces us to develop techniques of management to process, read, delete, skip over, or engage this ceaseless stream of requests for our attention.

This quandary of abundance drives us toward what social theorist Georg Lukacs called reification: a process where "a relation between people [that] takes on the character of a *thing*."[8] Through reification, I move closer to treating the dynamic between you and me as a "thing." And I also become inclined to objectify the people I love and the messages they post as mere tasks to complete, or as a means to be used or manipulated to boost my numbers and my ego. Through reification, I "relate" less and I "broadcast" more. Through reification, I mechanize the complex dance that social interaction involves and prefer the pre-packaged templates of emojis and likes. When the dynamic between you and me becomes closer to a "thing," I can go on to Facebook, Instagram, or Twitter and just as easily gossip, announce a milestone, offer a compliment, or heap verbal violence upon you with little or no difference in emotional cost or effect.

---

8. Lukacs, "Reification," 83–222.

3. The Drive to Control

Because there is so much digital stimulation such that we can never give each iota of data its due, for the sake of efficiency and productivity we have to decide what is not essential, or put more crudely—what is considered waste. This drive to control is often mechanized and preemptive. As we get habituated into the industrialized ecology of social media, where we take for granted the desire to become more efficient and better trained in our drives to quantify and reify, we also subconsciously make decisions about what we view as waste.

In the context of our digital age, social theorist Zygmunt Bauman writes, "Making eye contact and thereby acknowledging the physical proximity of another human being spells waste: it portends the necessity of spending a portion of precious, yet loathsomely scarce time on deep diving [into embodied interaction]."[9] Bauman does not spare us his indictment, but the truth is: we know that we have all been there. We have all made that split-second decision to ignore the person next to us in order to attend to our screens. We all know that meaningful embodied interactions with family, friends, colleagues, and neighbors take a lot of work and that the payoff can be great. It is, as Bauman puts it, a form of deep diving. But when we are preoccupied and tired, and are *still looking for some kind of payoff*, it is often more appealing to indulge in social media's promise of a dopamine hit or to answer one more email in order to bring down our anxiety by a notch. To tend to those who are physically proximate to us, Bauman writes, is "a decision that would interrupt or pre-empt" our hungry ritual of clicking through so many other potentially more interesting or more productive possibilities. Taken together, when we daily train in the drives to quantify, reify, and control, we arguably begin to live into a distinctive story of what it means to be human, a social imaginary that fundamentally positions the self at the center of reality.

In his account of the historical transformation of personal identity in Western civilization, Charles Taylor's book *Sources of the Self* argues that the sources of identity have shifted from external transcendent sources to internal subjective sources of the individual.[10] Even in our most recent history, with the decline of local community as an orienting factor to modern individuals, contemporary Americans have increasingly come to understand "community" in terms of multiple networks of friends, contacts, and acquaintances which span time and place—but which orient around the self.

---

9. Bauman, *44 Letters*, 14.
10. Taylor, *Sources of the Self*.

In this context, social media platforms feel like seamless additions to modern life because they fit who we are and what our social institutions have already become in the early twenty-first century. Sociologist Barry Wellman calls this phenomenon "networked individualism," and he recognizes how social media is organized around networked individualism's key premise that there is no meaningful source of orientation external to the self.[11] The network radiates out from the center—a center that is not a location, a cause, or a common identity—it is simply you.

Indeed, as we engage in digital media's permanent connectivity, the plausibility of this networked individualist gains a foothold as we discover that, while each of us is at the center of our networks, we are also competing against each other—vying for attention, people's time, and positive reinforcement—driven to quantify, reify, and control. And in doing so, despite the fact that so many of us enjoy material abundance, we are a people trained to see our world in terms of scarcity. Here, I again turn to Tish Harrison Warren to juxtapose two contrary social imaginaries that American Christians must begin to acknowledge and wrestle with.

> In contemporary America, our daily formation [through our habits of consumption] is often at odds with our formation in word and sacrament. In this alternative economy of the true bread of life, we are turned inside out so that we are no longer people marked by scarcity, jockeying for our own good, but are new people, truly nourished, and therefore able to extend nourishment to others. The economy of the eucharist is true abundance. There is enough for me, not in spite of others, but because we receive Christ together as a community.[12]

Indeed, the promise of the gospel speaks of a radical promise of abundance, and the work of the church is to be a demonstration plot of how to live into this promise. As our soul formation (or more accurately, deformation) is taking place every day in our digital ecology, the church is supposed to counter-form us. We are supposed to learn how this new economy of the Eucharist and the inexplicable multiplication of bread and loaves can subvert the zero-sum game of our society. How do we get ourselves turned inside out so that we no longer feel compelled to jockey for our own good? How do we get closer to that promised reality where we can lay down our sword and follow the lamb and cease feeling driven by the predatorial instincts of the warrior or the lion? How do we let go of the former things and submit ourselves to becoming a new people?

11. Wellman and Rainie, *Networked*.
12. Warren, *Liturgy of the Ordinary*, 73.

In this way, I think the iconic computer scientist Jaron Lanier was onto something very true when he wrote that living in the flow of social media and its practices means you "implicitly accept a new spiritual framework . . . You have agreed to change something intimate about your relationship with your soul . . . You have probably, to some degree . . . effectively renounced what you might think is your religion, even if that religion is atheism."[13] Lanier views social media's spiritual framework to be characterized by optimization. He argues that social media shapes us so that we come to view time, place, others, and even ourselves instrumentally; we come to think that everything in this world is merely fodder for us to use and manipulate for our own pleasure and good. Therefore, every time we begin to even think in terms of optimizing our identities or optimizing our relationships by optimizing our online presence for more views, more likes, and more followers, Lanier argues that we have effectively renounced our formal religious commitments and begun to serve a new master. "You have been baptized," he proclaims.[14]

If Lanier is right, the story embedded in contemporary digital ecologies not only competes against the spiritual frameworks we profess, it also distorts and undermines our capacity to commune with God and others in the ways that we were created because it "baptizes" us into utilitarian and industrialized conceptions of time, place, relationship, and the human condition. This is a serious contention for those of us in faith communities who only see technology as a tool. It reveals how we profoundly underestimate the deeply spiritual function that digital technologies actually play in our struggles against isolation, fear, and meaninglessness. It also reveals how profoundly we underestimate the ways in which our faith is socially situated within and often distorted when understood through the lens and framework of Western consumer culture.

The Call on the Church in This Digital Age

For a long while, I had thought that the way to motivate resistance against the impoverishing effects of the digital was to seek a more truthful understanding of technology's fundamental nature—that is, the truth about its moral valances and its social, cultural, and political power. I thought that resistance could be summoned when a proper understanding of the theology of technology was attained—when everyone could see clearly how

---

13. Lanier, *Ten Arguments*, 126.
14. Lanier, *Ten Arguments*, 126.

it functions as an artifact of our God-given creative powers, but is also bound up in the fallenness of creation.

But I have personally observed how such understanding does little to help me tame my own life habits and properly situate the digital in my life. As a result, I have come to think that maybe what we need is not so much more knowledge about technology, but a deeper understanding of being human and a far more serious and more creative attempt at living more deeply into that understanding. This would require establishing a sufficiently robust theological anthropology that asserts that human beings were created to enjoy communion with God, our neighbor, and the created order within the possibilities and limitations of place and time. To this end, one starting point that I have found particularly generative is the Augustinian understanding of Christian formation and bodily practices as James K.A. Smith has described in his works, *Desiring the Kingdom* and *You Are What You Love*. In these works, Smith argues that rather than assuming that we are formed primarily by knowledge or beliefs, we should better appreciate how we are shaped by our loves—what churns in our guts—as indicated most often through what we do with our corporeal bodies.

To me, this theological anthropology that Smith proposes is especially helpful in illuminating how, despite what knowledge we may have about how corporations are manipulating us through the addictive designs of our apps and devices, or how corrosive the verbal violence on Facebook or Twitter can be to our souls, despite our intuitive sense that aspects of our digital habits are impoverishing our lives, few of us intentionally work to curb these habits. We *know* a lot about how we should live, but that knowledge doesn't often translate into a transformed life. No. Our problem is not a lack of knowledge. Our problem is a lack of recognition in the formative powers of the visceral and the bodily. If we take to heart this assertion that what we do with our bodies indicates and trains our loves, then we can begin to see how we are being formed and trained in our daily lives—in each little routine—towards some goal, some *telos*. In all of our digital practices of checking our emails, reading our social media feeds, responding on Twitter, when we first wake up, right before we go to bed, in between meetings, waiting in lines, our desires and our souls are being formed in a particular direction. Like a vine on a trellis, we are being trained towards becoming some sort of person.

Unfortunately, when we are unreflective about our practices and simply following the taken-for-granted norms in our society, we inevitably find ourselves engaging in what Smith calls "secular liturgies," personal and cultural habits that we routinely practice with our bodies, which have the effect of *mis*-forming our desires. These secular liturgies ultimately misdirect our desires towards those things that falsely claim to fulfill our longings and that manage to draw us away from the very communion with God for which our souls thirst. So, what are we to do—especially when it comes to our digital practices? We need to recognize them as secular liturgies and awaken to how our bodily behaviors both signal and shape something about our loves and who we are becoming. We need to be asking: In our everyday senses and digital routines, are we cultivating the capacity to recognize the glory of the divine that is often everywhere, but hidden for only those who have eyes to see and ears to hear? Or are our routines comprised of secular liturgies that are setting up blinders and obstacles to hearing the still small voice of our Lord?

After becoming conscious of how our secular liturgies are framing our lives, Smith encourages us to identify and exercise "counter-liturgies" that push back against the mis-formations of the heart. Instead of simply removing the bad, we ought to fill ourselves with something good. Why? Because, as Saint Augustine famously intuited: our hearts are restless and will remain so until we find our rest in God. So, in response to our digital secular liturgies—checking our phones whenever we're bored, our soothing daily wind-down of thirty minutes with Candy Crush or Instagram—we should ask: How can we disrupt these digital habits and open ourselves up to the opportunity to taste a different kind of living? Can we seek out generative approaches to developing practices and routines that can redirect our loves *back* to experiencing communion with God and others in our lives?

An obvious place to begin looking for counter-liturgies is within our Christian heritage of spiritual disciplines. The disciplines of solitude, silence, scriptural reading, prayer, fasting—all of them can be practiced in their traditional forms or adapted to the digital context (such as fasting from particular apps or devices). They can be seen anew as counter-liturgies that serve to push back against the subtle but real mis-formations of the heart when our lives are framed by the dictates of the digital. Another approach to counter-liturgies is to think in terms of experiments, which can create situations that have the potential to reveal to ourselves the dependence we have on our digital devices. Experiments can be modest and contained ways to begin encouraging ourselves to step out of our comfort zones and try developing a taste for something new that, though frightening at first, might actually become a precious source of life and vitality. Here are two very basic experiments to try:

- Over and against our secular liturgies of digital multi-tasking: What if we engaged in experiments in mono-tasking? When we drive, only driving? When we are waiting in line, just waiting? When we are doing our laundry, just doing laundry? In those moments of mono-tasking, we could pay attention to what happens to our brains if we stop filling them with content or an agenda? Do we become more aware of the places and locations where we are? What do we hear in our souls or from God when there is quiet?

- What if we committed to turning off our phones for an hour once a week and went about our lives with it hidden away in a desk drawer or car trunk? Would we feel anxiety and panic? Or liberation and restoration? Whatever we experience, how might that reaction help us discover what lies in our very being and what we need to wrestle with before our merciful Lord?

A third way to approach counter-liturgies is to think in terms of creatively guarding essential aspects of our personhood. For example, in an attempt to better respect the reality of our embodiment or presence, we might begin by guarding sacred spaces. Some of us might already do this when we commit to guarding our dining table as a sacred space for mutual presence, conversation, and eating. We might work to keep our phones and digital devices away from that space during meals. Others of us might decide that our bedrooms at night are sacred spaces for rest and stillness. To protect that space then, we might all commit to setting our phones to charge on a dock somewhere in our house that is far away from our bedrooms. As for guarding sacred time, and learning to inhabit time rather than spend it, we might decide to avoid our phones for the first thirty minutes of our waking hours and decide to devote our first brain synapses and wakeful attention on prayer and meditation, Scripture reading, and exercise.

While we can each practice these new possibilities as individuals, what I particularly like about Smith's use of the terms "secular liturgy" and "counter-liturgy" is his choice of the word "liturgy." In its Greek origins, liturgy means "work of the people." Such a definition brings out the way that certain practices are not truly "individual" in nature but are actually the product of "the people"—that is, many people, a community, a culture. And when we consider how social media and so many of our digital practices actually work, we inevitably see that they retain their power and remain sustainable precisely because they are practiced *as* a people, a group, or a culture. So, if secular liturgies are practices that possess power because we engage in them together, then Christians need to find a way to engage in bodily counter-liturgies together. While personal acts of technological self-discipline and restraint are still essential, I believe it will ultimately be the communal effort in counter-liturgies—the work of the people—that proves effective and sustainable.

Conclusion

Several years ago, long-time political commentator Andrew Sullivan wrote an essay explaining why, after suffering a series of major health breakdowns, he had decided to leave his very successful career as a blogger and digital presence. In his poignant essay, "I Used to Be a Human Being," he reflects: "I am saturated in digital life, and I want to return to the actual world again . . . I want to read again, slowly, carefully. I want to absorb a difficult book and walk around in my own thoughts with it for a while . . . I want to spend some time with my parents, while I still have them . . . and rekindle the friendships that I have simply had to let wither."[15] Even though Sullivan was writing in the context of his own failing health and personal need to step away from an insanely demanding career commitment, I believe he was onto something important that speaks into our first-world modern condition: What would it be like to "walk around in our own thoughts about something for a while"? What would it be like to do anything slowly, carefully? To simply absorb and be absorbed by something delightfully difficult enough to nourish and feed the complex appetites of our souls? To spend time with people in such a way that honors the temporary nature of the gift of their company? To refuse to be swept away by life's winds, but to spend time gently and carefully rekindling a friendship like how one thoughtfully builds a fire that will endure and provide warmth to all who draw near? In many ways, Sullivan had the luxury to walk away from the digital realm. And I wholly appreciate that, for a variety of reasons, most of us do not. And yet, what I believe makes these rhetorical questions sound so impossible to us is because it tells a story, it speaks a social imaginary, that is quite contrary to the prevailing social imaginary of our digital environs.

I find it interesting that it has become more acceptable in the last three to four years to openly discuss the personal and cultural costs of our permanent connectivity. Christians and non-Christians alike have grown more tired and hungry for a different mode of living. As a culture, we lament digital addictions and the toxic nature of online discourse. We buy books like *How to Break Up with Your Phone* or *Digital Minimalism*, written not by curmudgeonly Luddites, but rather mainstream writers like Caroline Price and Cal Newport. And we willingly spend hundreds on digital detox retreats and try to regain a sense of discipline in our lives using productivity apps like Freedom or Moment.

We are clearly a culture that is restless and still hungry for something we can't put our finger on. At such a critical moment—when people in our society are searching for something different from the status quo, the

---

15. Sullivan, "I Used to Be a Human Being."

church has an opportunity to proclaim a refreshing gospel vision of what it means to be human and demonstrate the richness that in fact lies in Christian theology, heritage, and praxis. In light of this opportunity, Andrew Sullivan—himself a person of faith—brings a rather pointed indictment to the church when he writes,

> If the churches came to understand that the greatest threat to faith today is not hedonism but distraction, perhaps they might begin to appeal anew to a frazzled digital generation. Christian leaders seem to think that they need more distraction to counter the distraction. Their services have degenerated into emotional spasms, their spaces drowned with light and noise and locked shut throughout the day, when their darkness and silence might actually draw those whose minds and souls have grown web-weary.[16]

His point here is not to engage in the protracted debates over the superiority of traditional or contemporary worship, but to make the larger claim that maybe the church needs to stop trying to compete with the allure of media entertainment and all that is digital—"countering distraction with more distraction." Rather, the church ought to have confidence that people actually want the truth of what is naturally built into the DNA of Christianity—that the presence of Christ *in us* and *with us* when we gather together is life-transformative. And that we worship a God who is not only powerful in his merciful and loving redemption of us and all of creation, but also a God whose hiddenness requires those of us trained in contemporary sensibilities of our digital age to practice the quieting of our inner being, to learn how to trust the creaturely parameters of our bodies and brains, in order to hear the still, small voice that is already speaking to us.

The core problem is not distraction. The core problem is that our Christian communities do not see ourselves as active schools of love, training sites of confession, and theologies of abundance, places for training our appetites and imaginations that will inevitably run up against the grain of the digital. As Sullivan admonishes, to attempt to compete against the digital carnival is to miss out on how the gospel message has always been about playing a wholly different game. Jesus's promises in John 14 to his disciples pave a completely different way: I give to you not as the world gives. Don't be troubled or afraid. I won't leave you as orphans. I will come to you. We will come and make our home with them. Peace I leave with you. My peace I give you.

---

16. Sullivan, "I Used to Be a Human Being."

The truth of the matter is: what people want is something different from what the world is giving them. Something that frees them from the ensnarement of contemporary life that they feel so deeply bound in. Interestingly, CEOs in Silicon Valley understand this desire for something different when they send their children to tech-free schools. Leading edge art museums understand this when they hand out colored pencils and paper to visitors to draw and doodle as they come into the presence of art. Musicians and performers understand this when they have their audiences lock their digital devices in Yondr neoprene bags in order to be fully present in the live performance experience. Our Jewish brothers and sisters understand this when they ask congregants to turn off and put away all electronic devices in the synagogue because they see the synagogue as a holy place of worship where the word of God dwells, deserving reverence and respect. Practicing Buddhists understand this when they offer teachings and workshops on meditation and mindfulness.

What is the good news that Christians have to offer to this web-weary world? We have a social imaginary that is rooted in a theology of embodiment, in a creational theology, a Trinitarian theology, pneumatology, and much more. Most of all, we have an incarnational Savior who knew what it felt like to be pressed into the limits of time and space, but radically modeled to us how to live into that time and space—making those elements his friends, not his enemies—with love and mercy that brought forth the healing and transformation that all of humanity desires. May this be a season in the life of the church when we awaken and become reacquainted with what we profess to believe and what riches are already embedded in our spiritual traditions and practices.

Bibliography

Andrews, Sally, David A. Ellis, Heather Shaw, and Lukasz Piwek. "Beyond Self-Report: Tools to Compare Estimated and Real-World Smartphone Use." *PLoS ONE* 10.10 (2015).

Aranda, Julie H., and Safia Baig. "Toward 'JOMO': the Joy of Missing Out and the Freedom of Disconnecting." *MobileHCI '18: Proceedings of the 20th International Conference on Human-Computer-Interaction with Mobile Devices and Services* 19 (2018) 1–8.

Bauman, Zygmunt. *44 Letters from the Liquid Modern World.* Cambridge: Polity, 2010.

Conley, Dalton. *Elsewhere, U.S.A.: How We Got from the Company Man, Family Dinners, and the Affluent Society to the Home Office, BlackBerry Moms, and Economic Anxiety.* New York: Vintage, 2010.

Edmundson, Mark. "Dwelling in Possibility." *Chronicle of Higher Education* 54.27 (2008) B7.

Khazan, Olga. "How Smartphones Hurt Sleep." *Atlantic*, February 24, 2015. https://www.theatlantic.com/health/archive/2015/02/how-smartphones-are-ruining-our-sleep/385792/.

Lanier, Jaron. *Ten Arguments for Deleting Your Social Media Accounts Right Now*. New York: Henry Holt, 2018.

Lukacs, Georg. "Reification and the Consciousness of the Proletariat." In *History and Class Consciousness*, translated by Rodney Livingstone, 88–222. Cambridge: MIT Press, 1971. First published 1923.

Newport, Cal. *Digital Minimalism: Choosing a Focused Life in a Noisy World*. New York: Penguin, 2019.

Price, Caroline. *How to Break Up with Your Phone: The 30-Day Plan to Take Back Your Life*. New York: Ten Speed, 2019.

Smith, James K.A. *Desiring the Kingdom: Worship, Worldview, and Cultural Formation*. Grand Rapids: Baker Academic, 2009.

———. *You Are What You Love: The Spiritual Power of Habit*. Grand Rapids: Brazos, 2016.

Sullivan, Andrew. "I Used to be a Human Being." *New York Magazine*, September 18, 2016. https://nymag.com/intelligencer/2016/09/andrew-sullivan-my-distraction-sickness-and-yours.html.

Taylor, Charles. *Modern Social Imaginaries*. Durham: Duke University Press, 2004.

———. *Sources of the Self: The Making of the Modern Identity*. Cambridge: Harvard University Press, 1989.

Turkle, Sherry. *Alone Together: Why We Expect More from Technology and Less from Each Other*. New York: Basic, 2011.

———. *Reclaiming Conversation: The Power of Talk in a Digital Age*. New York: Penguin, 2015.

Warren, Tish Harrison. *Liturgy of the Ordinary: Sacred Practices in Everyday Life*. Downers Grove: InterVarsity, 2016.

Wellman, Barry, and Lee Rainie. *Networked: The New Social Operating System*. Cambridge: MIT Press, 2014.

14

Partnering with Pastors

How Early Modern Printers Advanced the Reformation

JENNIFER POWELL MCNUTT

Accelerated Technological Progress

BY ALL ACCOUNTS, WE are living through a time of unprecedented technological change. Ray Kurzweil, director of engineering for Google, has explained that unlike other periods of technological growth, our society's overall rate of progress is doubling every decade. He writes in *The Singularity Is Near*, "We won't experience one hundred years of technological advance in the twenty-first century; we will witness on the order of twenty thousand years of progress (again, when measured by today's rate of progress), or about one thousand times greater than what was achieved in the twentieth century."[1] No doubt we have all witnessed how technology has come to shape the moments of our lives in significant and everyday ways that are noticeable and even unnoticeable with the passing of time.

If there truly is such a thing, it has come to my attention that I am part of the "Xennial" generation also known as the "Oregon Trail Generation"[2]—a microgeneration between Gen X and the Millennials bridging the generational paradigm shifts of technology today thanks to an analog childhood and a digital adulthood.[3] I used rotary dial phones as a kid and then owned the ubiquitous Nokia cell phone by the end of college. I was one of those who

---

1. Kurzweil, *Singularity Is Near*, 11.
2. Garvey, "Oregon Trail Generation."
3. Stankorb and Oelbaum, "Reasonable People Disagree."

had a Myspace account and then abandoned it for Facebook. I understand the actual meaning behind common phrases such as "roll up the window" and "hang up the phone." In 1996, I was writing my high school senior thesis on an electric typewriter, using the card catalogue in the library, and writing my research quotes and data on notecards that were arranged on the floor. I still recall my parents talking about the benefits of the Xerox machine instead of the need for carbon paper. My entire research process and writing experience was straight out of the 1960s. Then just two months later, I started my bachelor's degree at Westmont College and was sitting in my first computer lab. I had an email address and access to the internet with no sense of what that meant. I recall struggling to choose what I thought would be my *one* password and then trying to get information from the internet when webpages still looked exactly like typed flyers. The web was mimicking the "memo culture" of the previous generation, and because there was no zoom function, the information was nearly impossible to read.

Nothing has been straightforward about navigating these technological shifts as they reshape our society and culture in ways that most of us could not have predicted today, including the way in which our dependence on technology has been accelerated by the COVID-19 pandemic.[4] During this global crisis, technology has proven to be a lifeline by allowing us to continue a level of work, fellowship, and social interaction not possible for generations before. As one recent *New York Times* article headline read, "Coronavirus Ended the Screen-Time Debate. Screens Won."[5] Out of necessity, church leaders were thrust into virtual church ministry, and survival left little room for reflection. How should pastors and churches effectively and faithfully navigate our world of accelerated technological change for the sake of the gospel?

As unprecedented as today's technological changes may seem, the church has managed the complications of shifting technologies and communication systems before. The Protestant Reformation of the sixteenth century was an era profoundly shaken and shaped by the moveable-type printing press. According to his *Table Talk*, Luther regarded the technological leap of the printing press as a source of God's blessing: "Printing is God's ultimate and greatest gift. Indeed, through printing God wants the whole world, to the ends of the earth, to know the roots of true religion and wants to transmit it in every language. Printing is the last flicker of the flame which

---

4. This portion was added after the conference and while editing during the outbreak of COVID-19.

5. Bowles, "Coronavirus Ended the Screen-Time Debate."

glows before the end of this world."[6] The capability to circulate identical copies of ideas *en masse* from mid-fifteenth-century Europe on was a game changer, and Luther's success and the spread of the Reformation cannot be understood apart from this technological shift. Yet, there is a human side to the story of the printing press's use that is all too easily overlooked.

This essay will explore how the Protestant Reformation managed the technological acceleration of its day through partnerships that developed between pastors and printers, the media makers of their time, and how those relationships were instrumental in shaping the future of the church and its ministry through the use of the press.

The "Xennial" Generation of Early Modern Print

The fact that Johannes Gutenberg's invention of the moveable type printing press in Mainz, Germany, was a milestone moment for the Western world is not up for debate. It has been estimated that the printing press led to more texts being published in the forty-year period from 1460 to 1500 (around thirty to thirty-five thousand different editions published estimated at fifteen to twenty million copies) than the entire medieval period combined.[7] The expansion of print in the sixteenth century, by comparison, reached one hundred fifty to two hundred million different copies published,[8] with Luther's works dominating the din. Monastic scriptoriums could not hold a candle to the output of the printing press in the sixteenth century, and yet, the success of print was hardly a foregone conclusion when it first emerged.

Any technological paradigm shift can be slow to catch on, especially when it disrupts normative patterns of human industry that intersect with social and economic systems. The process of printing was still labor-intensive, including casting metal type from a mold, setting the matrix, rolling the ink, and feeding the paper one at a time. Book binding was also unhelpfully elaborate at the start. The "Xennial" generation of early modern printers published books that mimicked medieval manuscripts in their formatting and style because those visual cues were still the markers of an authoritative document. Adding color and images required effort and expense, but they communicated a familiar look to the eye. Early on, printers used parchment or vellum rather than paper to print books. Parchment

---

6. Gilmont, "Introduction," 1. The quote is based on Luther, "Tischreden, 1. Band," 523.

7. Lindberg, *European Reformations*, 35; based upon conservative estimates of Febvre and Martin's *The Coming of the Book*, 262.

8. Febvre and Martin, *Coming of the Book*, 262.

had been the preferred writing support of the day due to its sturdy and enduring quality, but it did not suit the demands of the printing press.[9] Paper processed from old rags was slowly earning respect for its durability and flexibility, thanks to improved production processes and a significant drop in cost.[10] At one time, the use of paper unfairly demeaned the quality of the writing itself—the work was guilty by association. We can understand this when choosing to write a "thank you" note on expensive stationary rather than ruled school paper; only card stock truly shows you care. The high demand for books and the limited access to vellum transformed paper into a commercial commodity. In these ways, print benefited from time to grow into its function, form, and value.

As a result, the printing press was a bit of a slow burn until Luther came along. No one could have predicted that this unknown monk teaching at a brand-new university in an out-of-the-way town would have such a significant and enduring impact on the church and Western society, let alone the printing industry. Wittenberg's rise to prominence as a significant printing hub in Europe and the largest in Germany was as unexpected as Luther's rise to prominence, especially since the city did not even own a printing press until 1502, when the university was founded.[11] Nevertheless, within just five years from the moment that he wrote the *95 Theses*, Luther became the most published author in Europe ever.[12]

Printers issued nearly five thousand editions of Luther's works over the course of the century, primarily in Germany and in the German language, as well as three thousand other projects that included his involvement.[13] By the end of the century, Luther's writings "had been published more frequently than any known author in the history of Western letters."[14] With religious publications tending to dominate Europe's printing markets, Luther's voice helped generate a thriving industry that reached well beyond Germany. The Papal Nuncio Aleander's report from the Diet of Worms reflects a sense of panic over the rapid spread of Luther's writings to Spain,

---

9. The use of parchment required too many animal skins, was too expensive, and the demand was too high for the limits of the resource (Werner, *Studying Early Printed Books*, 26).

10. This process of papermaking first developed in China and then spread to the Arab world and Europe.

11. This is emphasized by Pettegree's *Brand Luther*, xi.

12. Pettegree, *Brand Luther*, xii.

13. Pettegree, *Brand Luther*, 334. Pettegree reports that 80 percent of Luther's works were published in the German language. Luther's publishing success outside of Germany defies expectation (Pettegree, *Brand Luther*, 109).

14. Pettegree, *Brand Luther*, 115.

Belgium (Ghent), Holland, and lower Germany (Munster, Utrecht).[15] He declared, "No one knows a way of confronting the heresy; even those who fear Luther speak in his favor." Aleander continued bemoaning Luther's role in "letting the dogs out," so to speak, stating, "Outside of this the whole world is our enemy, and the mad dogs, the Germans, are equipped with weapons of the spirit and of the body and know quite well how to boast that they no longer are stupid beasts like their ancestors but have now diverted the Tiber into their Rhine."[16] Notably, this was said before Luther even published his German Bible.

After Luther and his books received the imperial ban from Emperor Charles V at the Diet of Worms in 1521, Frederick of Saxony arranged for Luther's kidnapping to the Wartburg. While in hiding, Luther turned his attention to the translation of the Bible based on the second edition of Erasmus's Greek New Testament (1519), as well as with the assistance of his colleague and Greek language expert, Philip Melanchthon. After eleven weeks, the translation was complete. Luther's achievement was a folio that came to be known anonymously as the "September Testament," although his authorship was no mystery. Immediately, Duke George of Saxony (Frederick the Wise's cousin) banned Luther's New Testament, but it received the warmest of welcomes from the populace, selling out an unprecedented three thousand copies in the first run by December.[17] Johann Cochlaeus, Luther's opponent and anti-biographer, famously bemoaned the success of Luther's German Bible, saying that it was read by "tailors and shoemakers, even women and simpletons."[18] And yet, Luther's New Testament only became more accessible as it moved from exclusive sale in folio format to quarto size for better travel and use. By his death in 1546, Luther's German Bible in whole or in part had gone through nearly four hundred and fifty editions.[19] No matter how you look at it, the dynamic that developed between Luther and the printing press was extraordinary. As Pettegree argues, Luther could not have succeeded without the printing press, and the printing press could not have evolved without Luther.[20] This symbiosis was dependent, however, upon Luther's close proximity to and partnership with printers, even in cases when those partnerships proved frustrating.

15. He was the diplomatic representative of the pope at the Diet of Worms (1521).
16. Thuhn, "Papal Nuncio's Reports," 41.
17. Pettegree, *Brand Luther*, 186–88.
18. Johannes Cochlaeus, *Historia Martini Lutheri* (1582), 120, cited in Gow, "Challenging the Protestant Paradigm," 162–63.
19. Pettegree, *Brand Luther*, 188.
20. Pettegree, *Brand Luther*, 338.

Before the 95 *Theses*, Luther began to partner with the local Wittenberg printer, Johann Rhau-Grunenberg.[21] He was, in fact, the *only* printer in town because he alone had been convinced to take the job in 1508. When Luther's writing began to take Europe by storm, by all accounts, Rhau-Grunenberg was not up to the task. His inability to meet the rapid and frenzied turnover of Luther's writings proved a liability at key moments, leading to unnecessary controversy and misunderstandings involving Luther's works.[22] The process at the time required Luther to visit the printing house daily to ensure that no lost, stolen, or poorly printed pages crept into the publications. Although it was abundantly clear that Luther and Rhau-Grunenberg were unequally yoked, a remote printer created its own challenges. At times, Luther expressed appreciation for Rhau-Grunenberg's honesty and loyalty, despite a keen sense of exasperation for the slow pace of his work and remarkable lack of style and skill.[23] Luther's frustration with other printers is documented in a letter to George Spalatin where he bemoans how greed can lead to sloppy printing, though Scripture demands precision for the sake of the gospel message.[24]

The importance of collaborating with skilled printers deeply invested in expanding the evangelical message was not lost on him. It was only a matter of time until Luther actively recruited more printers to Wittenberg who fit the bill. The Lotter family (Melchior and sons Melchior the Younger and Michael) established a branch of their publishing house in Wittenberg after connecting with Luther at the Leipzig Disputation of 1519.[25] Their support lasted decades. Hans Lufft began printing in Wittenberg in 1523, producing thousands of Luther's Bible with highly regarded skill.[26] Six more printers arrived, including Joseph Klug, who was first to publish Luther's hymn, "A Mighty Fortress Is Our God." Meanwhile, Luther benefited greatly from close friendship and collaboration with Lucas Cranach the Elder (the godfather of his children), whose artistry became an identifiable mark for

---

21. He published Luther's *Theses against Scholastic Theology* (Sept. 1517).

22. The printer added two controversial woodcuts to a sermon that caused considerable fallout for Luther, though he did not approve it (Wengert, *Annotated Luther*, 226). Other examples of negligence are evident in the historical record.

23. Luther writes, "It is printed so poorly, so carelessly, and confusedly, to say nothing of bad typefaces and paper. Johann the printer is always the same old Johann and does not improve" (Lehman, *Luther's Works*, 292).

24. In a letter to George Spalatin dated August 15, 1521, Luther declared that it would be better for the Gospels and Epistles to stay hidden than to be misprinted (Smith, *Life and Letters of Martin Luther*, 124).

25. The Lotter family owned Latin and Greek type and bold-face Gothic.

26. Cole, "Reformation Printers," 334. He became the richest man in Wittenberg.

Luther's works in his Bible and his polemical pamphlets.[27] Cranach eventually opened up his own publishing house that partnered with Luther to advance his message.[28] As events unfolded, Luther's savvy instincts for the potential of print and his dedication to shaping style, format, and medium to its most effective form proved critical to helping the industry bridge this "Xennial" period between the Renaissance and the Reformation. The fact that he refused royalties for his publications[29] speaks to the true missional motivation behind his work of re-Christianizing Europe.[30]

Yet, even with this skill and drive, Luther's output was dependent on his partnerships with printers, regardless of their skill. As Richard Cole once wrote, "Individual authors and their specific works are only half of the story of the printing dimensions of Reformation times. The people who cast the type and rolled the ink are frequently overlooked by scholars because they are regarded as mere cogs in the wheel of the printing revolution."[31] Who were these printers, and why did they print what they did?[32] These questions are all the more compelling when recognizing what a risky business printing could be during the early modern period.

The Risky Business of Print

From its inception, printing was a financially risky enterprise. Its economic success was not a foregone conclusion, starting with German merchant Johannes Gutenberg himself. The forty-two-line Göttingen copy of the Gutenberg Bible printed on vellum is regarded by UNESCO's World Documentary Heritage Programme to be one of the most important documents of the world's written tradition and part of the Memory of the World Register.[33] For all that Gutenberg achieved, it did not protect him from dying penniless in his own time. As Pettegree explains,

---

27. See Ozment, *Serpent and the Lamb*.

28. The paper for Luther's Bible came from Cranach's papermill (Pettegree, *Brand Luther*, 187).

29. Pettegree, *Brand Luther*, 279.

30. Hendrix, "Rerooting the Faith," 558–77.

31. Cole, "Reformation Printers," 327.

32. Pettegree describes the early printers as "hard, practical men, often men of little education, to see the potential of a new method of copying that would bring many hundreds of texts simultaneously to the marketplace" (*Book in the Renaissance*, 21). Cole's article explores the challenges faced in uncovering the lives of printers ("Reformation Printers," 329).

33. Of the original thirty Bibles printed on vellum, only four have survived in their complete form with all their 1,282 pages. For instance, see UNESCO's 42-Line Gutenberg Bible.

Gutenberg could not make it pay. He died bankrupt and disappointed, defeated by the complexities of a market not yet adjusted to absorb many hundred copies of identical books. Making the new invention a commercial proposition was the crucial and most critical challenge facing the new book entrepreneurs. It would defeat many who plunged into the new art before the end of the fifteenth century.[34]

Even with a population hungry for learning, the commercial success of print was far from inevitable. Part of the challenge printers faced was the necessity of fronting the money for the production of books, which meant estimating the selling potential of every volume supplied.[35] The second generation of printers after Gutenberg were more cautious, and this is evident in John Calvin's publishing debut.

Certainly, the start of Calvin's publishing career was less than ideal. Abysmal failure would be a more appropriate description. Calvin completed his commentary on Seneca's *De Clementia* in February 1532, and it was printed in Paris during the following April. The printer required Calvin to pay the production costs, and so he became responsible for moving the copies. When course adoption at the university level proved out of reach, Calvin's first publication turned out to be a money pit that required him to liquidate part of his inheritance in order to pay the printer.[36] As Bruce Gordon writes in his biography of Calvin, "The deafening silence from the French intellectual world that greeted the Seneca commentary was wounding, and no doubt it came as a jolt to his pride."[37] This monumental defeat would prove effective in turning his attention from scholarly endeavors to the reform of the church. He never again faced the publishing setbacks known at his debut once he began to write for the church, and by the time he returned to Geneva in 1541 to launch the second phase of his ministry there, he had published in Paris, Basel, and Strasbourg, which were three of the most significant printing centers in Europe. Calvin's *Institutes* benefited from his partnerships with some of the finest printing houses in Europe before Geneva became a major printing center itself, and its success in the worldwide market continues to have an impact today.[38]

34. Pettegree, *Book in the Renaissance*, 21.

35. Subscription was another way to cover costs (Cole, "Reformation Printers," 334). Piracy and plagiarism were other concerns, since it was easier to copy a bestselling book than to predict one.

36. Pettegree, "Calvin and Luther," 27.

37. Gordon, *Calvin*, 30.

38. The first Chinese translation of Calvin's *Institutes* appeared in the 1950s in Hong Kong (Gordon, *John Calvin's Institutes*, 189).

Supporting or not supporting the Protestant Reformation in print was more than just a matter of financial risk since many printers could (and did), in the end, become wealthy by printing Luther's works. The risks that shaped the lives of printers also involved gambling one's livelihood over a controversial publication in a context where censorship was enforced. Fostering partnerships under these circumstances tended to be more missional than transactional.

Margarethe Prüss (d. 1542) was a female printer born into the world of the printing press. Kirsi Sterjna wrote that she "grew up with the smell of ink and the steady clacking sound of the press at work."[39] She was the daughter, the wife, and the mother-in-law of printers. Print was in her blood. Although Prüss lived at a time when guild regulations had tightened to exclude women from apprenticeships,[40] she inherited the family printing business after her father died, a business she could pass on to her husband as long as she married a printer.[41] And so she did, three different times. Because widows were given special privileges for managing a printing house independently after the deaths of their husbands through guardianships, Prüss was also able to direct publications in support of Protestant Reformers like Luther and the more radical voices of the Reformation. Strasbourg was a remarkably tolerant city for its time, and consequently, it became a haven for radical Protestants, especially Anabaptists and Spiritualists, who made up a substantial portion of the population.[42] This took her family's press in a very different publishing direction than during her father's time, but the business thrived under her care and doubled its output.

Prüss used the printing press to elevate the contributions of women Reformers by publishing the hymnbook of Strasbourg's "Church Mother," Katharina Schütz Zell.[43] Additionally, during the 1520s in a time of social and economic unrest among the peasants of Germany, Prüss published the prophetic visions of Ursala Jost (d. 1532/39). Jost was a follower of Melchior Hoffman and experienced seventy-seven apocalyptic visions between 1525 and 1532. Prüss printed Jost's *Prophetic Visions and Revelation*

---

39. An accessible overview is given by Sterjna's "Dangerous Pamphlets," 34. See also Sterjna's *Women and the Reformation*.

40. Women were excluded since they were not able to hold citizenship or guild membership on their own though both could be conferred through them to their sons or husbands.

41. Exceptions include Walburga Wähninger, who bought a printing shop and citizenship though she never published in her own name. Meanwhile, Charlotte Guillard published under her own name.

42. See Roth and Stayer, *Companion to Anabaptism and Spiritualism*.

43. For further reading, see Zell, *Church Mother*.

of the Works of God in these End Times (1530), but the risks were considerable since the radical Reformation had gained powerful enemies. Threats of arrest befell her third husband (Balthasar Back), who was almost certainly an Anabaptist himself, followed by censorship and confiscation that contributed to significant financial loss. Weathering these storms and more, Prüss's publishing house continued to print radical reformation writings under the remarkable benevolence of Strasbourg at the time.[44] Nevertheless, her story can illustrate the way in which printers chose to print risky books if they were willing to pay the cost.

The story of printer Johannes Oporinus also reflects the risks involved when publishing controversial books. Oporinus had served under Hieronymus Froben, the famous printer of Erasmus at Basel, before he began partnering with the Reformer, pastor, professor, and printer Theodor Bibliander. Bibliander translated the Qur'an into Latin and published Europe's first printed edition in Basel in 1542. Whether or not this was a permitted publication become a matter of broad discussion throughout Europe and even attracted the attention and response of Luther. Oporinus had been thrown in jail for the publication, but Luther intervened to secure his freedom by writing to the Basel Council.[45] Luther even wrote a preface in support of the publication. Printers could not always be saved so easily.

Risky printing led to the loss of livelihood and even one's life. During the French Reformation, the same year as the Qur'an was being published and censored in Basel, Calvin's *Institutes of the Christian Religion* became the focus of censorship laws in Paris. Printers were threatened with hanging if they did not surrender in three days the *Institutes* as well as any other books prohibited by the court. To the great frustration of the book trade industry, no books were to be sold that were not approved by censorship processes.[46] Facing the very real possibility of financial ruin, printers in Paris requested that an *errata* page be included for those books advancing "Lutheran" views so that they could still move their product. Because printing and binding books were separate processes at the time, adding a page of errors was a doable suggestion, though these were not actually printing errors but errors of conviction and reasoning. For French printers publishing Protestant works in France,

---

44. Sterjna, *Women and the Reformation*, 17.

45. Pettegree, *Brand Luther*, 185.

46. Printers stood to lose considerable capital since they had already fronted the money for books either on sale or in the press. To avoid the destruction of books and the devastation of the industry while still respecting the practice of censorship, it was suggested that a page of *errata* be included to indicate the portions that were most concerning within the book. Normally, this was a page at the end of a book dedicated to listing errors of printing. In this case, it was used to list "errors" of thinking.

this option worked only for a time. During the ebb and flow of Protestant persecution, the books themselves were more likely burned along with the heretic, their trial records, and sometimes even the printer.[47]

When we think about the costs of advancing the Protestant Reformation, the martyrdom of printers is not the first thing that comes to mind, but it is a component of the Reformation story of the printing press that deserves attention as an indicator of how much printers were willing to risk for the advancement of Protestant literature. Their sacrifices would be added to the martyrologies of their day as exemplars of what it meant to advance the true church.[48] For example, in 1534, the Protestants of France—including Calvin—were caught up in the persecution that resulted from the Placard Affair, an orchestrated public denunciation of the theology of the Mass. Arrests, mob violence, and royal executions followed. King Francis I's January edict forbade the printing of any new work, which lasted until February the following year when the German Protestant princes intervened.[49] On November 10, 1534, a printer of the Rue St-Jacques in Paris was condemned for printing and selling Luther's books and burned at the stake. A bookseller was executed the next day for binding and selling books by Luther. They were both burned alive at the Place Maubert, and another printer was burned Christmas Eve 1534.[50] In France, one needed royal support in order to print Protestant works without fear of consequence, and it was through the permission and the financing of Queen Jeanne of Navarre—the most significant female ruler supporting Protestantism in Europe next to Queen Elizabeth—that the printing presses of La Rochelle were able to publish the printing of Bibles, tracts, and political broadsheets in favor of the Huguenot cause.

If a printer harbored Protestant convictions in an unfriendly country and without noble protection, the decision to embrace the life of the religious refugee was in some cases far preferred to the alternative of risking spiritual hypocrisy (as a Nicodemite), financial ruin, or loss of life. The worst wave of French heresy persecutions took place in the mid-1540s. At the time, Calvin was encouraging Protestant believers to leave France rather than falsely participate in the worship life of the Roman Catholic Church. In this decade, France's "brain drain to Geneva" escalated.[51] Robert Estienne was among

47. Monter, *Judging the French Reformation*, 196.

48. Crespin, *Histoire des martyrs*. Consider the accounts of the martyrdoms of Nicolas Nail and Guillame Dalençon, for example.

49. Armstrong, *Robert Estienne*, 167.

50. Armstrong, *Robert Estienne*, 167; Monter, *Judging the French Reformation*, 71.

51. Monter highlights the departure of Jean Crespin, Theodore Beza, and Laurent de Normandie (*Judging the French Reformation*, 115).

the most notable of printers who chose to flee. Estienne had made his name as a printer by printing editions of the Bible from 1532 during the reign of King Francis I. A few years later, he was honored as king's printer in Greek, Hebrew, and Latin. In addition to being named royal typographer, he was known as a biblical scholar in his own right and considered today to be the founder of Latin and French lexicography due to his critical edition of the entire Latin Bible, as well as his *Thesaurus Linguae Latinae* and accompanying bilingual dictionaries. His books were sold in Germany, Spain, and Northern Europe. When the Chambre Ardente banned his biblical editions, he moved to Geneva in November 1550. The next year, he worked out the versification of the Bible, which was published for the first time in his New Testament (1551) and used in Bibles today. The purpose of versification was to advance Bible study, and this was the focus of his work while in Geneva.

Because of Frenchman like Estienne, who were willing to embrace the refugee life, Geneva became an important printing center for Protestantism. Printers relied then on smuggling systems that used colporteurs—book peddlers—to transport forbidden literature abroad to churches.[52] By this system, Bibles, catechisms, Psalters, and more were illegally smuggled into France. The effort was financed by the *Bourse française*, a fund for poor refugees from France, and the risks were significant.[53] Colporteurs lost their lives for the books they were carrying and selling in France, and accounts of smuggling, hiding, and dying for the French Protestant Bible continued well into the eighteenth century. And so, an undeniable part of what made the Reformation's relationship with the printing press successful were the printers themselves, particularly those who believed in the mission behind what they were publishing.

The Swiss Reformation reflects these same patterns after Ulrich Zwingli started preaching on the New Testament verse by verse from his pulpit in the Grossmünster of Zurich. Events came to a head during Lent 1522 when, Gordon writes, the Swiss Reformation began "with an empty stomach."[54] Zwingli was visiting the home of the printer Christoph Froschauer to help him as he was working furiously to complete a new edition of the epistles of Paul. The Frankfurt Book Fair was looming, so there was not a moment to lose. They had been working an untenable schedule, and as the energy levels of his workers lagged, Froschauer served sausages to boost their efforts to complete the task. Although Zwingli was mindful to not join them in breaking the Lenten fast, given that he was already in hot water with certain

---

52. Olson, *Calvin and Social Welfare*, 50–69. See also Olson, "Quest for Anonymity," 33–55.

53. See Chung-Kim, "Aid for Refugees," 1–14.

54. Gordon, *Swiss Reformation*, 54.

leaders in the city, he did not discourage the event either. When it became known, Froschauer was duly arrested by the city council. He was the main printer of Zurich and a supporter of the evangelical cause. On March 23, Zwingli came to his defense in a sermon that was subsequently published as a pamphlet by Froschauer's workers entitled, *Freedom of Choice in the Selection of Food* (April 16, 1522). The piece is replete with echoes of Luther's *Freedom of a Christian* as Zwingli seeks to break the church's tyranny over food by teaching that only faith rather than food can make a person holy. In the end, Froschauer was fined, and the city ended up revoking the ordinance on Lenten fasting. The act of eating sausages during periods of fasting became a recognizable way to assert one's Protestant leanings. Only two weeks after Zurich's Affair of the Sausages, Wilhelm Reublin (1484–ca.1559), the People's Priest at St. Alban's Basel, broke the Lenten Fast on Palm Sunday with two other priests by partaking in a meal of suckling pig. There is no better image of the Protestant Reformation than sausages served at a printer's house during Lent inspired by a theology of grace as they labored over the publication of Paul during a visit from the pastor.[55]

Froschauer's contributions to the Reformation cause were significant over the course of his career. Not only did he publish Reformers like Zwingli[56] and Heinrich Bullinger, he also printed more than a hundred full or partial editions of the Bible, beautifully illustrated and decorated with a skill that reflected a deep commitment and care. As Gordon's work on the Swiss Reformation has shown,

> Not only did the printers have to make sober business decisions, they also often had profound sympathies with what they produced. The printing houses of Basle and Zurich not only played a crucial role in the dissemination, but the printers were themselves committed to the ideas . . . They were deeply involved in the struggle over beliefs, and as men of the world they often served as conduits between learned and lay cultures.[57]

Froschauer was no mere cog in the Reformation machine, but a printer with evangelical convictions dedicated to advancing Reformation ideas.[58]

55. By 1523, the city council had adopted the Protestant Reformation after a successful disputation won by Zwingli. By 1525, Zurich's city council abolished the Latin mass and established a Protestant seminary.

56. His partnership with Zwingli and the Zurich Reformation was so profound that when Zwingli died at the Battle of Kappel in 1531, he stopped the production of his religious publications for a time.

57. Gordon, *Swiss Reformation*, 334.

58. Indeed, Froschauer's conversion is noted by anonymous printings of Luther's works in 1520 (Gordon, *Swiss Reformation*, 334–35).

Pastoring through Technological Acceleration

The church is called to be on the ground, in the world, and living and proclaiming the gospel in word and deed. The good news of Jesus Christ is a universal message that does not change, but the transmission of that message often requires contextual innovation. Today, for the church to do that effectively, it must reach audiences in the places where minds and hearts can be shaped using modes that can effectively mobilize people's attention. During the time of Paul, the Roman roads paved the way. In the medieval period, it was due to monastic centers. During the time of the Reformation, it was through the printing press. In the recent past, pastors have taken to the radio, television, and now the podcast. Whether its tweeting, posting, blogging, or microblogging, this is the time for the church to strive to be nimble when navigating the technological terrain and building communication bridges among the generations for the sake of advancing the gospel. That is not to say that using technology creatively in pastoral ministry is a sure-fire recipe for "success." Pastoral ministry attuned to technological avenues is most akin to itinerant preaching insofar as you are likely not even around to witness the seeds that your ministry is planting. The goal is to create opportunities for the Holy Spirit to work freely in spreading the good news of Jesus Christ. The objectives of this work must be clear.

Firstly, engaging technology in ministry is not about "keeping up with the Joneses" or being cutting edge, but rather about finding ways to faithfully use the communication tools and channels of our day to spread Christ's ministry. In a pandemic, engaging technology in ministry is akin to survival. Secondly, incorporating technology in ministry is not about turning pastors into influencers, but about elevating the voice of Scripture that the Holy Spirit may be at work. Thirdly, applying technological innovation in ministry should never strive to take the place of the gathered body of the church community, which includes both preaching and participation in the sacraments commanded by Christ. Rather, technology is an avenue or tool for advancing Scripture and the work of the Holy Spirit to proclaim the good news of Jesus Christ in such a way that it should lead believers into the life of the gathered church. As the crisis of COVID-19 passes, we will need to remind our churches of this truth.

The Great Commission has bound the church to the mission of faithful proclamation of Jesus Christ to every corner of the earth. Today, those corners include the internet, and many of those corners are desperate for the light of the gospel. As we face a world of accelerated technological progress, it is worth remembering that this is not the first time that technology has transformed the life and ministry of the church in a significant way. The Reformers beginning with Luther saw the technological acceleration of their time as an opportunity to expand the reach of the church and the message of the gospel more effectively than before. They treated technology like a tool that was capable of expanding one's encounters with the gospel. Yet, there is more to their story.

The pastors of the Reformation could not have achieved what they did without fostering partnerships in ministry for the sake of the gospel with those around them. They were actually partnering with gifted people in this work, who believed in the mission behind what they were publishing and were willing to take risks to advance that message. Here was the priesthood of all believers at its best with each person using their gifts, training, and expertise to advance the ministry of the church. The Reformation story of pastors partnering with printers is, therefore, a reminder to us that the pastorate requires more than tools and cogs but true partnerships in order to advance the work of the church. There is a need for willing pastors and faithful media makers to partner together in order to steward the opportunities that technology presents to communicate the gospel on behalf of the church and to the glory of God alone. *Soli Deo gloria.*

Bibliography

Armstrong, Elizabeth. *Robert Estienne: Royal Printer*. Cambridge: Cambridge University Press, 1954.

Bowles, Nellie. "Coronavirus Ended the Screen-Time Debate. Screens Won." *New York Times*, March 31, 2020. https://www.nytimes.com/2020/03/31/technology/coronavirus-screen-time.html.

Chung-Kim, Esther. "Aid for Refugees: Religion, Migration, and Poor Relief in Sixteenth-Century Geneva." *Reformation and Renaissance Review* 20.2 (Jan. 2018) 1–14.

Cole, Richard C. "Reformation Printers: Unsung Heroes" *Sixteenth Century Journal* 15.3 (1984) 327–39.

Crespin, Jean. *Histoire des martyrs: Persécutez et mis à mort pour la vérité de l'Evangile, depuis le Temps des apostres jusques à Present*. London: Forgotten Books, 2018. First published 1619.

Febvre, Lucien, and Henri-Jean Martin. *The Coming of the Book: The Impact of Printing, 1450–1800*. Translated by David Gerard. London: Verso, 1997.

Garvey, Anna. "The Oregon Trail Generation: Life Before and After Mainstream Tech." *Social Media Week*, April 21, 2015. https://socialmediaweek.org/blog/2015/04/oregon-trail-generation/.

Gilmont, Jean-François. *The Reformation and the Book*. Translated by Karin Maag. New York: Routledge, 2016.

Gordon, Bruce. *Calvin*. New Haven: Yale University Press, 2009.

———. *John Calvin's Institutes of the Christian Religion: A Biography*. Lives of Great Religious Books. Princeton: Princeton University Press, 2016.

———. *The Swiss Reformation*. Manchester: Manchester University Press, 2002.
Gow, Andrew. "Challenging the Protestant Paradigm: Bible Reading in Lay and Urban Contexts of the Later Middle Ages." In *Scripture and Pluralism: The Study of the Bible in the Religiously Plural Worlds of the Middle Ages and the Renaissance*, edited by Thomas Heffernan, 161–91. Leiden: Brill, 2005.
Hendrix, Scott. "Rerooting the Faith: The Reformation as Re-Christianization." *Church History* 69 (2000) 558–77.
Kurzweil, Ray. *The Singularity Is Near: When Humans Transcend Biology*. New York: Penguin, 2005.
Lehman, H.T., ed. *Luther's Works*, vol. 48. Philadelphia: Fortress, 1963.
Lindberg, Carter. *The European Reformations*. 2nd ed. Oxford: Wiley Blackwell, 2010.
Luther, Martin. *D. Martin Luthers Werke*. Weimar: Verlag Hermann Böhlaus Nachfolger Weimar, 1912.
Monter, William. *Judging the French Reformation: Heresy Trials by Sixteenth-Century Parlements*. Cambridge: Harvard University Press, 1999.
Olson, Jeannine. *Calvin and Social Welfare: Deacons and the Bourse Française*. Plainsboro, NJ: Associated University Presses, 1989.
———. "The Quest for Anonymity: Laurent de Normandie, His Colporteurs, and the Expansion of Reformed Communities through Worship" In *Semper Reformanda: John Calvin, Worship, and Reformed Traditions*, edited by Barbara Pitkin, 33–56. Gottingen: Vandenhoeck & Ruprecht, 2018.
Ozment, Steven. *The Serpent and the Lamb: Cranach, Luther, and the Making of the Reformation*. New Haven: Yale University Press, 2011.
Pettegree, Andrew. *The Book in the Renaissance*. New Haven: Yale University Press, 2010.
———. *Brand Luther*. New York: Penguin, 2015.
———. "Calvin and Luther as Men of the Book." In *Calvin and the Book: The Evolution of the Printed Word in Reformed Protestantism*, edited by Karen Spierling, 17–32. Refo500 Academic Series. Göttingen: Vandenhoeck & Ruprecht, 2015.
Roth, John, and James Stayer, eds. *A Companion to Anabaptism and Spiritualism, 1521–1700*. Leiden: Brill, 2007.
Smith, Preserved. *The Life and Letters of Martin Luther*. London: John Murray, Albemarle St., 1911.
Stankorb, Sarah, and Jed Oelbaum. "Reasonable People Disagree about the Post-Gen X, Pre-Millennial Generation." *Good Magazine*, September 25, 2014. https://www.good.is/articles/generation-xennials.
Sterjna, Kirsi. "Dangerous Pamphlets." *Christian History Magazine* 131 (2019) 34–37.
———. *Women and the Reformation*. Oxford: Blackwell, 2009.
Wengert, Timothy, ed. *Annotated Luther*, vol. 1. Minneapolis: Fortress, 2015.
Werner, Sarah. *Studying Early Printed Books, 1450–1800: A Practical Guide*. Hoboken, NJ: Wiley-Blackwell, 2019.
Zell, Katharina Schütz. *Church Mother: The Writings of a Protestant Reformer in Sixteenth-Century Germany*. The Other Voice in Early Modern Europe. Translated by Elsie McKee. Chicago: University of Chicago Press, 2006.

Subject Index

Affair of the Sausages, the, 233
AI, x, xvii–xviii, 5, 48, 111–19, 124–25, 128–35, 137, 140–42, 144–46, 148–49
alchemy, 55–58, 181
Anabaptists, 229–30
anxiety, 93, 208, 211, 216
Apostles' Creed, 135, 178
art, 98, 103, 114, 118
artificial intelligence, x, 5, 48, 53, 111–12, 118, 124–25, 129, 131, 137, 139–41, 145n19
ascension, 129–30, 136
autonomous, 9–10, 37–39, 47, 50–51, 58, 129–30, 134, 137

baptism, 30, 73, 85–86, 135
beauty, 57, 100–103, 107, 164, 189, 194, 196
bioethics, 153, 173
biology, 67, 153, 172, 174, 176–77, 179n18
blessedness, 99–100
body of Christ, 21, 73, 135, 165, 204
brain, 4, 17, 48–49, 53, 92–93, 114, 119, 123, 131, 145, 159n32, 175, 182, 184, 190–91, 197, 208–9, 216, 218, 231
Brave New World, 172

Cambridge Analytica, 132

capacities, 6, 13, 41–42, 47, 90, 144, 155, 158–61, 163n52, 165, 168, 182
catechism, 111–13, 126n27, 232
century of biology, 172
chimera, 183–84
chimeric, 183–84
Chinese room, 113
civilization, 7, 80–81, 83, 88, 211
cloning, 183
colporteurs, 232
community, 12–14, 18, 20, 30n48, 37, 44, 59, 83–84, 87, 90, 97, 111, 135–37, 147, 159n32, 166n63, 192, 204, 211–12, 216, 234
Confessions, 94, 96
consciousness, 7, 18, 111, 113–14, 116–17, 119–21, 140, 142–47, 149, 205–6
contemplation, 101–3, 199–200
creation, xvi, 4, 10, 33, 39–40, 46, 52, 56, 64, 78,–79, 81–83, 86–87, 89–90, 98, 103, 107, 115, 118–19, 125–27, 136, 140, 149, 154–57, 161–64, 167, 177, 182, 190, 214, 218–19
Creator, 81–83, 101–3, 107, 154, 155n16, 156, 160, 163–65, 200
CRISPR, 152, 154
cult of technology, 172
cultural mandate, 4n1, 81, 84

Da Vinci machine, 45

SUBJECT INDEX

dehumanization, 152, 156, 167
democracy, 8n13, 24, 202
depression, 93
deuterostomes, 179
Diet of Worms, 224–25
differentiation, 174–75, 180, 182–83
digital, the, 205–9, 213–15, 217–18
disenchantment, 88–89
distraction, 98–99, 101, 107, 200, 218
DNA, 47, 172, 180, 218
dystopian, 74, 81–82, 172

ELIZA effect, 148–49
embryonic development, 172–73, 174n4, 175–78
embryonic stem cells (ES cells), 180–82
embryos, 152, 154–55, 166n63, 172, 175–81, 183–84
emergent, 114, 119–20, 122
emotion, 95, 115, 149, 158, 198
enframing, 67–68
entertainment, 33, 93, 95–97, 106, 218
ES cells. *See* embryonic stem cells
Eucharist, 21, 28, 135, 137, 212
eucharistic, 27, 29–30
excellency, 101, 103, 157n20

Facebook, 33, 52, 55, 61, 105, 132, 202–3, 205, 210, 214, 222
feeling(s), 28, 41, 62, 87, 95–96, 104, 114, 119, 143, 190, 198, 202–3, 212
fertilization, 174, 176, 178–81,
flourishing, 45, 55, 87, 89–90, 92–94, 96, 99, 104–7, 129–30, 134, 137
focal practices, 20
focal things, 19–20, 44

garden, 11, 64, 81–84, 164, 178, 189
gastrulation, 175
gastruloids, 182
gene editing, 151–52, 154, 156, 166n63,
genetics, 53–54
Gestell, 67
gladiatorial games, 98
gnostic, 139, 146
Google, 5, 17, 31, 131–32, 208, 221
Google Translate, 131

gospel, the, 33, 58, 64, 72, 74, 87, 90, 105, 212, 218, 222, 226, 234–35
Great Awakening, 100
Great Commission, the, 234

happiness, 10–11, 56, 99, 100n25, 104–5, 107
Hierarchical Paradigm, 131
Holy Spirit, 103, 105, 135–36, 204, 234
Homo adorans, 79, 82–87
homo deus, 46, 56, 78n2
Homo faber, 79, 81–87
human body, 86, 174, 198
humanism, 6, 10, 11
humanity, xvi, 4n1, 5–10, 14, 37, 47, 55, 56n20, 65, 67–68, 78–79, 82, 85–87, 129–30, 132–34, 136–37
humanzees, 183
Hybrid Deliberative/Reactive Paradigm, 131
hyper-real/hyper-reality, 93, 103–4

ICM. *See* inner cell mass
icon, 20, 103, 107
image, xv–xvi, 22, 23n34, 31, 43, 64, 66, 71, 73, 77–79, 81–85, 90, 93, 98, 102–4, 115, 117, 119, 122, 126–27, 137, 147, 151, 155–65, 167–68, 177, 184, 186, 188–90, 198, 223, 233
image of God, xvi, 78, 81–85, 103n35, 115, 117, 119, 122, 126, 151, 155–61, 163–65, 167–68
image-bearer, 82, 85, 90, 161, 165, 177, 184
imago Dei, 65, 83, 87, 124, 155n15, 161–62, 177
Incarnation, 147, 189
individuals, 8–10, 18, 21, 166, 177, 181, 204, 211, 216
induced pluripotent stem cells (iPS cells), 181–82
inner cell mass (ICM), 175, 180
inner spiritual essence, 5–6, 10–12, 14
Institutes, The, 230
instrument(s), 23n34, 25–27, 43, 45, 46, 48, 77, 80–81, 85–88, 130
instrumentalist, 17

SUBJECT INDEX 239

iPS cells. *See* induced pluripotent stem cells
isolation, 93, 191, 213

joy, 24, 30, 33, 94–95, 100, 104–5, 107, 112, 147
justification, 136

language, 12, 37, 40, 52, 65, 72, 84, 118, 131, 133, 142, 149, 159n32, 161, 188, 190, 192–93, 195–97, 200, 222, 224–25
Leipzig Disputation, 226
liberalism, 6, 8–10, 166
linear, 190–91
literature, 17, 21, 74, 146, 166n63, 172, 193–97, 199–200, 206–7, 231–32
liturgy, 25, 27, 29, 130, 134, 137, 202, 216
Lord's supper, 73, 86, 87n17, 90
Lordship, 4, 12–14, 154
love, 19, 26, 30, 52, 70, 94–95, 99–102, 106–7, 114, 130, 134–37, 168, 179, 187, 199, 205–6, 210, 214–15, 218–19

machine learning, 48, 51–52, 118
Manichean, 96
martyrdom, 83, 231
material, 19–20, 22–23, 25–26, 31, 33, 39–40, 45, 77–79, 83, 89, 112, 116–17, 119–20, 122–23, 147–48, 151–52, 154, 156, 167, 174, 212
materialism, 116, 120–22
metaphor, 24–25, 40–41, 164, 196–97
monastic scriptoriums/centers, 223, 234
monism, 122–23
monozygotic twins, 179
Moore's law, 141
moral agency, 140, 143, 145
moral beauty, 103
morphogenesis, 174, 176
MySpace, 222

nature, 4n1, 8–10, 12–13, 48, 56, 67–68, 70n33, 77–79, 81–87, 89, 101, 103, 112, 116, 119–21, 126, 130, 143, 147, 149, 154, 158n23, 159–60, 165, 166n63, 177–78, 184, 189, 194, 196–97, 199, 213, 216–17
95 Theses, 224, 226
NRP (non-reductive physicalism), 122–23

oocyte, 174, 180–81
Oregon Trail Generation, 221
organoids, 182

pastor theologian, 4–5, 11, 13, 184
PDRs. *See* personal data records
Pelagianism, 13
personal data records (PDRs), 133
personal digital technology, 93
PGD. *See* preimplantation genetic diagnosis
Phaedrus, 42, 187
Placard Affair, the, 231
Platonic, 69, 94n4, 95, 147
pluripotent stem cells, 180–82
polar body, 180
political, 8, 9n14, 19, 62, 166, 195, 202, 213, 217, 231
politics, 8, 26, 62, 67
Preimplantation genetic diagnosis (PGD), 153n10, 179
printing press, 222–25, 229, 231–32, 234
profaning technology, 12

qualia, 122, 140, 142–43, 145
Qur'an, 230

R.U.R. (Rossum's Universal Robots), 130
Ramsey Colloquium, 176
Reactive Paradigm, 131
reading, 18, 62, 71–72, 87, 102, 189–91, 193–97, 200, 214
Redeemer, 101
Reformation, the, 163, 222–23, 227, 229–33, 235
robot, 47, 111, 130–31
"Runaround," 133

sacrament, 21, 23, 27, 77–79, 84–91, 136, 212, 234
sacramental imagination, 78, 85, 87, 89–90
sacramental theology, 85
sanctification, 136
screens, 5, 71, 78, 103, 199, 206–7, 211, 222
Scripture, xvi, 21n27, 47, 63, 65, 80, 87, 93n1, 102–3, 106, 123–26, 134–35, 146, 177, 189, 216, 226, 234
selfie individualism, 10
September Testament, 225
singularity, 46, 48, 50, 52–54, 141, 144, 221
social imaginary, 77, 88, 203–5, 208–9, 211, 217, 219
social media, 5, 18, 61, 93, 102, 105–6, 202–3, 205–6, 208–14, 216,
Socrates, 42, 139–40, 187–88
soul, 45–46, 52, 61, 94–97, 101–2, 105, 112, 114–15, 117, 120, 122–25, 134, 137, 139, 156, 158–59, 161, 165, 173, 187, 191, 198–99, 212–18
soulishness, 122–24
Soylent, 147
spiritual essence, 5–7, 10–12, 14
Spiritualists, 229
symbol, 22, 98, 103, 113n7, 130, 189, 200
synthetic embryo, 182

Tay Sachs disease, 180
technē, 17, 22, 37, 41–44, 58
technical necessity, 7, 13
technique, 6–7, 10, 26, 33, 56, 62, 87–90, 210
technological ideology, 4n1, 5–6, 8, 10–14
technological Pelagianism, 13
telemanipulator, 131
telos, 10, 71, 136, 214
test-tube baby, 172
The Island of Doctor Moreau, 184

therapeutic, 153, 166
Three Laws of Robotics, 133
tool, 6–7, 17, 19, 22, 32–33, 37–41, 46, 67, 77–81, 83, 87–88, 90, 125, 140, 149, 152n4, 181, 193, 213, 234–35
tradition, xvi, 20, 23–25, 32, 42, 49, 57, 74, 78, 80, 92, 93n1, 102, 106, 111, 113, 117, 123, 158, 161, 166, 204, 219, 227
transcendence, 87, 139, 143, 147, 195
transhuman, 16, 111, 137
Trinity, 99–100, 126, 153, 178
tripartite structure, 104
trophoblast, 175, 180, 182
Turing Test, 52, 124, 131, 142
twins, 166n63, 179

virtual, 124, 127, 222
virtual reality (VR), 5
virtue, 8–9, 20, 95–96, 100, 103–6, 130, 145, 198
vocation, xv, 3, 79, 81, 136, 155–56, 160–61, 163n52, 164–65

Wartburg, 225
well-being, 93, 100n25, 104–5, 107, 166
Western liberalism, 6, 8
wisdom, xi, xvi, 21, 24–25, 27, 72, 74, 92–94, 101, 105–7, 111, 117, 125, 139, 143, 158, 167, 177, 187
Wittenberg, 224, 226
wonder, 19, 25, 87, 102, 146, 173, 207
word of God, the, 21, 86, 193, 199–200, 219
worship, xvi, 17, 21–30, 32, 65, 71, 79, 82–84, 90, 103–4, 126, 137, 161, 207, 218–19, 231

Xennial, 221, 223, 227

Yamanaka factors, 181

zygote, 174, 176

Name Index

Allmen, J. J. von, 27
Alypius, 96–97
Anderson, V. Elving, 177
Aquinas, Thomas. *See* Thomas Aquinas
Arendt, Hannah, 66
Asimov, Isaac, 133
Augustine, Saint, 9, 85, 92–96, 98–100, 106–7, 134, 158, 215

Barash, David, 183
Barth, Karl, 3, 123, 136
Bass, Clarence, 3
Bauman, Zygmunt, 71, 211
Bayerque, Nicolas, 132
Beale, G. K., 82n11, 164
Berry, Wendell, 22, 44
Billings, Todd, 87n17
Borgmann, Albert, 18–21, 41, 43–44, 63n6, 66, 79n5
Bostrom, Nick, 141, 143–44, 146–48
Brown, Louise, 172

Calvin, John, 85–86, 135–36, 157n20, 159, 163, 228, 230–31,
Capek, Karel, 130
Cassuto, Umberto, 80
Chauvet, Louis-Marie, 86, 130
Cochlaeus, Johann, 225
Cole, Richard, 227
Cranach, Lucas, 226–27

Crisp, Oliver, 178
Croasmun, Matthew, 104n36, 105

Deneen, Patrick, 8
Duke George of Saxony, 225

Edwards, Jonathan, 92–93, 100, 102, 107
Ellul, Jacques, 6–7, 12, 63n7, 79n5, 88
Emperor Charles V, 225
Erasmus, 225, 230
Estienne, Robert, 231–32
Evans, John, 173

Foucalt, Michel, 66
Frederick of Saxony, 225

Gay, Craig M., 55, 80
Goebbels, Joseph, 61, 69, 70n34
Gordon, Bruce, 228, 232–33
Greenman, Jeffrey, 7
Gutenberg, Johannes, 223, 227–28

Harari, Yuval, 11, 46, 56
Heidegger, Martin, 22, 66–71, 74
Hobson, George, 4n1, 5, 11–12
Huxley, Aldous, 172

James, P. D., 16
Jobs, Steve, 39–41
Jost, Ursula, 229

NAME INDEX

Kingsley, Charles, 176–77
Kurzweil, Ray, 48–50, 54, 221

Leithart, Peter, xi, 29
Levering, Matthew, 95
Lints, Richard, 161–62, 163n52, 164
Luther, Martin, 163n53, 222–27, 229–31, 233, 235
Lyotard, Jean-François, 66

McLuhan, Marshall, 18, 66, 71, 188–89, 195, 199
Melancthon, Philip, 225
Middleton, J. Richard, 81n9
Mishra, Pankaj, 10
Musk, Elon, 129, 145

Niebuhr, Reinhold, 143, 147

Owen, John, 159

Pagden, Anthony, 9
Papal Nuncio Aleander, 224
Pascal, Blaise, 82, 156
Pettegree, Andrew, 224n11, 225, 227
Pichai, Sundar, 131
Plato, 42, 47, 69, 126, 140, 187–88
Postman, Neil, 189
Prüss, Margarethe, 229

Queen Jeanne of Navarre, 231

Ramsey, Paul, 173
Rhau-Grunenberg, Johann, 226

Schmemann, Alexander, 28, 79, 137
Siedentop, Larry, 9
Spalatin, George, 226
Sterjna, Kirsi, 229

Tegmark, Max, 113, 145
Thomas Aquinas, 158
Thomson, James, 181
Torrance, T.F., 3, 126n28
Turkle, Sherry, 93n3, 149, 205–6

Vico, Giambattista, 9
Volf, Miroslav, 92, 94, 104–5, 107

Wainwright, Geoffrey, 130, 135
Waltke, Bruce, 157, 162–64
Walton, John H., 82n11
Webb, Amy, 132–33
Weber, Max, 68n23, 70n32, 89, 209
Weizenbaum, Joseph, 148
Wells, H.G., 184
Williams, Rowan, 86

Yamanaka, Shinya, 181

Zwingli, Ulrich, 232–33

www.ingramcontent.com/pod-product-compliance
Lightning Source LLC
Chambersburg PA
CBHW030823230426
43667CB00008B/1355